CITIZENS' GUIDE TO CRIMINAL LAW

MONICA SAKHRANI

HRLN
Human Rights Law Network (India)

Universal
Law Publishing Co. Pvt. Ltd.

HRLN Vision

To protect fundamental human rights, increase access to basic resources for the marginalised communities, and eliminate discrimination

To create a justice delivery system that is accessible, accountable, transparent, efficient and affordable, and works for the underprivileged. Raise the level of *pro bono* legal expertise for the poor to make the work uniformly competent as well as compassionate.

Professionally train a new generation of public interest lawyers and paralegals who are comfortable in the world of law as well as in social movements, and who learn from social movements to refine legal concepts and strategies.

Citizens' Guide to Criminal Law, Reprint 2009

ISBN : 978-81-7534-801-1

Text Editor
Abid Shah

Cover Design
Shyam Jagota

Layout
Hardeo Sharma

Published by
Universal Law Publishing Co. Pvt. Ltd.
C-FF-1A, Dilkhush Industrial Estate
(Near Azadpur Metro Station)
G.T. Karnal Road, Delhi-110 033
Tel.: 011- 42381334, 27215334, 27438103
Fax : 011-27458529
E-mail (For sales inquiries):sales@unilawbooks.com
Website : www.unilawbooks.com

Under special arrangement with
Human Rights Law Network (HRLN)
A division of Socio Legal Information Centre
576, Masjid Road, Jangpura
New Delhi - 110014, India
Ph.: +91-11-24379854/55/56
E-mail:publications@hrln.org

Printed at Vishal Binding Housc, New Delhi

"Criminal law has its own basic philosophy, entirely outside the legal system. Criminal law is like war...That is the reason why all attempts to 'humanise' the criminal law have failed so far..."

[Herman Bianchi, 'Abolition: assensus and sanctuary' in Anthony Duff and David Garland (eds.) A Reader on Punishment (Oxford: Oxford University Press) (1994)]

"The reform of criminal law must be read as a strategy for the rearrangement of the power to punish, according to modalities that render it more regular, more effective, more constant and more detailed in its effects; in short, which increase its effects while diminishing its economic cost (that is to say, by dissociating it from the system of property, of buying and selling, of corruption in obtaining not only offices, but the decisions themselves) and its political cost (by dissociating it from the arbitrariness of monarchical power). The new juridical theory of penalty corresponds in fact to a new 'political economy' of the power to punish."

[Michel Foucault, Discipline and Punish: The Birth of the Prison (Translated from French by Allan Sheridan) (Middlesex: Penguin Books) (1977) Pages 80-81]

FOREWORD

This book is what it promises to be — Citizens' guide to criminal law for the beginner and the uninitiated. To that extent, it makes a very tidy addition to the existing plethora of books on the subject. The book stands apart from the crowd since in its Preface and the first two Chapters, it raises certain disquieting questions regarding the recent trend in the Apex Court of toppling earlier settled precedents like ninepins besides recent attempts to narrow down human rights. Malimath Committee Report might appear to have been cold-shouldered by the State. But the indifference seems to be more apparent than real. Some of the latest amendments to criminal law -- both substantive as well as procedural -- and the pronouncements of the Supreme Court, which are binding in view of Article 141 of the Constitution of India, leave nothing to imagination.

The issue has been raised in conferences and seminars of lawyers giving rise to a lot of heartburning and to its visible manifestation -- breast-beating. I am afraid this quite misses the fundamental point -- the nature of the State. The so-called human rights guarantees were ostensibly espoused by the bourgeois revolution in France and the due process clause propagated by its trans-Atlantic cousin -- the American revolution. Not that there were no opportunities to incorporate "due process " clause into the Constitution. But due process met repeated and early deaths-- in the Constituent Assembly, in AK Gopalan (AIR 1950 S,C. 27), and in Shiv Kant during the Emergency. It is not because of judicial or executive somnambulance but the class character of the agencies involved. Human rights are not a heaven-sent blessing. They are the social opportunities offered by a given socio- economic system of class society and formulated in legal rules and institutions. We cannot forget that the State is an organ of class rule, and an organ for the oppression of one class by another. It creates " order" which legalises and perpetuates this oppression by moderating the collisions between classes. Moderation does not mean conciliation of classes. If it were so, the State could neither arise nor continue to exist. To sustain this order, the ruling class created organs for the enforcement of legal rules. These organs included the judicial system as well. For making similar statements EMS Namboodripad was fined by the highest court of the land.

How times have changed! Some of the judges from the same court have conceded this historical truth; as also for the so-called police reforms. The police force is one more arm of the State to suppress the masses and any talk of making it "people- friendly" forgets the raison d'etre of its existence.

As for the clamour that crime is on the increase, a more detailed discussion is required elsewhere. But it is axiomatic that crime is on the increase throughout the capitalist world. The increase in crime is not an isolated chance phenomenon. It has roots in the socio-economic structure of society. Poverty, unemployment, despair about the future, revolt against inequality in society, ever-widening gulf between the so-called "feel good" section and the vast majority of the disadvantaged, cynicism generated by "instant "methods of growing big in power and money, self-centered careerist tendencies which are the hallmark of an exploitative system, tendency to treat women as "chattel" and a thing for acquisition and enjoyment have all led to such a situation. The US may be an affluent society for some but at the same time it is one of the most unequal societies. Such a situation puts the individual in opposition to the collective and society. A social system whose foundations are laid on social inequality and injustice, on the exploitation of man by man and on the disharmony between social and personal interests becomes the breeding ground for crime. With the removal of these causes even excesses like crime will disappear. We cannot make such a disappearance a time-bound programme. But we know for sure that they will disappear. A survey carried out by the John Hopkins University noted that for every one percent increase in unemployment there was a 4.1% rise in suicides, 5.7% increase in admissions into mental asylums, 3,4% increase in admissions into jail, 28.7% increase in drug addicts and 5.7% increase in murders.

This is not to say that personal conduct of an individual does not influence his actions on some occasions. But the root cause lies in the socio-economic conditions available in a given society. To forget this is like missing the forest for the trees. The danger is this mistaking trees for the forest is deliberate. I am glad that Monica Sakhrani's book has given rise to this discussion. More power to her!

—***Dhairyasheel Patil***
Former Chairman, Bar Council of India

CONTENTS

PREFACE

The Citizens' Guide to Criminal Law is not meant to be a substitute to Criminal Major Acts. It attempts to work as a guide for lay persons and people who need some basic information on the subject of the working of the criminal justice system. The guide is not a comprehensive one as it would require many more volumes to cover all the aspects of criminal law. The paucity of space and the purpose of the book have also resulted in some issues being left out.

The selection of the material has been such so as to give an overall knowledge of how the system operates, without any illusions of demystifying law for lay persons. Law remains mysterious for all alike, lay people as well as lawyers. In the last decade there has been considerable change in criminal law and the jurisprudence has been developed mainly through law. The hitherto well settled principles of criminal law have been unsettled in a series of judgments and so conflicting judgments co-exist uneasily with each making the law a grey area. But the trend is clear -- the march is backward.

This brings me to the other objective of this exercise -- to raise certain issues concerning the efficacy of the criminal justice system and critique the ends it seeks to achieve and the manner in which it does so.

The system is a relic of our imperial past and it treats citizens not as subjects of a democratic system but as objects of governance. These colonial laws have been brought under the constitutional framework influenced by post-revolution France and United States of America with its commitment to equality, justice and the promise of the rule of law. However, till date constitutionally guaranteed human rights remain a distant dream for most. The least of the citizens are deprived of their fundamental freedoms. No blueprint of an alternative plan is laid out here. Solutions have to evolve after a lot more debate and discussion, not just by lawyers but also others who are affected by the system.

Some of the references have been mentioned at the footnotes, but there are too many books and influences that do not find a direct reference point in the book, but are scattered all over.

Lastly an apology for any flaws and mistakes here -- the author takes full responsibility for them.

Monica Sakhrani
January 2008

CHAPTER 1

ON CRIME AND PUNISHMENT

The difference in civil and criminal law lies not so much in the nature of infringement but in the relief granted. The infringement of civil law gives rise to a remedy under the law while infringement of criminal law leads to punishment for the offence. An act or an omission can be both a civil wrong and a criminal offence. An example of this is cases of cruelty to married women by the husband or his family. The woman can register a criminal case against the husband under Section 498A of the Indian Penal Code and the husband will be liable to be sentenced to imprisonment upto a term of three years and also file for divorce in a civil or family court. The latter would amount to a civil remedy.

Criminal and civil law overlap in very few cases. The rationale behind criminal law is that such acts are dangerous to the society at large and hence should be actively discouraged. It is seen as one of the sovereign functions and hence the State prosecutes the serious offences and these are considered offences against the State. The machinery of the State is involved in the investigation, prosecution and prevention of offences, as these are considered necessary for the maintenance of law and order, which is a State function. Civil remedies have to be pursued by the parties themselves while this is not true of all criminal wrongs where the state continues with the prosecution of the offence even where the victim does not want to pursue the prosecution or is not in a position to do so.

Apart from the nature of the relief, criminal law also demands a more stringent proof of "beyond reasonable doubt" rather than the civil "preponderance of probabilities" as here the person is punished and loses his freedom. There is a shaming/blaming/labeling function of criminal law, which has led to the principle of "presumption of innocence" and the onus on the prosecution as the positive can be proved but not the negative. The burden in criminal law shifts to the accused only upon the prosecution proving its case. However, over the last few decades, while there has been a public debate of crime and criminal law, there has been a shift in the evidentiary rules of practice with the gap between the burden and extent of proof diluting and coming closer to the civil law standards.

Modern law has its origins in the Renaissance and the Age of Reason. As the role of the state changed, there emerged the Rule of the Law. This law and its rule were different in the different areas of life. With the industrial revolution and the rise of capitalism, the function of law was seen as facilitating economic activity. Law's role was sought to be confined to maintenance of law and order for creation of an environment for the market to decide on issues of economy (*laissez faire*). This was done through the mechanism of criminal law in matters such as infringement of public wrongs that affect the market, such as theft, violence, etc of private persons that impact the general climate of the economy. The emphasis here was punishment to not merely to penalise and thereby stop the wrong doer from committing the same wrong again, but also to deter others from committing similar offences in future. The other wrongs which only had a direct bearing on the parties concerned was regulated by civil law, where the aggrieved person approached the court for a legal remedy for the wrong committed. The domain of civil law was mostly confined to economic affairs, as the purpose of the state was not to interfere in every aspect of the person's life.

The British brought this rationale for the legal system with them in India. This was perhaps even more strictly adhered to in India, as the purpose of the political invasion was an economic one. The British were admittedly here to carry on trade. So the contractual aspects of trade needed regulating uniformly. With the Crown taking over India after the mutiny, the anger and resistance of the Indian people was obvious. Hence, administration of criminal law both to quell resistance and to maintain law and order for the carrying on of trade and continuance of power became the prime consideration of the legal system in India. Hence the emphasis was on criminal law. This emphasis on criminal administration of justice continues till date.

The English initially set up a system of law, which recognised indigenous law but administered it through its system of courts. These courts began introducing the principles of English law and hence the common system of law came to be implemented in India. In 1858, when India became a part of the British Empire, the first set of laws to be introduced were the criminal laws, which were codified and made universally applicable. The Criminal Laws in India to date continue to be the same with certain changes and additions. The main laws are:

- Indian Penal Code, which codifies the offences and prescribes the maximum (and in some cases minimum) penalty for them
- Criminal Procedure Code, which provides the procedures for investigation and trial of offences
- Indian Evidence Act, which is common to both civil and criminal trials, and provides the rules for the evidence in the trials.

These apart, there are several other laws that specifically provide for criminal law sanctions for other offences. Once the criminal law in India was codified, it led to the repeal of traditional criminal law in India. The criminal law in India is universally applicable to all crimes committed within the territory of India be it by foreigners or Indians. Thus we have the rule of uniform criminal law.

The focus of the criminal law system is the individual who commits the offence with the requisite *mens rea* or intention. Thus, physical and mental culpability are both prerequisites for punishment. Since individual freedom is sacrosanct, deprivation of freedom became the real punishment. This has led to the change in the type of punishment. Earlier, imprisonment was used as an interim measure till the infliction of punishment in Europe, but now imprisonment has become the principal type of punishment. Rusche and Kirchheimer, two eminent Marxist criminologists in their seminal work, *Punishment and Social Structures* written in 1939 have pointed out that the type of punishment depends on the economic need of the society. In feudal society when labour was not valued, corporal punishment was the norm, but in the industrial society labour came to be valued and the type of punishment shifted to incarceration, with its emphasis on discipline.

There are two aspects of criminal law -- substantive and procedural. Substantive law defines the offences and prescribes the punishment for the same while procedural law sets out the procedure to be followed on infringement of the law. Though the system of criminal legal system existing in India today is by and large a legacy of the British, there have been post-Independence changes. Yet these changes do not reflect any growing sense of people friendliness vis-à-vis law. The definitions and punishment for political crimes have broadened and post 1947 preventive detention laws are harsher. State interference through penal action is more intensive and extensive than it was during the pre-independence era. Moreover, with the development in international law, there have been certain other changes in the law. The Human Rights Conventions and the Constitution have brought in certain procedural safeguards in the criminal justice system and certain laws such as the Juvenile Justice Act have been enacted to conform with treaty obligations. But there is also a counter movement to do away with the traditional procedural safeguards through the introduction of specialised legislation such as the anti-terror laws like TADA and POTA, the Narcotic and Psychotropic Substances Act. While the development of International law in the field of criminal legal system has also led to the standardisation and universalisation of the adversial system of criminal justice all over the world, certain legislations try to introduce the inquisitorial system by shifting the onus of proof on the accused and introducing presumptions against the accused.

The Government of India constituted a Committee on Reforms of Criminal Justice System (Malimath Committee Report, March 2003) which came out with its recommendations which though not accepted in toto have informed many recent rulings and the changes in the criminal law. The Committee sought to do away with traditional safeguards and took the stringent crime control model to its extreme. The terms of reference of the report was to examine the fundamental principles of criminal jurisprudence, to simplify procedure, to suggest means of reducing delay, to see the feasibility of introducing the concept of 'Federal Crime' and 'to suggest ways and means of developing such synergy among the Judiciary, the Prosecution and the Police as to restore the confidence of the common man in the Criminal Justice System by protecting the innocent and the victim and by punishing unsparingly the guilty and the criminal'. The recommendations include the doing away of the right of silence of the accused, change the adversarial system to the inquisitorial, reduction of the burden of proof from "beyond reasonable doubt" to the standard of "courts conviction that it is true", subserving legal prosecution to police investigation, increase in the number of cases brought under summary procedure, reduction in the number of court holidays, deletion of death penalty and increasing period the life imprisonment, increase in the fines and reclassification of offences. The Committee stated that it wanted to make "quest for truth to be the foundation of the criminal justice system".

While this may not have happened in exactly the manner the Committee envisaged, the Supreme Court in the progressive Best Bakery judgment where the Gujarat government had made a travesty of law held that, "The concept of fair trial entails familiar triangulation of interests of the accused, the victim and the society and it is the community that acts through the State and prosecuting agencies...If a criminal Court is to be an effective instrument in dispensing justice, the Presiding Judge must cease to be a spectator and a mere recording machine by becoming a participant in the trial evincing intelligence, active interest and elicit all relevant materials necessary for reaching the correct conclusion, to find out the truth, and administer justice with fairness and impartiality both to the parties and to the community it serves...It has to be unmistakably understood that a trial which is primarily aimed at ascertaining truth has to be fair to all concerned...It will be not correct to say that it is only the accused who must be fairly dealt with. That would be turning Nelson's eyes to the needs of the society at large and the victims or their family members and relatives. Each one has an inbuilt right to be dealt with fairly in a criminal trial. Denial of a fair trial is as much injustice to the accused as is to the victim and the society. Fair trial obviously would mean a trial before an impartial Judge, a fair prosecutor and atmosphere of judicial calm. Fair trial means a trial in which bias or prejudice for or against the accused, the witnesses, or the cause which is being tried is eliminated."[1]

Over the last decade, we have witnessed the dilution of some of the fundamental principles of law such as the shifting of the burden of proof from the prosecution on to the accused in certain cases, with almost all the new criminal legislations or new amendments in recent years doing so starting from the 1983 amendments in rape and dowry cases to the NDPS Act, TADA, Prevention of Corruption Act, Section 138 of the Negotiable Instruments Act, POTA and the state enacted

1 Zahira Habibulla H. Sheikh v. State of Gujarat, AIR 2004 SC 3114 at 3125-6

control of organised crimes acts. Principles such as the evidentiary value of confessions, the need for independent witnesses in panchnamas and the need for Test Identification Parade have also been diluted in recent judgments. Thus, the adversarial system of criminal justice and the test of beyond reasonable doubt have been gradually eroded in the last decade. There has been an increase in the number of criminal laws and police power has grown. Despite the public hue and cry over the human rights judgments and their role in tying the hands of the police, human rights jurisprudence has had little impact at the ground level. Almost every human rights judgment of the Supreme Court including the DK Basu guidelines have been violated by the State.

American Criminologist Herbert Packer in 1964 formulated two models of criminal justice: Crime control and Due Process models. The first sees the real role of criminal administration as control of crime and its success as the effective control of crime. This model, which is advocated by many law enforcement agencies emphasises on stringent laws, deterrent sentences and more powers to the law enforcement agencies. The second places emphasis on the human rights of the accused, the presumption of innocence, the need for procedural safeguards to ensure that the innocent are not penalised and punishment that is proportionate to the offence and not cruel, degrading and inhuman. Most of the debate that surrounds criminal justice system is centered towards the posited opposition of these two dominant strands of thinking. However, these are not really opposed to each other. Both the models do not question the rationale for punishment or the right of the State to punish. The only points of dispute are *how* (should corporal punishment and death penalty be abolished and what constitutes cruel, inhuman and degrading treatment) and *to what extent* (should punishment be proportionate or deterrent and what constitutes either). The Due Process model does not deny the role of the criminal justice system from the point of view of crime control -- it merely states that observance of due process of law makes way for more effective crime control by arguing that stringent punishments are not really deterrent and that following due process of law through respect for human rights makes for good and more effective governance by lending legitimacy to the system and creating respect for the laws, including criminal laws. Crime control also recognises that the legitimacy of law as being morally superior to retribution and the moral right of the State to punish is corroded by contempt of the law by the law enforcement agencies inviting anarchy. The balance is seen as the true purpose of the Rule of Law, which is just, equitable, determinate, impartial and universal.

The recent development of criminal law shows a broadening of the areas of substantive law and a narrowing of the scope of procedural safeguards many of which have been hard won battles of the human rights movement. The recent amendments to Criminal Procedure Code reflect the dynamics of this struggle for justice between the traditional role of the law as an instrument of effective crime control and focus on individual rights by seeking to control unbridled state power. Within this arena, has recently entered the debate on victim jurisprudence and their right to redressal of their grievance and the right to public safety versus the rights of the accused. The core issue, however, is the extent to which the state can impinge upon the individual's life and personal liberty in order to control crime. Should an innocent person be punished due to the society's need to be crime free? Should a person be punished disproportionately in order to satisfy the victim's need for justice? What should be the role of law and what should be the limits of state power? It would be pertinent here to remember the words of a leading criminologist, " *...if we think that institutions of punishment are necessary and desirable, and if we are morally sensitive enough to want to be sure that we have the moral right to punish before we inflict it, then we had better first make sure that we have restructured society in such a way that criminals genuinely do correspond to the only model that will render punishment permissible- i.e., make sure that they are autonomous and that they do benefit in the requisite sense. Of course, if we did this then... crime itself and the need to punish would radically decrease entirely."*[2]

2 Jeffrie G. Murphy 'Marxism and Retribution' in Anthony Duff and David Garland (eds.) *A Reader on Punishment* (Oxford: Oxford University Press) (1994) 47 at pg. 65

CHAPTER 2

STRUCTURE OF CRIMINAL LAW IN INDIA

The purpose of the criminal law in any state is crime prevention and crime punishment. The traditional methods of both have been similar and two-fold: internment and externment. Logically crime prevention activities of the state should address basic causes of crime such as poverty, lack of education, lack of employment, corruption of the polity and other such known social factors at the political level. However, all governments prefer to leave the task of crime prevention and crime control to the police.

Outline of Criminal Law in India

The basic substantive law is the Indian Penal Code, 1860 that stipulates offences and punishments. Major categories of offences prescribed are offences against the state, offences by or relating to public servants, offences relating to elections, offences against public justice, offences affecting public health, safety and morals, offences affecting the human body, offences against property and offences relating to documents.

Juvenile is defined as a person who has not attained the age of 18 years. A minimum age limit of criminal responsibility is 7 years. A person above 18 years of age but less than 21 years of age is considered a youthful offender, and receives different treatment from an adult offender. The Juvenile Justice (Care and Protection of Children) Act, 2000 was enacted for the care, protection, treatment, development rehabilitation and adjudication of children in need of care and protection and children in conflict with the law.

The main law on criminal procedure is the Code of Criminal Procedure, 1973. The Code classifies offences into two categories, cognizable offence and non-cognizable offence. For cognizable offences, the police officer may arrest the offender without warrant. As for the investigation procedure, the police must forward an arrested suspect to the nearest magistrate within 24 hours, by whom the legality of arrest and necessity of detention is examined. The magistrate may authorise detention of the suspect in police custody for a term not exceeding 15 days. The magistrate may also authorise pre-trial detention of a suspect in judicial custody for a period not exceeding 90 days in respect of offences punishable with death/life imprisonment or imprisonment for not less than 10 years and 60 days in respect of other offences. The suspect can be released on bail at any stage. On completion of investigation, the police submit the chargesheet to the public prosecutor with reports and documents.

The public prosecutor examines the case and sometimes gives advice to the police on legal issues or sufficiency of evidence, but it is not binding. The case is prosecuted in court by the public prosecutor.

Regarding the courts system, the Supreme Court, is the highest judicial organ and has jurisdiction over the whole nation and whose legal judgment is binding upon all the lower courts. Each state has a High Court, which is the highest court in the state and adjudicates appeals from subordinate courts. A state consists of several sessions, which are also divided into several districts. In each session there is a session court and in each district there are magistrate courts.

The maintenance and development of prisons is a state subject and the state governments have their own prison manuals. Prisons are categorised as follows: central prisons; district jails; state jails for women; special jails; open jails and sub-jails. Jails having accommodation for more than 500 prisoners are called central prisons. Prisoners sentenced to imprisonment over 2 years are detained in central prisons. Prisoners sentenced to imprisonment up to 2 years are confined in district jails. Special jails are opened whenever necessary for the confinement of such prisoners as the state government may order. Sub-jails are for under trial prisoners. The suspension of sentence and release of offenders on probation has been accepted as the most constructive alternative to imprisonment in India. According to the Code of Criminal Procedure and the Probation of Offenders Act, 1958, the courts have been empowered to release on probation, in all suitable cases, an offender found guilty of having committed an offence not punishable with death or life imprisonment. Where the sentence is up to seven years imprisonment, the courts should firstly consider the desirability of release on probation. The courts, while releasing the offender, may pass a supervision order directing that the offender remain under the supervision of a probation officer for not less than a year and may impose certain conditions regarding residence, abstention from intoxication, etc. If the offender has failed to observe any of the conditions, the court may sentence him/her for the original sentence. In India, about 13 000 persons are sentenced to imprisonment every year for a period not exceeding six months and about 12 000 more for a period not exceeding one year. Thus, about 25 000 persons per annum can easily be released on probation for good conduct and placed under the supervision of probation officers.

Supreme Court of India

a) Writ jurisdiction under Article 32
b) Appellate jurisdiction over orders passed by the High Court
c) Power to transfer any case pending in any Indian court

High Courts

a) Writ jurisdiction under Article 226 and Article 227
b) Appellate jurisdiction over sentences and appeals passed by Sessions Courts
c) Inherent powers under Section 482 to pass any orders
d) References and Revision powers over orders of lower courts
e) Bail, Cancellation of Bail, Modification of Bail, Anticipatory Bail
f) Power to transfer any case pending in subordinate court
g) Power to try any case pending in lower court
h) Confirmation of death sentence

Sessions Courts

a) Trial of offences punishable with over 7 years imprisonment
b) Appeals from lower courts
c) References and Revision powers over orders of lower courts
d) Bail, Cancellation of Bail, Modification of Bail, Anticipatory Bail
e) Power to transfer any case in subordinate court

Chief Judicial / Metropolitan Magistrates

a) Try offences and can pass sentence upto 7 years
b) Power to transfer cases pending in Magistrates courts within its jurisdiction
c) Bail, cancellation of bail and remand

Metropolitan/ Judicial Magistrates of the First Class

a) Try offences and pass sentence upto 3 years and Rs.10,000 fine
b) Bail, Cancellation of Bail and remand

Juvenile Courts

a) Remand and Trial of cases of Juveniles including right to grant bail

Judicial Magistrates of the Second Class

a) Try offences and pass sentence upto 1 year and Rs. 5,000 fine
b) Bail, Cancellation of Bail and remand

Structure and Hierarchy of the Criminal Courts

The Code of Criminal Procedure, 1973 (CrPC in short) lays down the procedure to be followed when an offence is committed. The CrPC has 484 provisions contained in 37 chapters with two schedules, the first of which classifies offences laid down in the Indian Penal Code and other laws and the second contains 56 forms related to the provisions of the CrPC. The CrPC lays down the framework of the hierarchy of the courts that can try and hear criminal cases.

I. Supreme Court of India

Writ Jurisdiction

It has the original jurisdiction to hear cases of violations of fundamental rights under Article 32 of the Constitution of India and award compensation in such cases. The Supreme Court has the power to issue directions, orders or writs against the State and any of its instrumentalities and agencies.

The writs include habeas corpus, mandamus, prohibition, quo-warranto and certiorari. The writ of Certiorari is issued when an authority acts without jurisdiction or in excess of its powers and the court cancels or quashes the act/order. The writ of mandamus is issued to direct a public authority to act in accordance with law and the writ of prohibition prohibits a public authority from acting against the law. The writ of quo-warranto questions the legality of any claim to a public office and ousts a person whose claim is not well founded. The writ of habeas corpus is essentially a procedural writ to secure release of a person who is illegally restrained of his remedy. Unlike other writs, it can be issued even against a private person and is seen as a criminal law remedy against illegal detention. It is a command addressed to a person who is alleged to have another person unlawfully in his custody requiring him to bring the body of such person before the court in order to determine the circumstances of his detention and enforce his freedom. All writs began as common law remedies issued by the courts in England in the interest of justice, equity and good conscience in cases where no legal remedy was available to the victim. Writ remedy is a fundamental right under the Constitution of India for protection of the fundamental rights and the same is a discretionary remedy, which is generally issued when no other efficacious alternative remedy exists. It can be issued against all administrative orders of the State that have civil consequences. Writs are also issued on failure of the authorities to comply with the principles of natural justice. The principles of natural justice require that an order of the authority should be passed after giving the aggrieved parties an adequate opportunity to be heard, which means that notice of the proceeding should be given along with a fair and impartial hearing by a person who is not personally interested in the case. Writ remedy can be used to challenge the legislative competence to pass a statute and also to challenge the constitutional validity of any act of the legislature. The principle of res judicata, that prohibits a party from approaching a court twice for the same cause of action except by way of appeal, revision or review or any other remedy permissible under the law applies to writs except where the writ has been disposed of on technical grounds and in the case of writs of habeas corpus where the rule of res judicata does not apply.

The effects of the exercise of writ jurisdiction on a criminal proceeding are:

a) To enforce a fundamental right against the State agency or even a private individual and award compensation for the violation of the fundamental right to the victim or his family.[3]

b) When a person has been arrested in exercise of a power conferred by a law or order, or for having committed an offence created by a law that violates a fundamental right, the person so arrested may obtain his release by an application for the writ of habeas corpus.[4]

c) Where a prosecution has been initiated for the violation of an unconstitutional law, the Court would issue mandamus directing the appropriate authority to withdraw the prosecution or would quash the proceeding because no valid charge could be founded upon an unconstitutional law[5].

d) Where a person has been convicted under an unconstitutional statute or the proceeding otherwise violates a fundamental right of the accused, the conviction would be quashed by a writ of certiorari and the prisoner would be released forthwith and the fine imposed by the sentence, if realised, should be refunded.[6]

e) Since the invalidity of a law that violates a fundamental right goes to the root of the power of the Legislature and vitiates the prosecution founded on it, it is not open to the accused to waive his fundamental right and get convicted.[7]

Appeals

The court can also hear appeals from the decisions of the High Courts and also review its own judgments. Under Article 132 of the Constitution, an appeal shall lie to the Supreme Court from any judgment, decree or final order of a High Court in the territory of India whether in a civil, criminal or other proceeding, if the High Court certifies under Article 134A that the case involves a substantial question of law as to the interpretation of the Constitution. Under Article 134, an appeal shall lie to the Supreme Court from any judgment, final order or sentence in a criminal proceeding of a High Court if the High Court has on

3 Rudal Sah vs. State of Bihar, AIR 1983 SC 1086; Sebastian M.Hongrey vs. Union of India, AIR 1984 SC 956; Joginder Kumar vs. State of Uttar Pradesh, (1994) 4 SCC 260; D.K.Basu vs. State of West Bengal, 1997 Cri.L.J. 743; People's Union for Civil Liberties vs. Union of India, 1997 (3) SCC 433; Sube Singh vs State of Haryana (2006)3SCC178. Also see Bodhisattva Gautam vs Subhra Chakraborty, (1996)1 SCC 490 where the writ was issued against a private individual

4 Harish vs. Union of India, AIR 1973 SC 258; Ram vs. State of West Bengal, AIR 1975 SC 623; Sadhu Singh vs. State of Punjab, (1984) 2 SCC 310; State of Bihar vs. Saldanha 1970 Cri.L.J. 98

5 Rashid vs. Municipal Board, 1950 SCR 566; Behram vs. State of Bombay, (1955) 1 SCR 613

6 Jagjit vs. State of Punjab, 1953 SCR 744

7 Behram vs. State of Bombay, (1955) 1 SCR 613; Olga Tellis vs. Bombay Corporation, AIR 1986 SC 180

appeal reversed an order of acquittal of an accused person and sentenced him to imprisonment for life or to imprisonment for a period of not less than ten years, or has withdrawn for trial before itself any case from any court subordinate to its authority and has in such trial convicted the accused and sentenced him to imprisonment for life or to imprisonment for a period of not less than ten years (Section 379 CrPC). The Supreme Court also hears appeals against convictions on a trial conducted by the High Court in its extraordinary original jurisdiction (Section 374(1) CrPC). However no appeal lies against the decisions of the High Court in cases where the accused has pleaded guilty (Section 375(a) CrPC)or where the punishment awarded is of imprisonment not exceeding six months or fine not exceeding Rs.1000 or both (Section 376(a) CrPC).

Under Article 136, the Supreme Court may, in its discretion, grant special leave to appeal from any judgment, decree, determination, sentence or order in any case or matter passed or made by any court or tribunal in the territory of India except that relating to the Armed forces. The Supreme Court grants special leave to appeal in criminal cases when exceptional and special circumstances exist, when it is shown that grave and substantial injustice has been done and that the case in question presents features of sufficient gravity to warrant a review of the decision appealed against. In Ramakant Rai vs Madan Rai, the Supreme Court has held that in cases of acquittal by the Court, if the state fails to file an appeal, the private party can file appeal in the Supreme Court under Article 136 even where the private party does not have any right to appeal under the CrPC.[8]

The judgments of the Supreme Court are binding on all courts within India by virtue of Article 141.

Transfer

Under Section 406 of the CrPC, the Supreme Court can transfer case or appeal from one High Court to another High Court or from a criminal court subordinate to one High Court to another criminal court of equal or superior jurisdiction subordinate to another High Court. The High Courts do not have the jurisdiction cases from courts that do not come under their jurisdiction whereas the Supreme Court can transfer cases from any court to any other court in the country subject to the provisions of Section 406.[9] In the Jayalalitha case, a political opponent of the accused Chief Minister filed the transfer application to the Supreme Court on ground that there was reasonable apprehension of likelihood of bias in dispensation of criminal justice, the Court held that he had the locus to do so as being a political opponent he was vitally interested in the run of the Government and in administration of criminal justice.[10] In Jayendra Saraswathy Swamigal Vs. State of Tamil Nadu[11], where the Accused had reasonable apprehension

8 2004 CrLJ 36

9 See Zahira Habibulla H. Sheikh v. State of Gujarat, AIR 2004 SC 3114 at 3125-6

10 K.Anbazhagan vs Superintendent of Police, 2004 CrLJ 583

11 (2005)8SCC771

that he would not get a fair trial in the state, the Supreme Court ordered the transfer of the trial to Pondicherry.

II. High Courts

Writ Jurisdiction

The High Courts can also exercise writ jurisdiction under Articles 226 and 227 of the Constitution of India in cases of violation of fundamental rights similar to the powers of the Supreme Court under Article 32. In the case of the High Courts, this power is wider as the High Courts can issue writs not just for the violation of a fundamental right but also for violation of all legal rights, subject to the rule of lack of alternative effective remedy. However, it is not necessary to exhaust the writ remedy under Article 226 or 227 before approaching the Supreme Court in cases of violation of fundamental rights. At the same time though the rule of constructive res judicata applies to writs and upon approaching the High Court, the party can then approach the Supreme Court not by way of another writ but by way of a special leave petition.

Inherent Powers

The High Courts also have inherent powers under Section 482 of the CrPC to pass any order as may be necessary to give effect to any order under this Code, or to prevent abuse of the process of any court or otherwise secure the ends of justice.

The Supreme Court in the case, State of Haryana Vs. Bhajan Lal[12], has stated that the High Court in exercise of powers under Article 226 or under Section 482 of the CrPC may interfere in proceedings relating to cognizable offences to prevent abuse of the process of any court or otherwise to secure the ends of justice, in the rarest of rare cases, where

a) The allegations made in the First Information Report or the complaint, even if they are taken at their face value and accepted in their entirety do not prima facie constitute any offence or make out a case against the accused.

b) The allegations made in the First Information Report and other materials, if any, accompanying the FIR do not disclose a cognizable offence, justifying an investigation by police officers under Section 156(1) of the Code except under an order of a Magistrate within the purview of Section 155(2) of the Code.

c) The uncontroverted allegations made in the FIR or the complaint and the evidence collected in support of the same do not disclose the commission of any offence and make out a case against the accused.

d) The allegations in the FIR do not constitute a cognizable offence but constitute only a non-cognizable offence, no investigation is permitted by

12 AIR 1992 Supreme Court 604

a police officer without an order of a Magistrate as contemplated under Section155 (2) of the Code.

e) The allegations made in the FIR or complaint are so absurd and inherently improbable on the basis of which no prudent person can ever reach a just conclusion that there is sufficient ground for proceeding against the accused.

f) There is an express legal bar engrafted in any of the provisions of the Code or the concerned Act (under which a criminal proceeding is instituted) to the institution and continuance of the proceedings and/or where there is a specific provision in the Code or the concerned Act, providing efficacious redress for the grievance of the aggrieved party.

g) A criminal proceeding is manifestly attended with mala fide and/or where the proceeding is maliciously instituted with an ulterior motive for wreaking vengeance on the accused and with a view to spite him due to private and personal grudge.

The Supreme Court reiterated principles for quashing of complaints in M/s Indian Oil Corporation vs M/s NEPC India Ltd[13], wherein it stated:

(i) A complaint can be quashed where the allegations made in the complaint, even if they are taken at their face value and accepted in their entirety, do not prima facie constitute any offence or make out the case alleged against the accused. For this purpose, the complaint has to be examined as a whole, but without examining the merits of the allegations. Neither a detailed inquiry nor a meticulous analysis of the material nor an assessment of the reliability or genuineness of the allegations in the complaint, is warranted while examining prayer for quashing of a complaint.

(ii) A complaint may also be quashed where it is a clear abuse of the process of the court, as when the criminal proceeding is found to have been initiated with mala fides/malice for wreaking vengeance or to cause harm, or where the allegations are absurd and inherently improbable.

(iii) The power to quash shall not, however, be used to stifle or scuttle a legitimate prosecution. The power should be used sparingly and with abundant caution.

(iv) The complaint is not required to verbatim reproduce the legal ingredients of the offence alleged. If the necessary factual foundation is laid in the complaint, merely on the ground that a few ingredients have not been stated in detail, the proceedings should not be quashed. Quashing of the complaint is warranted only where the complaint is so bereft of even the basic facts which are absolutely necessary for making out the offence.

A given set of facts may make out: (a) purely a civil wrong; or (b) purely a

13 (2006) 6 SCC 736: AIR 2006 SC 2780

criminal offence; or (c) a civil wrong as also a criminal offence. A commercial transaction or a contractual dispute, apart from furnishing a cause of action for seeking remedy in civil law, may also involve a criminal offence. As the nature and scope of a civil proceeding are different from a criminal proceeding, the mere fact that the complaint relates to a commercial transaction or breach of contract, for which a civil remedy is available or has been availed, is not by itself a ground to quash the criminal proceedings. The test is whether the allegations in the complaint disclose a criminal offence or not.

In G. Sagar Suri vs State of UP[14], the Supreme Court observed: "It is to be seen if a matter, which is essentially of civil nature, has been given a cloak of criminal offence. Criminal proceedings are not a short cut of other remedies available in law. Before issuing process a criminal court has to exercise a great deal of caution. For the accused it is a serious matter. This Court has laid certain principles on the basis of which High Court is to exercise its jurisdiction under Section 482 of the Code. Jurisdiction under this Section has to be exercised to prevent abuse of the process of any court or otherwise to secure the ends of justice."

In BS Joshi vs State of Haryana[15] the Supreme Court held that in case of non compoundable offences, where the parties had settled the matter, they could approach the High Court in the exercise of its jurisdiction under Section 482 Cr PC and the court could quash the proceedings in the interest of justice.

Bail, Transfer and Confirmation

The High Court has powers under Section 439 of the CrPC to grant bail or modify order of bail and cancel bail. Under Section 407, the High Courts can transfer cases and appeals from one court to another of equal or superior jurisdiction within its jurisdiction and also before itself provided that it appears to it that a fair and impartial inquiry or trial cannot be had in any criminal court subordinate to it or that some question of law of unusual difficulty is likely to arise or that an order under this section is required by any provision of the code or will tend to the general convenience of the parties or witnesses or is expedient for the ends of justice. Thus, the High Court can try cases under this section. Apart from that the High Court has to confirm the death penalty in all cases where the Sessions Court conducts the trial and the Sessions Court has passed a death sentence (Section 366). The sentence will come into effect only after the High Court confirms the same. The High Court has the power to make further inquiry into such matters or record further evidence on any point bearing upon the guilt or innocence of the convicted person by itself or directs the Sessions Court to do so. The High Court should come to its own conclusion about the same and should be cautious, circumspect and careful in confirming the death sentence, which is to be awarded in the rarest of the rare cases.[16]

14 (2000) 2 SCC 636

15 (2003) 4 SCC 675

16 See Rajendra Prasad's case, AIR 1974 SC 799, Bachan Singh's case, (1980) 2 SCC 604 and Santa Singh's case, (1976) 4 SCC 190

Appeals

The High Court also hears appeals against convictions by the Sessions Judge or an Additional Sessions Judge and in cases where the sentence has been for a term more than seven years against the appellant or his co-accused (Section 374). However no appeal lies against a conviction where the accused has pleaded guilty except as to the extent or legality of the sentence (Section 375). Appeals do not lie also in the case of a conviction by the Sessions Court where it passes only a sentence of imprisonment for a term not exceeding three months or of fine not exceeding two hundred rupees, or of both such imprisonment and fine (Section 376(b). Appeals against convictions filed by the prosecution regarding the adequacy of the sentence lie in the High Court only in cases where the sentence has not been passed by a Magistrate in which case appeal will lie in the Sessions Court. In all other cases, including in cases where the offence has been investigated by the Delhi Special Police Establishment, constituted under the Delhi Special Police Establishment Act, 1946 (25 of 1946), or by any other agency empowered to make investigation into an offence under any Central Act the appeals lie in the High Court. In such cases the High Court shall not enhance the sentence except after giving to the accused a reasonable opportunity of showing cause against such enhancement and while showing cause, the accused may plead for his acquittal or for the reduction of the sentence (Section 377). Appeals against acquittals can be heard by the High Court only in cases where the same is from an original or appellate order of an acquittal will lie to the High Court except in cases of acquittal by the High Court itself or from an order of acquittal passed by a Magistrate in respect of a cognizable and non-bailable offence (in which case the court of appeal shall be the Sessions Court) or an order of acquittal passed by the Court of Session in revision and where the appeal is filed by the Complainant after obtaining leave to appeal by the High Court. This has to be filed within six months where the appellant is the State and in every other case, within sixty days (Section 378). The High Court has to give reasons for not granting leave to appeal in cases of appeals against acquittal and decisions of the High Court without assigning any reasons are illegal.[17] Notwithstanding anything contained in the Chapter relating to appeals, when more persons than one are convicted in one trial, and an appealable judgment of order has been passed in respect of any of such person, all or any of the persons convicted at such trial shall have a right of appeal (Section 380).

Powers of the High Court are extensive in the case of an appeal and the court can reassess the entire evidence and also call for recording of additional evidence by itself or the trial court or direct the retrial of the case in cases where it deems it necessary. Under Section 386, the Appellate Court may, if it considers that there is no sufficient ground for interfering, dismiss the appeal, or may in an appeal from an order of acquittal, reverse such order and direct

17 State of Punjab vs Bhag Singh, 2004 CrLJ 916

that further inquiry be made, or that the accused be re-tried or committed for trial, as the case may be, or find him guilty and pass sentence on him according to law. In an appeal from a conviction, it may reverse the finding and sentence and acquit or discharge the accused, or order him to be re-tried by a Court of competent jurisdiction subordinate to such Appellate Court or committed for trial, or alter the finding, maintaining the sentence, or with or without altering the finding, alter the nature or the extent, or alter the nature and extent of the sentence, but not so as to enhance the same. In an appeal for enhancement of sentence, the Appellate Court may reverse the finding and sentence and acquit or discharge the accused or order him to be re-tried by a Court competent to try the offence, or alter the finding maintaining the sentence, or with or without altering the finding, alter the nature or the extent, or the nature and extent, of the sentence, so as to enhance or reduce the same and in an appeal from any other order, alter or reverse such order. The Court may make also any amendment or any consequential or incidental order that may be just or proper provided that the sentence shall not be enhanced unless the accused has had an opportunity of showing cause against such enhancement and also the Appellate Court shall not inflict greater punishment for the offence which in its opinion the accused has committed, than might have been inflicted for that offence by the Court passing the order or sentence under appeal.

Appeals against convictions should not be dismissed in limine and in cases where the appellant is in custody. It shall not be dismissed unless the appellant or his pleader is given an opportunity to be heard. In cases where the accused is an indigent person entitled to legal aid and his case has been unrepresented by a lawyer, then the conviction is liable to be set aside.[18]

In a series of judgments the Supreme Court has laid down the principles that govern and regulate the hearing of appeal by the High Court against an order of acquittal passed by the trial court:

a) In an appeal against an order of acquittal, the High Court possesses all the powers it possesses while hearing an appeal against an order of conviction.

b) The High Court has the power to reconsider the whole issue, reappraise the evidence and come to its own conclusion and findings in place of the findings recorded by the trial court, if the said findings are against the weight of the evidence on record, or in other words, perverse.

c) Before reversing the finding of acquittal, the High Court has to consider each ground on which the order of acquittal was based and to record its own reasons for not accepting those grounds and not subscribing to the view expressed by the trial court that the accused is entitled to acquittal.

18 See Khatri vs. State of Bihar (1981) 1 SCC 627, Tyron vs. State of Goa, 1994 SCC (Cri) 1716 and Surendra Kumar vs State, 1996 Cri LJ 3217 (Delhi)

d) In reversing the finding of acquittal, the High Court has to keep in view the fact that the presumption of innocence is still available in favour of the accused and the same stands fortified and strengthened by the order of acquittal passed in his favour by the trial court.

e) If the High Court, on a fresh scrutiny and reappraisal of the evidence and other material on record, is of the opinion that there is another view that can be reasonably taken, then the view that favours the accused should be adopted.

f) The High Court has also to keep in mind that the trial court had the advantage of looking at the demeanour of witnesses and observing their conduct in the Court especially in the witness box.

g) The High Court has also to keep in mind that even at that stage, the accused was entitled to benefit of doubt. The doubt should be such as a reasonable person would honestly and conscientiously entertain as to the guilt of the accused.[19]

The principle to be followed by appellate Court considering the appeal against the judgment of acquittal is to interfere only when there are compelling and substantial reasons for doing so. If the impugned judgment is clearly unreasonable and relevant and convincing materials have been unjustifiably eliminated in the process, it is a compelling reason for interference.[20]

In the Best Bakery case, while setting aside the order of acquittal, the Supreme Court held that, "It is no doubt true that the accused persons have been acquitted by the trial Court and the acquittal has been upheld, but if the acquittal is unmerited and based on tainted evidence, tailored investigation, unprincipled prosecutor and perfunctory trial and evidence of threatened/terrorised witnesses, it is no acquittal in the eye of law and no sanctity or credibility can be attached and given to the so-called findings. It seems to be nothing but a travesty of truth, fraud on legal process and the resultant decision of courts - coram non judis and non est. There is, therefore, every justification to call for interference in these appeals."[21]

The appellate court has the power to suspend the sentence or to grant bail to the accused/appellant whenever it thinks fit. In case of appeals against acquittals, the court can direct the accused to be arrested and brought before it or the subordinate court and the court before which he is brought may commit him to prison or release him on bail (Section 390).

---

19 See Sanwat Singh vs. State of Rajasthan AIR 1961 SC 715 and Ajit Savant Majagvai vs. State of Karnataka (1997) 7 SCC 110; Bhagwan Singh and Ors. v. State of Madhya Pradesh (2002 (2) Supreme 567; Pulicherla Nagaraju @ Nagaraja Reddy vs State of A.P.(2006) 11 SCC 444

20 Shivaji Sahabrao Bobade and Anr. v. State of Maharashtra (AIR 1973 SC 2622), Ramesh Babulal Doshi v. State of Gujarat (1996 (4) Supreme 167), Jaswant Singh v. State of Haryana (2000 (3) Supreme 320), Raj Kishore Jha v. State of Bihar and Ors. (2003 (7) Supreme 152), State of Punjab v. Karnail Singh (2003 (5) Supreme 508 and State of Punjab v. Pohla Singh and Anr. (2003 (7) Supreme 17); V.N. Ratheesh vs State of Kerala (2006) 10 SCC 617

21 Zahira Habibulla H. Sheikh v. State of Gujarat, AIR 2004 SC 3114

Reference

Any subordinate court can refer a case pending before it which in its opinion involves a question as to the validity of any Act, Ordinance or Regulation or any provision thereof the determination of which is necessary for the disposal of the case and the subordinate court is of the opinion that the said provision or Act or Ordinance or Regulation is invalid but has not been declared so by the High Court to which the said court is subordinate or the Supreme Court (Section 395).

Revision

The High Court has the powers of revision, that it can call for and examine the record of any proceeding before any inferior criminal court situated within its local jurisdiction for the purpose of satisfying itself as to the correctness, legality or propriety of any finding, sentence or order recorded or passed and as to the regularity of any proceedings before such inferior court. The High Court can also suspend the execution of any order during the pendency of the revision proceedings (Sections 397 and 401). However, revision does not lie against an interlocutory order. Interlocutory order means an order that is not a final order and an order that is made during the pendency of the case, which does not decide any of the issues involved in the case. A bail order is held to be an interlocutory order and a revision does not lie against it.[22] Revision lies not just against the final orders but against any order which conclusively decides on any issue relating to the case such as the order of issue of process against the accused,[23] order in a discharge application of the accused,[24] dismissal of a complaint and in cases where no appeal lies after the trial court's order. The complainant in cognizable cases does not have the right to file an appeal and can file a revision against the order of acquittal. This is interfered with only in exceptional cases where the interests of public justice require interference for the correction of a manifest illegality, or for the prevention of gross miscarriage of justice. The revisional jurisdiction cannot be invoked merely because the lower court has not appreciated the evidence properly.[25] However, the High Court shall not pass any order to the prejudice of the accused or any other person unless he has had an opportunity to be heard. Revisional powers are exercised only in exceptional cases where there is glaring defect in the procedure or there is a manifest error on point of law and consequently there is a flagrant miscarriage of justice.[26] The accepted rule is that the object of revisional jurisdiction is to confer upon the criminal courts a kind of paternal or

22 Chitra Shankarnarayanan vs. State, (1995) 2 ALT (Cri) 710
23 AIR 1977 SC 2185
24 AIR 1961 AP 117; AIR 1962 AP 236
25 AIR 1975 SC 1854; (1997) 4 Supreme 211
26 AIR 1973 SC 799

supervisory jurisdiction in order to correct miscarriage of justice arising from a misconception of law, irregularity of procedure, neglect of proper precautions, or apparent harshness of treatment which has resulted in some undeserved hardship to the individual or illegality in the order. The High Courts have as a matter of practice recognised a rule that ordinary finding of fact or an order of acquittal should not be interfered within revision.[27]

III. Sessions Court

The Sessions Courts have the same powers as the High Courts in cases of revision and bail. The Sessions Courts can also transfer cases falling within its jurisdiction. The jurisdiction of these courts lies within the territorial limits of the district.

Original Jurisdiction

The Sessions Courts conduct trials of cases specified in the first schedule of the Code of Criminal Procedure, and in case of those offences, which are not listed; the Sessions Court conducts trials where the maximum punishment is imprisonment for a term exceeding 7 years. The Sessions Court, however, has to submit for confirmation to the High Court the proceedings wherein it passes a death sentence.

A case can relate to the commission of more than one offence in the course of the same transaction and these are prosecuted together. Persons accused of more than one offence of the same kind (punishable under the same section) committed within the space of twelve months from the first to the last of offences, whether in respect of the same person or not, can be tried at one trial for any number of them not exceeding three under Section 219 of the CrPC. According to Section 220 of the CrPC, if in one series of acts so connected together as to form the same transaction, the same person commits more than one offence, he may be charged with and tried at the same trial for every such offence. An example of this is that if a person is wrongfully confined and grievous injury is caused to him by another person, then the latter becomes an accused who could be charged with both offences at the same trial. It also states that if the acts alleged constitute an offence falling within two or more separate definitions of any law in force as offences, the accused may be charged with and tried for each of these offences in the same trial. Causing hurt to a child is punishable both under the relevant sections of the Indian Penal Code and under Section 23 of the Juvenile Justice Act, and the accused can be tried under both sections at the same trial. If several acts of which one or more than one would by itself or themselves constitute an offence, as also when combined constitute a different offence, the accused may be charged with and tried at one trial for the offence constituted by such acts when combined and for any offence constituted by

27 AIR 1954 Hyd 129

one or more of the acts. Causing hurt while committing robbery is a separate offence while both the acts individually too are offences. An accused can be charged for all three offences in the same trial. However, under Section 71 of the Indian Penal Code, the accused if convicted should not be sentenced for a period exceeding the maximum penalty imposable by the gravest offence when charged and tried thus.

Under Section 221 of the CrPC, if a single act of series of acts is of such a nature that it is doubtful which of several offences can be proved, the accused may be charged with having committed all or any of such offences. Where a person is charged with one offence and the evidence reveals that he has committed another offence with which he was not charged he might be convicted for the offence with which he is not charged. An example of this is where a woman dies, her husband may be charged with committing murder under Section 302 IPC, for cruelty under Section 498A IPC, for dowry death under Section 304B IPC and after the trial maybe convicted under any of these provisions and even in the event of failure of the court to charge him for any of these or other offences such as Abetment of suicide, if the evidence on record reveals the commission of this offence, he may be convicted for the same. Under Section 72 of the Indian Penal Code, when in such cases, the court concludes that the accused is guilty, but is unsure as to which of the offences he is guilty of, he shall be punished for the offence for which the lowest punishment is provided.

More than one person can commit an offence and they are to be tried jointly even if they are charged under different sections as per the role played by them. Under Section 223 of the CrPC, the following persons maybe charged with and tried together:

a) Persons accused of the same offence committed in the course of the same transaction;

b) Persons accused of more than one offence and persons accused of abetment of, or attempt to commit such offence;

c) Persons accused of more than one offence of the same kind within the meaning of Section 219 committed by them jointly within the period of twelve months;

d) Persons accused of different offences committed in the course of the same transaction;

e) Persons accused of an offence which includes theft, extortion, cheating, or criminal misappropriation, and persons accused of receiving or retaining, or assisting in the disposal or concealment of, property possession of which he is alleged to have been transferred by any such offence committed by the first named persons, or of abetment of or attempting to commit any such last-named offence;

f) Persons accused of offences of dishonestly receiving stolen property knowing it to be stolen (Section 411 IPC) or assisting in its concealment knowing it to be stolen (Section 414 IPC) and wherever the possession of stolen property has been defined as a separate offence;

g) Persons accused of any offence under Chapter XII of the IPC (Offences relating to Coins and Government Stamps) relating to counterfeit coin and persons accused of any other offence under the said Chapter relating to the same coin or of abetment of or attempting to commit any such offence.

Appeals

The Sessions Court can also hear appeals of orders of chapter proceedings held under Chapter VIII of the CrPC (Section 373). Under Section 374, any person convicted on a trial held by a Metropolitan Magistrate or Assistant Sessions Judge or Magistrate of the first class or of the second class, or sentenced under section 325 by the Chief Judicial Magistrate, or in respect of whom an order has been made or a sentence has been passed for release on bond of good behaviour under section 360 by any Magistrate, may appeal to the Court of Session. The Sessions Court can also hear appeals preferred by the State Government against judgments passed by Magistrates convicting the accused for enhancement of sentence. Appeals from an order of acquittal passed by a Magistrate in respect of a cognizable and non-bailable offence by the State shall also lie in the Court of Session (Section 378). The powers of all appellate courts are similar.

IV. Magistrates' Courts

Magistrates' courts are of two types- Executive and Judicial. Executive Magistrates are generally police officers of the rank of the Assistant Commissioner of Police who have certain powers to conduct proceedings under Chapter VIII of the CrPC wherein they have the powers to ask any person to furnish security for keeping peace and for good behaviour. Executive magistrates come under District Magistrates and are appointed by the State government.

Judicial Magistrates are of the first class and of the second class. The First Schedule of the CrPC enlists the cases to be tried by the different categories of magistrates. In cases where the same is not specified, the Magistrate of the first class can try offences which are punishable with imprisonment for 3 years upwards, but not more than 7 years and the Magistrate of the second class can try those offences which are punishable with imprisonment for less than 3 years or with fine only. In every district the High Court shall appoint one Judicial Magistrate of the First Class as the Chief Judicial Magistrate. The High Court may also appoint any Judicial Magistrate of the first class to be an Additional Chief Judicial Magistrate and Sub-divisional Magistrates who shall have all or any of the powers of a Chief Judicial Magistrate as the High Court may specify.

The powers of the Chief Judicial Magistrate include defining the local limits to the areas within which the Magistrates may function, distribute the business among the Judicial Magistrates and exercise general control over them. The Chief Judicial Magistrate is subordinate to the Sessions Judge. The High Court may also appoint any Magistrate as the Special Judicial Magistrate to try any particular case or particular class of cases in a local area.

In metropolitan areas, i.e. areas that have a population of over one million and are notified to be metropolitan areas by the state government, the High Court may appoint Metropolitan Magistrates. It may also appoint a Metropolitan Magistrate to be the Chief Metropolitan Magistrate and any Magistrate to be an Additional Chief Metropolitan Magistrate who shall have the powers of the Chief Metropolitan Magistrate as the High Court may specify. It may also appoint Special Metropolitan Magistrates. In Metropolitan areas, the judicial magistrates are called metropolitan magistrates and they exercise all their functions. All Metropolitan Magistrates are Judicial Magistrates of the First Class (Sections 11 to 18).

The Chief Judicial Magistrate and the Chief Metropolitan Magistrates can pass any sentence authorised by law except a sentence of death or of life imprisonment or of imprisonment for a term exceeding 7 years. The Metropolitan Magistrate or the Judicial Magistrate of the First Class may pass a sentence of imprisonment for a term not exceeding 3 years or of fine not exceeding Rs 10,000 or of both, while a Judicial Magistrate of the Second Class may pass sentence of imprisonment for a term not exceeding 1 year or of fine not exceeding Rs.5,000 or both. The court can award sentence in lieu of fine which should not exceed the substantive sentence and where there is no substantive sentence not more than one-fourth of the term of imprisonment the magistrate is competent to impose (Sections 29 and 30). Whenever a Magistrate is of opinion, after hearing the evidence that the accused is guilty and ought to receive a punishment different in kind, form or more severe than that which he is empowered to inflict, he may record the opinion and submit the proceedings and forward the accused to the Chief Judicial Magistrate, who may examine any party, or recall any witness or take any further evidence and then pass such judgment, sentence or order in the case as he thinks fit, and as is according to law (Section 325).

Apart from trying offences, the Judicial Magistrates also have the powers to grant remand to custody of accused persons and to release them on bail in both bailable and non-bailable offences (Section 436, 436A and 437). The custody of no accused person can be extended beyond a period of 24 hours without the order of remand granted by the magistrate and failure to obtain such order or detention in case of refusal to grant the remand, the custody renders the detention illegal (Section 167 and Article 22(2).. Even in cases, which are triable by the Sessions Courts, the remand is before the magistrate except in cases, which are triable by the Special Courts for, specified offences wherein it is specified that the accused be produced before the Special Judge. In sessions triable cases the cases are committed to the Sessions Court by the Magistrate after the filing of the chargesheet, i.e. after the completion of investigation when it is apparent that the case is a sessions triable one and then the papers are sent over to the concerned Sessions Court where the trial is held (Section 209). The Judicial Magistrates can also record statements of witnesses and confessions of accused persons whether he has the jurisdiction to try the case or not under Section 164 of the CrPC. The Magistrate recording a confession or statement shall forward it to the Magistrate by whom the case is to be tried. The committing magistrate has no powers to discharge and can only ascertain as to whether the case as disclosed by the police report appears to show an offence triable solely by the Sessions Court.[28]

Trials of offences committed by juveniles are conducted by the Juvenile Justice Board. If an adult and a juvenile are charged as being co-accused in an offence, then their trial should be separate.[29]

On Punishment

From the above, it can be seen that the hierarchical structure of the courts is based on the power to punish. It is Section 53 of the Indian Penal Code, which lays down the permissible punishments. They are death, imprisonment for life, imprisonment that can be rigorous i.e., with hard labour or simple, forfeiture of property and fine. Life imprisonment is imprisonment for a term not less than 14 years and can extend upto life. The Government can commute the sentence of death for any other punishment provided in the Indian Penal Code, a sentence for imprisonment for life to imprisonment for a term not exceeding 14 years (except in cases where death is one of the penalties for the offence for which the convict has been sentenced), rigorous imprisonment to simple imprisonment or fine and a sentence of simple imprisonment for fine.[30] When a person has been convicted for more than one offence in the same trial, the court can specify whether the sentences are to run concurrently or subsequent to each other. If a person is convicted for another offence while undergoing imprisonment in a case, the subsequent sentence shall run after the previous sentence has been undergone. The Government can also suspend the sentence. In case of a convict being sentenced to death, he can seek pardon from the President of India or the Governor of a state. The Supreme Court has held that the powers conferred

28 Sanjay Gandhi vs Union of India, 1978 CrLJ 642
29 Juvenile Justice (Care and Protection of Children) Act, 2000
30 Sections 433 and 433A of the CrPC

on the Executive under Articles 72 and 161 of the Constitution of India are not fettered by the statutory provisions and are wider.[31] The Supreme Court has held in Standard Chartered Bank's case[32] where large scale financial irregularities were done by the corporations that there is no immunity from prosecution for companies merely because the prosecution is in respect of offences for which the punishment is mandatory imprisonment. As the company cannot be sentenced to imprisonment, the court cannot impose that punishment, but when imprisonment and fine is the prescribed punishment, the court can impose fine.

Guidelines on Capital Punishment

Capital Punishment has been upheld by the Supreme Court of India but mandatory sentence of death has been struck down as it is not just and fair, taking away the discretion of the Court in the matter of awarding the sentence after giving the accused an opportunity to show cause why the death penalty should not be awarded to him.[33] However, death by way of public hanging has been invalidated, as it constitutes a barbaric penalty that would be a disgrace to any modern civilised society.[34] The sentence of death should not be executed in a cruel, barbarous or degrading manner. The Courts have repeatedly held that death penalty is not unconstitutional and does not offend Article 21 of the Constitution of India. In *Machhi Singh v. State of Punjab*[35], a three-Judge Bench of this Court following the decision in Bachan Singh, observed that in rarest of rare cases when collective conscience of the community is so shocked that it will expect the holders of the judicial power centre to inflict death penalty irrespective of their personal opinion as regards desirability or otherwise of retaining death penalty. The community may entertain such a sentiment in the following circumstances:

I. When the murder is committed in an extremely brutal, grotesque, diabolical, revolting or dastardly manner so as to arouse intense and extreme indignation of the community. For instance, when the house of the victim is set aflame with the end in view to roast him alive in the house when the victim is subjected to inhuman acts of torture or cruelty in order to bring about his or her death; and when the body of the victim is cut into pieces or his body is dismembered in a fiendish manner.

II. When the murder is committed for a motive which evinces total depravity and meanness. For instance when a hired assassin commits murder for the sake of money or reward or a cold-blooded murder is committed with

31 State of Punjab vs Joginder Singh, 1990 CrLJ 1464

32 Standard Chartered Bank vs Directorate of Enforcement, AIR 2005 SC 2622

33 Bachan Singh v. State of Punjab, AIR 1980 SC 898

34 Attorney General vs. Lachma, AIR 1986 SC 467

35 1983(3) SCC 470

a deliberate design in order to inherit property or to gain control over property of a ward or a person under the control of the murderer or vis-a-vis whom the murderer is in a dominating position or in a position of trust, or a murder is committed in the course for betrayal of the motherland.

III. When murder of a member of a Scheduled Caste or minority community etc., is committed not for personal reasons but in circumstances. etc., which arouse social wrath. For instance when such a crime is committed in order to terrorise such persons and frighten them into fleeing from a place or in order to deprive them of, or make them surrender, lands or benefits conferred on them with a view to reverse past injustices and in order to restore the social balance. In cases of 'bride burning' and what are known as 'dowry deaths' or when murder is committed in order to remarry for the sake of extracting dowry once again or to marry another man on account of infatuation.

IV. When the crime is enormous in proportion. For instance when multiple murders say of all or almost all the members of a family or a large number of persons of a particular caste, community, or locality, are committed.

When the victim of murder is (a) an innocent child who could not have or has not provided even an excuse, much less a provocation, for murder (b) a helpless woman or a person rendered helpless by old age or infirmity (c) when the victim is a person vis-a-vis whom the murderer is in a position of domination or trust (d) when the victim is a public figure generally loved and respected by the community for the services rendered by him and the murder is committed for political or similar reasons other than personal reasons.

The Court further observed that in this background the guidelines indicated in the case of Bachan Singh will have to be culled out and applied to the facts of each individual case and where the question of imposing death sentence arises, the following proposition emerge from the case of Bachan Singh:

The extreme penalty of death need not be inflicted except in gravest cases of extreme culpability.

(ii) Before opting for the death penalty the circumstances of the 'offender' also require to be taken into consideration along with the circumstances of the `crime'

(iii) Life imprisonment is the rule and death sentence is an exception. In other words death sentence must be imposed only when life imprisonment appears to be an altogether inadequate punishment having regard to the relevant circumstances of the crime, and provided, and only provided, the option to impose sentence of imprisonment for life cannot be conscientiously exercised having regard to the nature and circumstances of the crime and all the relevant circumstances.

(iv) A balance sheet of aggravating and mitigating circumstances has to be drawn up and in doing so the mitigating circumstances have to be accorded full weightage and a just balance has to be struck between the aggravating and the mitigating circumstances before the option is exercised.

The Court thereafter observed that in order to apply these guidelines the following questions may be answered :

(a) Is there something uncommon about the crime which renders sentence of imprisonment for life inadequate and calls for a death sentence?

(b) Are the circumstances of the crime such that there is no alternative but to impose death sentence even after according maximum weightage to the mitigating circumstances which speak in favour of the offender?

In recent judgments the Supreme Court stressed on the need for proportionality of punishment stating that "The criminal law adheres in general to the principle of proportionality in prescribing liability according to the culpability of each kind of criminal conduct. It ordinarily allows some significant discretion to the Judge in arriving at a sentence in each case, presumably to permit sentences that reflect more subtle considerations of culpability that are raised by the special facts of each case. Judges in essence affirm that punishment ought always to fit the crime; yet in practice sentences are determined largely by other considerations. Sometimes it is the correctional needs of the perpetrator that are offered to justify a sentence. Sometimes the desirability of keeping him out of circulation, and sometimes even the tragic results of his crime. Inevitably these considerations cause a departure from just deserts as the basis of punishment and create cases of apparent injustice that are serious and widespread."[36]

Cruelty and torture are not legal means of punishment in India. The punishments that have been specified for each offence is generally the maximum penalty prescribed for the particular offence and the courts have the discretion to sentence a lesser term except in cases where the mandatory minimum term is prescribed by statute. However, as stated earlier the main method of punishment is imprisonment. Convicts are entitled to remission of sentence for good conduct. Remissions are of three types -- ordinary,

36 Shailesh Jaswantbhai vs State of Gujarat (2006) 2 SCC 359; Siddarama vs State of Karnataka (2006) 10 SCC 673; State of MP vs Babbu Barkare (2005)5SCC413. Also see State of UP vs Virendra Prasad (2004) 9 SCC 37 and State of Karnataka vs Puttaraja (2004)1 SCC 475

which is granted to most prisoners; special, which is granted to prisoners under exceptional circumstances; and State remission granted by the State on important occasions. Parole and furlough leave are also granted to convicts to visit home periodically and on special occasions. Though these are discretionary, they are generally granted upon execution of a bond and furnishing of surety. Undertrials are not entitled to these benefits. Fines are also prescribed as a mandatory penalty in certain offences and in the case of failure to pay fine, the convict has to undergo imprisonment in lieu of fine. However, while the accused is entitled to set off imprisonment undergone as an undertrial in cases where the court awards imprisonment, no set off is awarded in case of sentence in lieu of fine though the undertrial imprisonment term may cover the same. There is a growing trend to compensate the victim by awarding heavy fines which are partly directed to be paid to the victim, especially in rape cases and cases of deaths caused due to a rash and negligent act such as drunken driving, which enables the rich to escape criminal liability by bypassing the punitive sanctions which supposedly form the core difference between civil and criminal law.

CHAPTER 3

CLASSIFICATION OF OFFENCES

The Code of Criminal Procedure classifies offences in various ways according to their degree of gravity.

Cognizable Offences

Cognizable offences are those in which the police can arrest without a warrant (Section 2©). This definition includes the right to investigate on the part of the police. Cognizable offences are serious offences in which the state undertakes the responsibility of prosecuting the offender as these are considered crimes against the State being the representative of public in general in order to prevent the breakdown of law and order. The First Schedule of the Code of Criminal Procedure lays down which offences are cognizable in nature. Examples of these are murder, rape, theft, rioting, robbery, and sedition. Generally, offences punishable with imprisonment of three years or more are cognizable, though certain offences against public order are also cognizable though they are not punishable severely.

In cognizable cases, the victim is not the complainant and does not have to prosecute the offender. Further it is not necessary that only the victim can set the criminal prosecution in motion. Every person knowing or having reason to believe that an offence has been committed is legally bound to give that information to the police and failure to do so is an offence under Section 202 of the Indian Penal Code. Similarly giving false information in order to screen offender or causing disappearance of evidence is also punishable under Section 201 of the IPC. The information received by the police regarding the commission of a cognizable offence may be oral or written. If oral it has to be reduced into writing by the officer in charge of the police station read over to the informant for verification and the signature or thumb impression of the informant obtained (Section 154). This is known as the **First Information Report** or the **FIR** and sets the process of investigation by the police in motion. The first informant need not be the victim or eyewitness to the commission of the offence. Any person having information or knowledge that an offence has been committed who is the first in point of time to give information of the same to the police is the first informant. The police should give a copy of the FIR to the first informant free of cost. A copy of the FIR should be forwarded to the nearest Magistrate immediately (Section 157(1). Any person can peruse the copy of the FIR, which is kept in a file in the court within whose local jurisdiction the police station falls.

In case the police fail to register an FIR on receiving information of the commission of a cognizable offence, then the informant may send the copy of the information to the Superintendent of the Police (and in cities the Assistant Commissioner of Police) who, if satisfied that the information discloses the commission of a cognizable offence, shall either investigate it himself or direct it to be investigated by any officer subordinate to him (Section 154(3)). The informant can also approach the Magistrate having jurisdiction to try the case and ask for a direction to the police to investigate the case (Section 156(3).

The police cannot refuse to register an FIR because the particular police station does not have the jurisdiction to investigate the offence, but should register the FIR and forward it to the police station, which has the jurisdiction to try the same.[37]

Non-Cognizable Offences

Offences, which are not cognizable, i.e. in which the police do not have the power to investigate or arrest, are non-cognizable offences (Section 2(l). These are considered to be petty offences more in the nature of private wrong than a public wrong. The victim has to bring in the prosecution in these cases personally and the State is not the prosecutor. It is not necessary to inform the police in the case of a commission of a non-cognizable offence and if the same is reported, then the police have to enter the substance of the information in a N.C. Register and give a receipt of the same to the informant. A police officer can only investigate a non-cognizable offence if he receives an order to do so from a Magistrate empowering him to do so. However, if the case registered by the police relates to two or more offences, of which at least one is cognizable, then the police officer can investigate notwithstanding the fact that the other offences are non-cognizable (Section 155). In the case of prosecution of a non-cognizable offence, the complainant or complainants, in case there is more than one, should file a private complaint before the Magistrate having jurisdiction to try the said offence. Calling the accused person to the police station upon receipt of information of a non-cognizable offence is illegal and the concerned officer is liable to be prosecuted for unlawful restraint or confinement. The police have absolutely no powers to take any steps without the specific directions of the Magistrate and attempts to settle civil disputes and non-cognizable offences in police stations amounts to usurping of judicial powers by the police which amounts to criminal contempt as it undermines the dignity of the courts. It is not mandatory to launch prosecution in the case of commission of non-cognizable offences unlike cognizable offences, nor is it necessary to inform the police of the same. However, in certain cases it is advisable to lodge an N.C with the police as a precaution for future action. This should be done when a person receives threats from another, where if subsequently harm is caused; it helps in proving enmity and motive. Or in

37 State of Andhra Pradesh vs. Punati Ramulu, AIR 1993 SC 2644

cases of domestic violence, where subsequently these N.C. form a part of the evidence in a divorce case or if a subsequent serious incident gives rise to the commission of a cognizable offence. The Assistant Commissioner of Police who also has the powers of an Executive Magistrate can initiate chapter proceedings against someone against whom several N.C. have been filed which that the person is likely to commit a breach of the peace or disturb the public tranquility.

Generally in non-cognizable cases, the accused is not arrested but summoned to the court to answer the charge. The court after verifying the complaint, issues summons to the accused to appear before the court on a specific date and the accused has to remain present before the court on all the dates when the case is being heard unless his presence has been exempted by the court. However, if the accused fails to remain present or if there is a reasonable apprehension that the accused is likely to abscond and avoid the process of the court, the court may at any time issue a warrant of arrest against the accused. This warrant may be bailable or non-bailable. A bailable warrant is one in which the court specifies that the accused may be released on furnishing bail of a specified amount while in case of a non-bailable warrant, there is no direction for release on bail.

Bail

As stated earlier, a cognizable offence is one where the police can arrest without a warrant. This means that a person can be detained on the allegation of the commission of an offence before the same is proved against him. The rationale for the same differs from case to case. Generally the police do this in order to facilitate investigation. By removing the accused from the place, there is no apprehension of tampering or disappearance of evidence or intimidation to witnesses. It also prevents the likelihood of commission of further offences by the accused. It also enables the police to interrogate the accused in custody. It is also considered necessary for maintenance of public order and to prevent the accused from absconding in order to avoid the proceeding and punishment. An accused that is in legal detention remains in custody till granted bail. Bail is not defined under the Criminal Procedure Code. Put simply, bail is release of accused pending the trial of the offence. According to the Law Lexicon, the word "Bail" is understood as security for the appearance of prisoner at the time of trial of the case and can be defined as meaning to set at liberty a person arrested or imprisoned on security being taken for the appearance on a day and at a certain place and such a security is called bail because the party arrested or imprisoned is delivered into the hands of those who bind themselves for his forthcoming in order that he may be safely released from jail. Bail is of three types-

a) **Surety** - the accused is directed to furnish surety of a specified sum of money. A surety is a person who stands as a guarantor for the accused and undertakes to keep the accused present in court whenever directed, assist in the investigation of the case and comply with any other condition specified in the bail order. In case of his failure to do so, the surety will be summoned to the court and forfeits the sum of money specified in the surety bond. The court has the discretion to grant forfeiture of a lesser sum, but the surety has to show solvency and ability to pay the sum specified in the bond. Generally bail is granted on furnishing of surety. A surety in order to show solvency has to show that he is gainfully employed and earning the sum specified, or having property of the specified sum. Apart from this, the surety has to show that he is a resident of the area within the local jurisdiction of the court, has no criminal antecedents and has not stood as a surety in any pending case. This last requirement is incorporated in order to prevent professional sureties from perpetuating. The surety has to be a person who personally knows the accused and has to furnish details of the relationship with the accused. The court may accept surety on perusal of the documents furnished by the surety including any identification papers, or direct a police verification of the details furnished. The requirements of the documents to be furnished by the surety vary in different areas. Under Section 441A, every person standing surety to an accused person for his release on bail, shall make a declaration before the Court as to the number of persons to whom he has stood surety including the accused, giving therein all the relevant particulars. The Supreme Court has held that rejection of surety on ground that he is from different district or his property is situated in a different district is discriminatory and illegal.[38]

b) **Cash Bail** -- the accused furnishes the cash amount specified in the bail bond in order to be released on bail. In case of the failure of the accused to comply with any condition of bail or failure to remain present in court, the cash amount remitted by him is forfeited entirely or in part. If the accused complies with the directions of bail order, after the completion of trial the amount is refunded to him.

c) **Personal Recognisant Bond** -- this is release of the accused on his own bond. The accused undertakes to remain present in court till the completion of trial and co-operate with the investigating agency in the investigation of the case. In case of his failure to do so, he undertakes to forfeit a specified sum of money to the court. Every accused released on bail has to furnish this undertaking along with the cash or surety furnished. However, release only on Personal Recognisant Bond is generally given to persons who are accused of non-serious or technical offences. The courts are extremely reluctant to grant PR bond in most cases, as they fear that there will be no pressure on the accused to remain present even in minor offences. The Supreme Court has in several judgments stated

38 Motiram vs. State of Madhya Pradesh, AIR 1978 SC 1584

that PR bond should be granted to poor people who lack the resources to furnish surety or cash. The Court has deprecated the property-oriented approach towards grant of bail, which effectively leads to denial of bail to the poor. The Court has advocated a community-oriented approach to bail, which takes into account the roots of the accused in his community and a policy in favour of grant of bail.[39] In Hussainara Khatoon's case,[40] the Supreme Court has held that it should use the following criteria to satisfy itself that the accused has his roots n the community which would deter him from fleeing if released on his personal bond:

i. The length of his residence in the community;

ii. His employment status, history and financial condition;

iii. His family ties and relationships;

iv. His reputation, character and monetary condition;

v. His prior criminal record including any record of prior release on recognisance bond;

vi. The identity of responsible persons in the community who would vouch for his reliability;

vii. The nature of the offence charged and the apparent probability of conviction and the likely sentence insofar as these factors are relevant to the risk of non-appearance; and

viii. Any other factors indicating the ties of the accused to the community or bearing on the risk of wilful failure to appear.

However, the Court has failed to lay down in unambiguous terms grant of bail on PR bond in certain specific cases or to specific underprivileged classes and left the same to the discretion of the individual authority, which has resulted in the under-utilisation of this provision except in cases of bailable offences.

The Supreme Court has held that refusal to grant bail to the accused only on the ground that he is from a different state and may abscond from the jurisdiction of the court is not justified.[41]

Section 229A of the IPC enacted by the Code Of Criminal Procedure (Amendment) Act, 2005 makes it an offence if the person charged with an offence and released on bail or on bond without sureties, fails without sufficient cause (the burden of proving which shall lie upon him), to appear in Court in accordance with the terms of the bail or bond, shall be punished with imprisonment of either description for a term which may extend to one year, or with fine, or with both. The said offence is cognizable and non bailable. The punishment under this

39 Ibid. Also see the Hussainara Khatoon judgments I to VII reported in (1980) 1 SCC 81,91,93,98,108 and 115 and (1995) 5 SCC 326

40 (1980) 1 SCC 91

41 Sanjay vs State of Gujarat (2002) 10 SCC 403

section is in addition to the punishment to which the offender would be liable on a conviction for the offence with which he has been charged and without prejudice to the power of the Court to order forfeiture of the bond.

Bail can also be granted under Section 167(2) of the Cr.P.C upon failure to file chargesheet on completion of investigation within the stipulated period. Thus, investigation has to be completed and chargesheet filed within 90 days of the date of arrest of the accused, where the investigation relates to an offence punishable with death, imprisonment for life or imprisonment for a term of not less than 10 years and in any other offence, for a period not exceeding 60 days. This right of the accused to be released on bail can be claimed by the accused till the filing of the chargesheet and if the same were not claimed before the filing of the chargesheet, even if it is filed after the lapse of the stipulated period, the accused would not be entitled to bail.[42] However, the Supreme Court in *Aslam Babulal Desai's case*[43] has held that bail granted under the proviso to Section 167(2) of the CrPC cannot be cancelled on subsequent filing of the chargesheet.

Bailable Offences

Certain offences are not considered very grave and it is not considered necessary to keep the accused in prolonged custody till trial to protect public interest or facilitate investigation. In such cases the accused has a right to be granted bail immediately on arrest. These offences are known as Bailable offences. Examples of bailable offences are unlawful assembly, rioting (Sections 143 to 148 and 150 to 153), causing death by rash and negligent act (Section 304A), voluntarily causing hurt (Sections 323), wrongful restraint or confinement (Sections 341 to348), assault (Sections 352 to 358) and kidnapping (Section 363). The accused has a right to be released by either the police officer in charge of the police station or the Magistrate when he is produced before them upon arrest upon his readiness and ability to furnish bail. Provided that when such accused is indigent and is unable to furnish surety, the person may be discharged on his executing a bond without sureties for his appearance. When a person who has been released on bail is unable to furnish the same within a week of the date of his arrest, the police officer or Court shall presume that the person is indigent and release him on his personal recognizant bond (Section 436). In case a person has been arrested for a bailable offence, the officer arresting him has to inform him that he is entitled to be released on bail (Section 50). Upon granting bail, the officer or the court can impose any conditions other than attendance of the case, such as bar on leaving the district without the permission of the court or attendance to the police station. The court has the powers to cancel bail in the case on the violation of any of the conditions including failure to remain present in court.

42 Abdul Wahid vs. State of Maharashtra, 1992 Mh.L.J. 595
43 AIR 1993 SC 1

Non-Bailable Offences

In certain cases, the offence is considered so grave that the law considers it expedient not to release an accused unless circumstances so warrant. Such offences are categorised as Non-Bailable offences. The first schedule of the Code of Criminal Procedure specifies which of the offences in the Indian Penal Code are bailable and which are non-bailable. It also specifies that in other penal statutes, all offences punishable with imprisonment of less than three years or fine only are bailable while the other more serious offences are non-bailable. This does not mean that bail is generally not to be granted in non-bailable offences. It is discretionary to release the accused on bail and it is not to be granted as a matter of of right. Generally, in a non-bailable offence also, bail should be granted by the Magistrate except in the following cases-

a) If there are reasonable grounds for believing that he has been guilty of an offence punishable with death or with life imprisonment

b) When the accused is arrested for a cognizable offence and he had been previously convicted of an offence punishable with death, imprisonment for life or imprisonment for seven years or more, or he had been convicted previously on two or more occasions of a cognizable offence punishable with imprisonment for three years or more but not less than seven years.

However, even in the above cases the Magistrate may grant bail if the accused is below 16 years of age (under the Juvenile Justice Act, bail has to be mandatorily granted except if it is not in the best interest of the juvenile), woman or is sick or infirm. The court can also grant bail if it considers it just and proper for any other special reason. Bail should not be denied only on ground that the accused is to be identified by the witness and hence should remain in custody. However the court should not grant bail to a person alleged to have committed an offence punishable with death, imprisonment for life, or imprisonment for seven years without giving an opportunity of hearing to the Public Prosecutor. When a person is accused or suspected of the commission of an offence punishable with 7 years or more or of an offence under Chapter VI (Offences Against the State), Chapter XVI (Offences affecting the Human Body) and Chapter XVII (Offences against Property) of the Indian Penal Code, or abetment or conspiracy or attempt to commit any such offence, is released on bail then the court shall impose the following conditions:

- that such person shall attend in accordance with the conditions of the bond executed under this Chapter,

- that such person shall not commit an offence similar to the offence of which he is accused, or suspected, of the commission of which he is suspected, and

- that such person shall not directly or indirectly make any inducement, threat or promise to any person acquainted with the facts of the case so as to dissuade him from disclosing such facts to the Court or to any police officer or tamper with the evidence
- and may also impose, in the interests of justice, such other conditions as it considers necessary.[44]

Under Section 436A, an undertrial who is charged with an offence not punishable with death has undergone detention for a period extending up to one-half of the maximum period of imprisonment specified for that offence, he shall be released by the Court on his personal bond with or without sureties unless the court after hearing the Public Prosecutor, for reasons to be recorded by it in writing, order the continued detention of such person or release on bail other than personal bond. But in no case shall the person be detained for longer than the maximum imprisonment. In computing the period of detention under this section for granting bail the period of detention passed due to delay in proceeding caused by the accused shall be excluded.

The Sessions Court and the High Court have wider powers to grant bail and there are no similar bars on their discretion. These courts also have the powers to modify a bail order passed by this or a lower court including reduction of bail amount and any other conditions. These courts can also cancel bail already granted (Sections 439 and 440(2). Bail can be cancelled only when it is shown that the conditions of bail are violated, the accused has interfered with the investigation, tampered with evidence, threatened witness, is likely to flee to another country or on the arising of any other material circumstance subsequent to the grant of bail which justify the cancellation of bail including subsequent investigation revealing the commission of a more serious offence than that disclosed by the FIR. Cancellation of bail should not be done mechanically. The fact that the accused has while on bail committed another offence is not a ground for cancellation of bail.[45] The victim in the non-bailable offence can oppose grant of bail or move for cancellation.

The court while granting bail in non-bailable cases especially where the trial has not yet commenced takes into account the following considerations:

a) The nature and seriousness of the offence;

b) The character of the evidence, i.e. whether there are reasonable grounds for believing that the accused is guilty of such an offence;

c) Circumstances which are peculiar to the accused, such as age, gender, health, family responsibilities, motive for the commission of the offence and the criminal antecedents of the accused;

44 Section 437

45 Bhagirathsinh vs State of Gujarat, AIR 1984 SC 372

d) Reasonable possibility of the presence of the accused not being secured at the time of the trial;

e) Reasonable apprehension of witnesses being tampered with if the accused is released on bail;

f) Frivolity in prosecution and doubt as to the genuineness of the prosecution;

g) The larger interest of the public and the State;

h) Similar other considerations which arise in the case.[46]

The power of granting bail is a matter of judicial discretion and the chief consideration in the exercise of that discretion is the likelihood of the person failing to appear at the trial. A detailed examination of merits and demerits of the case is not required and the court should examine whether a prima facie case is made out.[47]

In Kalyan Chandra Sarkar's case[48] the Supreme Court held that personal liberty is a constitutional guarantee. However, Article 21 which guarantees the above right also contemplates deprivation of personal liberty by procedure established by law. Under the criminal laws of this country, a person accused of offences which are non bailable is liable to be detained in custody during the pendency of trial unless he is enlarged on bail in accordance with law. Such detention cannot be questioned as being violative of Article 21 since the same is authorised by law. But even persons accused of non bailable offences are entitled for bail if the court concerned comes to the conclusion that the prosecution has failed to establish a prima facie case against him and/or if the court is satisfied for reasons to be recorded that in spite of the existence of prima facie case there is a need to release such persons on bail where fact situations require it to do so. In that process a person whose application for enlargement on bail is once rejected is not precluded from filing a subsequent application for grant of bail if there is a change in the fact situation. In such cases if the circumstances then prevailing requires that such persons to be released on bail, in spite of his earlier applications being rejected, the courts can do so. Though the principles of res judicata and such analogous principles are not applicable in a criminal proceeding, the courts are bound by the doctrine of judicial discipline having regard to the hierarchical system prevailing in our country. The findings of a

46 Capt. Jagjit Singh AIR 1962 SC 253; Gurcharan Singh v. State (Delhi Admn.) AIR 1978 SC 179; Jayendra Saraswathi Swamigal vs State of Tamil Nadu (2005)2 SCC 13

Also see Prahlad Singh Bhati vs. NCT, Delhi (2001) 4 SCC 2805; Ram Govind Upadhyay vs. Sudarshan Singh (2002) 3 SCC 598; Jayendra Saraswathi Swamigal vs State of Tamil Nadu (2005) 2 SCC 13

47 Puran vs Rambilas, (2001)3 LRI 103

48 (2005) 2 SCC 42

higher court or a coordinate bench must receive serious consideration at the hands of the court entertaining a bail application at a later stage when the same had been rejected earlier. In such an event, the courts must give due weight to the grounds which weighed with the former or higher court in rejecting the bail application. Ordinarily, the issues which had been canvassed earlier would not be permitted to be re-agitated on the same grounds, as it would lead to a speculation and uncertainty in the administration of justice and may lead to forum hunting.

Anticipatory Bail

The Sessions and the High courts have the power to grant **anticipatory bail**. This is granted in non-bailable cases prior to arrest. Anticipatory bail is granted discretionally depending on the circumstances of the case. It is not a right and is not granted as a rule. It is not a direction to the police not to arrest, but to release the accused on bail upon arrest. Any person who is apprehending arrest for the commission of a non-bailable offence may make an application for anticipatory bail. The apprehension should be based on some reasonable grounds, though it is not necessary that a FIR should have been filed. But a person cannot be granted a blanket bail order and the offence in respect of which the bail order will be effective should be specified by the court though the normal rule is not to limit the operation of the order in relation to a period of time. There is no foreclosure of categories for which anticipatory bail cannot be granted and the courts have wide discretionary powers to grant the same in any case that it thinks fit.[49] Anticipatory bail can be granted by that court within whose local jurisdiction the applicant resides, even though the offence may be relating to the area not under its local jurisdiction. Generally anticipatory bail should not be granted without hearing the Public Prosecutor. While granting anticipatory bail, the court may, after taking into consideration, inter alia, the following factors, namely:

(i) the nature and gravity of the accusation;

(ii) the antecedents of the applicant including the fact as to whether he has previously undergone imprisonment on conviction by a Court in respect of any cognizable offence;

(iii) the possibility of the applicant to flee from justice; and

(iv) where the accusation has been made with the object of injuring or humiliating the applicant by having him so arrested,

either reject the application forthwith or issue an interim order for the grant of anticipatory bail. Before passing the final order the Public Prosecutor shall

49 Gurbaksh Singh vs. State of Punjab, AIR 1980 SC 1632

be heard after being given notice at least seven days in advance. The Accused has to remain present in the court when the matter comes up for hearing. The Court while granting anticipatory bail may impose any of the conditions it does while granting ordinary bail and in addition it may impose any of the following conditions-

1. That the person shall make himself available for interrogation by a police officer as and when required;
2. That the person shall not, directly or indirectly make any threat, inducement or promise to any person acquainted with the facts of the case so as to dissuade him from disclosing such facts to the Court or to any police officer;
3. That the person shall not leave India without the previous permission of the Court.[50]

Anticipatory bail can be filed only when there is reason to believe that the person apprehends arrest and the grounds for this apprehension should be capable of being examined. Mere fear or vague apprehension is not sufficient ground. The order of bail cannot be a blanket order and should not be an order restraining arrest but orders release on bail when arrested. The Supreme Court has held in several recent judgments that anticipatory bail does not last until the end of the trial but is only for a duration and thereafter the regular court should grant bail on the basis of the chargesheet filed or evidence before it.[51] There is no limit to the number of bail applications that a person can make. Rejection of bail once is no bar to subsequent bail application in the same court where the accused can show a change in the circumstances since the previous application that can include factors such as long period of detention, completion of investigation, lack of material against him and others. An accused need not approach the lowest court at the first instance, though rejection of bail by the higher court would be a bar to approaching the lower court at a later date, except in case the earlier order was in an anticipatory bail application or where the higher court gives the accused the permission to approach the lower court. But the convention is to place the subsequent bail applications made to the same court before the same judge if available in order to prevent abuse of the judicial process.[52] There is nothing in the Code of Criminal Procedure stating that a bail application should be written or should be made only through a lawyer, though the practice is generally that. Interim bail is permissible but in serious cases the prosecution may, wherever possible be heard. Bail should not be refused nor

50 Section 438, CrPC

51 Salauddin Abdulsamad Shaikh vs State of Maharashtra, AIR 1996 SC 1042; K.L. Verma vs State (1996) 7 SCALE 20; Nirmal Jeet Kaur vs State of MP (2004)7 SCC 558; Sunita Devi vs State of Bihar, AIR 2005 SC 498; Adri Dharan Das vs State of West Bengal, (2005) 4 SCC 303: AIR 2005 SC1057

52 Shahgad Hassan Khan vs., Istiaq Hassan Khan, 1987 Cri.L.J. 157

prohibitive bail insisted upon merely on the ground that the police desire it but the court may take into consideration the information supplied and the reports made by the police. Generally, if there are more than one accused in a case and bail is granted to one or more accused, the rest of the accused should be granted bail too on grounds of parity unless the nature of the evidence against the accused differs or because of certain circumstances peculiar to the accused, such as past criminal history or where the co-accused has been granted bail on special grounds.

Cancellation of Bail

In *Gurcharan Singh vs State (Delhi Administration)* [53] the Supreme Court held that bail can be cancelled if the order of grant of bail is perverse and passed by ignoring the material and evidence on record. Bail can be cancelled when it is shown that the conditions of bail are violated, the accused has interfered with the investigation, tampered with evidence, threatened witness, is likely to flee to another country or on the arising of any other material circumstance subsequent to the grant of bail which justify the cancellation of bail including subsequent investigation revealing the commission of a more serious offence than that disclosed by the FIR. Cancellation of bail should not be done mechanically. The fact that the accused has while on bail committed another offence is not a ground for cancellation of bail.[54] In Ram Govind Upadhyay vs. Sudarshan Singh[55], the Supreme Court has held that the conditions for cancellation of bail are different from those for the grant of bail. The basic criteria for cancellation is interference or attempt to interfere with the administration of justice and/or abuse of privilege granted. The Court in Raghubir Singh's[56] case has held that the conditions for cancellation of both regular bail and anticipatory bail are the same, i.e. (i) the accused misuses his liberty by indulging in similar criminal activity; (ii) interferes with the course of investigation; (iii) attempts to tamper with evidence or witnesses; (iv) threatens witnesses or indulges in similar activities which would hamper smooth investigation; (v) there is likelihood of his fleeing to another country; (vi) attempts to make himself scarce by going underground or becoming unavailable to the investigating agency; (vii) attempts to place himself beyond the reach of his surety etc. The court held that these grounds are illustrative and not exhaustive. But cautioned that it must be remembered that rejection of bail and cancellation of bail stand on different footing and the latter is a harsh order because it interferes with the liberty of the individual and hence must not be lightly resorted to.

53 (1988) 1 SCC 118: AIR 1988 SC 179

54 Bhagirathsinh vs State of Gujarat, AIR 1984 SC 372

55 2002 Cri. L.J 1849. Also see State through C.B.I.Vs. Amarmani Tripathi, (2005)8SCC21; Union of India. vs. Rajesh Ranjan Alias Pappu Yadav 2004 7 SCC 539 (I) and Kalyan Chandra Sarkar vs. Rajesh Ranjan Anr. 2004 7 SCC 528 (II)

56 Raghubir Sing vs State of Bihar, (1986) 4 SCC 481. Also see Mehboob Dawood Shaikh vs State of Maharashtra (2004)2 SCC362

Compoundable and Non-Compoundable Offences

Section 320 of the Code of Criminal Procedure allows for the settlement of criminal prosecutions between the accused and the victim. This is known as compounding the case. Not all offences can be compounded, but even in some of the cognizable cases the parties have the right to compound the cases by themselves and in certain other cases with the permission of the court. Examples of the former are causing hurt, wrongfully restraining the person, assault or use of criminal force, criminal trespass, house trespass, criminal breach of contract of service and adultery. Examples of the latter are voluntarily causing hurt by dangerous weapons or means, voluntarily causing grievous hurt, wrongfully confining a person for ten days or more, assault or use of criminal force against woman with the intent to outrage her modesty, theft, including theft by servant or receiving stolen property where the value of the property stolen does not exceed Rs.250, dishonest misappropriation of property, criminal breach of trust including that by carrier or servant where the value of the property does not exceed Rs.250, cheating and bigamy.

The abetment of a compoundable offence is also compoundable. In case the person competent to compound the offence is dead, a minor or insane, his legal representative can compound the offence on his behalf with the permission of the court. When the accused has been committed for trial or when he has been convicted and an appeal is pending, composition of the offence will be allowed only with the permission of the court to which he has been committed or before which the appeal is to be heard. In a revision proceeding also, a court may allow for the composition of a compoundable offence. The effect of the composition shall be the acquittal of the accused in the case. However, no case shall be compounded if the accused is by reason of a previous conviction, liable either to enhanced punishment or to a punishment of a different kind for such offence. If a person has been accused in a case of both compoundable and non-compoundable offences, the Magistrate has the powers to refuse the composition of any of the offences. It is also the obligation of the court to not grant permission without inquiring whether the complainant has entered into compromise voluntarily. Though the courts have allowed compounding in several non-compoundable offences, in Ram Lal vs State of Jammu and Kashmir, the Supreme Court held that same is not permissible in law though the settlement between the parties can be taken into consideration while sentencing the accused.[57] In B.S. Joshi vs State of Haryana[58] the Supreme Court held that in case of non-compoundable offences, where the parties had settled the matter, they could approach the High

57 In the said case, the Court held that its earlier judgments in Mahesh Chand vs. State of Rajasthan, AIR 1988 SC 2111 and Y. Suresh Babu vs State of A.P (1987)2 JT(SC) 361 were per incurium. In a later judgment, Jetta Ram vs State of Rajasthan, (2006) 9 SCC 255 the Court has confirmed that sentence can be reduced in case of a settlement

58 (2003) 4 SCC 675

Court in the exercise of its jurisdiction under Section 482 Cr PC and the court could quash the proceedings in the interest of justice.

In cognizable offences where the Public Prosecutor or the Assistant Public Prosecutor are conducting the prosecution, he may with the consent of the court, at any time before the judgment is pronounced, withdraw the prosecution of the case against any accused either generally or in respect of any one or more offences. The Supreme Court has laid down the following guidelines for the exercise of this discretion by the Public Prosecutor:

a) Under the scheme of the Code of Criminal Procedure, the prosecution of an offender for a serious offence is primarily the responsibility of the Executive;

b) The withdrawal from the prosecution is an executive function of the Public Prosecutor;

c) The discretion to withdraw from the prosecution is that of the Public Prosecutor and none else, and so, he cannot surrender that discretion to someone else;

d) The Government may suggest to the Public Prosecutor that he may withdraw from the prosecution but none can compel him to do so;

e) The Public Prosecutor may withdraw from the prosecution not merely on the ground of paucity of evidence, but on other relevant grounds as well as in order to further the broad ends of public justice, public order and peace. The broad ends of justice will include appropriate social, economic and political purposes;

f) The Public Prosecutor is an officer of the court and responsible to the court;

g) The court performs a supervisory function in granting its consent to the withdrawal;

h) The court's duty is not to re-appreciate the grounds which led the Public Prosecutor to request withdrawal from the prosecution but to consider whether the Public Prosecutor applied his mind as a free agent uninfluenced by irrelevant and extraneous considerations. The court has a special duty in this regard, as it is the ultimate repository of legislative confidence in granting or withholding its consent to withdrawal. [59]

In Abdul Karim vs State of Karnataka[60] too the Court reiterated that the Public Prosecutor has to independently apply his mind to all the relevant material and reach his own satisfaction regarding the need for withdrawal from prosecution in good faith disregarding any decision, order or direction of the Government

59 Rajender Kumar Jain vs. State, 1980 Cri.L.J 1084 at Para 25 on Page 1096

60 (2000) 8 SCC 710; Also see S.K. Shukla vs State of U.P (2006)1 SCC 314

in that regard. He must briefly set out the material considered by him in his application or affidavit. The Court has to be satisfied that on the basis of such material PP's satisfaction was bona fide, in public interest and will not thwart or stifle the process of law or cause manifest injustice and thereafter grant an informed consent for withdrawal.

In Rahul Agarwal vs Rakesh Jain's case,[61] the Supreme Court discussed the entire case law regarding when a case maybe permitted to be withdrawn and held that the court should permit withdrawal only in the interest of justice. Even if the Government directs the Public Prosecutor to withdraw the prosecution and an application is filed to that effect, the court must consider all relevant circumstances and find out whether the withdrawal of prosecution would advance the cause of justice. If the case is likely to end in an acquittal and the continuance of the case is only causing severe harassment to the accused, the court may permit withdrawal of the prosecution. If the withdrawal of prosecution is likely to bury the dispute and bring about harmony between the parties and it would be in the best interest of justice, the court may allow the withdrawal of prosecution. The discretion under Section 321 Code of Criminal Procedure is to be carefully exercised by the Court having due regard to all the relevant facts and shall not be exercised to stifle the prosecution which is being done at the instance of the aggrieved parties or the State for redressing their grievance. Every crime is an offence against the society and if the accused committed an offence, society demands that he should be punished. Punishing the person who perpetrated the crime is an essential requirement for the maintenance of law and order and peace in the society. Therefore, the withdrawal of the prosecution shall be permitted only when valid reasons are made out for the same.

61 (2005)2 SCC 377

CHAPTER 4

INVESTIGATION OF OFFENCES

Registration of the First Information Report (FIR)

The police are empowered under the law to investigate cognizable offences. As stated earlier, the investigation process begins with the receipt of information of the occurrence of a cognizable offence upon which the police have to lodge a FIR or First Information Report. The FIR need not name the accused -- it can even state that unknown persons have committed the offence. Where unknown persons commit the offence, their description should be stated where the witness has seen the accused. The FIR should as far as possible have all the facts relating to the offence. While it is not necessary to record every detail, important facts should not be omitted as it will amount to contradictions and omissions that will affect the credibility of the witness and the benefit of this will go to the accused. However, the FIR is not meant to be encyclopaedia and its objective is to set the machinery of law into motion against the delinquent persons and as long as the broad features of the prosecution case are unfolded in the FIR, it hardly matters if details are absent in it.[62] The Supreme Court has held that mentioning of the names of witnesses in the FIR is not necessary.[63] It is the responsibility of the police to elicit proper and correct details from the informant and duly record all the important facts that they often fail to do so, weakening the prosecution case.

A telephonic message which discloses the commission of a cognizable offence can be considered an FIR when it is given to an officer in charge of a police station, the person giving the message is an ascertained one or is capable of being ascertained, the information is reduced into writing and the information is a complete one and not cryptic or incomplete in details.[64] In a case where information was furnished by a person without disclosing his identity but disclosing the name of the offender and the place of the offence and where the evidence of the crime was being destroyed, the information was allowed to be treated as an FIR.[65] A confessional FIR is not admissible in evidence.[66]

62 Bistar vs. State of Maharashtra, (1994) 3 BCR 675 (Bom)

63 Bhagwan Singh vs State of MP, AIR 2002 SC 1621; Chittarlal vs State of Rajasthan, AIR 2003 SC 3590; State of MP vs Man Singh, (2003) 6 Supreme 202; State of Madhya Pradesh vs Dahrkole, 2005 CrLJ 108

64 1989 Cri. L.J 1350

65 1977 Cr.L.J. 107; 1980 Cr.L.J. 1397

66 Bhenu Singh vs. State of Rajasthan, (1994) 2 SCC 467

Generally, the FIR should be recorded promptly. Delay in the recording of the FIR raises doubt as to thé truth of the allegation and give rise to the suspicion that the story is fabricated or improved upon, or at best the person is likely to have forgotten some important details. Inordinate delay in recording the FIR casts a cloud of suspicion regarding the truth of the prosecution case, but delay if properly explained will not be of much consequence. Generally, in rape cases, the courts are expected to take a lenient view as the hesitance on the part of the victim and her family is considered natural. However, in a case of delay of five years in lodging of the FIR against a Government servant for corrupt practices, after he was allowed to retire, the Supreme Court quashed the same[67]. Where there was a delay in the dispatch of the FIR but the court came to a conclusive finding that the same was not ante-timed on the basis of the evidence on record, the Supreme Court held that no adverse view can be taken.[68] However, in Kunju Muhammed vs State of Kerala,[69] the Supreme Court set aside the conviction by the High Court where there was a delay of 36 hours in dispatching the FIR to the Magistrate as the delay was not explained and the medical evidence raised a doubt as to the time of occurrence. Similarly in Gorle S Naidu vs State of AP[70], where the house of the eye witness was near the police and he could not explain the delay in the registration of the FIR, the prosecution story was considered doubtful. In Ram Jag and Ors. v. The State of U.P.[71] the Supreme Court held that "Whether the delay is so long as to throw a cloud of suspicion on the deeds of prosecution case must depend upon a variety of factors. Even a long delay can be condoned if the witnesses have no motive for implicating, the accused. On the other hand, prompt filing of the reports is not an unmistakable guarantee of the truthfulness of the version of the prosecution. It is true that witnesses cannot be called upon to explain every hour's delay in filing information and a commonsense view has to be taken in ascertaining whether the First Information Report was lodged after an undue delay so as to afford enough scope for manipulating evidence."

FIR is an important document but that by itself cannot be the basis to decide the culpability of the assailants in every case. The FIR is not a substantive piece of evidence, and can be used to corroborate or contradict the statement of the maker in the court.[72]

An FIR lodged by the police station not having territorial jurisdiction to register the criminal case cannot be quashed on this ground.[73] A continuing offence

67 State of AP vs. Pavithran, AIR 1990 SC 1266
68 Anil Sharma vs State of Jharkhand, 2004 CrLJ 2527
69 (2004)9 SCC 193
70 2004 CrLJ 924
71 MANU/SC/0150/1973; Also see Ravi Kumar Vs. State of Punjab, (2005)9SCC315
72 Apren Joseph vs. State of Kerala , AIR 1973 SC 1
73 Satvinder Kaur vs State (Govt. of NCT of Delhi) 1999 CrLJ 4566

committed in more than one local area could be filed in any of the areas.[74] Successive FIRs cannot be lodged with regards the same incident, but cross case is permissible.[75]

The investigation by the police generally comprises of --

a) Proceeding to the spot;
b) Ascertainment of the facts and circumstances of the case;
c) Discovery and arrest of the suspected offender;
d) Collection of the evidence relating to the commission of the offence which may consist of:
    i) An examination of various persons including the accused and recording of their statements if the Investigating Officer thinks it necessary
    ii) The search of places, seizure of things considered necessary for the investigation and to be produced at the time of trial;
e) Formation of opinion as to whether it is a fit case for the accused to be sent up for the trial and if so, taking steps to file chargesheet. [76]

Arrest of the Accused

In a cognizable offence, the police have the right to arrest anyone suspected of having committed the offence even if the FIR does not name the accused, irrespective of whether there are any eye-witnesses to the offence or not. Chapter V of the CrPC deals with Arrest of Persons. Section 41 specifies when the police officer can arrest without a warrant:

a) Who is concerned in any cognizable offence or against whom a reasonable complaint has been made or credible information has been received, or a reasonable suspicion exists, of his having been so concerned;
b) Who has in his possession without lawful excuse the burden of proving which excuse shall lie on such person, any implement of house-breaking;
c) Who has been proclaimed as an offender either under this Code or by order of the State Government;
d) In whose possession anything is found which may reasonably be suspected to be stolen property and who may reasonably be suspected of having committed an offence with reference to such thing;
e) Who obstructs a police officer while in the execution of his duty, or who has escaped, or attempts to escape, from lawful custody;

74 Sujata Mukherjee vs Prashant Kumar Mukherjee, (1997) 5 SCC 30

75 See T.T.Anthony vs. State of Kerala and Ors. 2001 (6) SCC 181 and Upkar Singh vs Ved Prakash, (2004) 13 SCC 296

76 H.N.Rishbud vs. State of Delhi, AIR 1955 SC 196

f) Who is reasonably suspected of being a deserter from any of the Armed Forces of the Union;

g) Who has been concerned in or against whom a reasonable complaint has been made or credible information has been received or a reasonable suspicion exists of his having been concerned in any act committed at any place out of India which if committed in India, would have been punishable as an offence and for which he is under any law relating to extradition, or otherwise, liable to be apprehended or detained in custody in India;

h) Who being a released convict commits a breach of rule under Section 356(5), in cases where the person is liable to inform the convicting court of any change of residence or absence from such residence after release for the specified period;

i) For whose arrest any requisition whether written or oral has been received from another police officer provided that the requisition specifies the person to be arrested and the offence or other cause for which the arrest is to be made and it appears therefrom that the person might lawfully be arrested without a warrant by the officer who issued the requisition;

j) A person specified under Sections 109 or 110 of the CrPC (Chapter cases dealt with in Chapter VIII).

Under Section 42, an officer can arrest any person who in his presence has committed or has been accused of committing a non-cognizable offence and who refuses to give his name and residence or gives a false name and address upon demand by the officer. But such arrest can be made only with a view to ascertain his real name and residence. A private person can also arrest a person who in his presence commits a non-bailable and cognizable offence or any proclaimed offender. However, he has to hand over the arrested person without any delay to a police officer or to the nearest police station (Section 43). Under Section 44, a Magistrate may arrest a person who commits an offence in his presence and within his local jurisdiction. Section 45 protects members of the Armed Forces of the Union from being arrested for anything done or purported to be done in the discharge of his official duties, notwithstanding anything contained in Sections 41 to 44, except with the previous consent of the Central Government. The Supreme Court has specified that arrest and custody are not synonymous. While custody is a necessary ingredient of an arrest, all detentions in custody do not amount to an arrest.[77] The court by making this distinction sought to differentiate between custodial detentions by various authorities such as the Customs, Directorate of Enforcement and those by the police and between preventive and punitive detention.

77 Directorate of Enforcement vs. Deepak Mahajan, (1994) 3 SCC 440

While making an arrest, the police officer shall not subject a person to more restraint than is necessary to prevent his escape (Section 49). If any police officer making an arrest or person executing a warrant of arrest, has reason to believe that the person to be arrested has entered into or is within any place, any person residing in or being in charge of such place shall on demand, allow the officer free ingress into the place and afford all reasonable facilities for a search therein. If they fail to do so, then the police or other officer is entitled to break into the place in order to prevent the accused from having an opportunity to escape (Section 47). In making the arrest, the police officer shall actually touch or confine the body of the person to be arrested, unless there be a submission to the custody by word or action. If such person forcibly resists or attempts to evade the arrest, such police officer may use all means necessary to effect the arrest. However, the police officer does not have the right to cause the death of the person who is not accused of an offence punishable with death or with imprisonment for life (Section 46). Hence, it is clear that the law permits the police officer making an arrest to use requisite force that could extend to the causing of the death of the person if he is even suspected with the commission of an offence punishable with death or imprisonment of life. There are around 50 offences in the Indian Penal Code, which provide for punishment upto life imprisonment including forgery. In all such cases the police are empowered to even kill a person who is suspected of having committed the offence. This provision allows for encounter killings. The practice is not to bring in any judicial inquiry into such deaths. A departmental inquiry is held by an officer belonging to the rank of the Deputy Commissioner of Police who upon exoneration, closes the file and the officer is not subjected to any legal action. The case made out is invariably that the police had gone to arrest the accused suspected of having committed an offence punishable with death or life imprisonment, the accused evaded arrest and attempted to use violence, which necessitated the use of counter force which resulted in the death of the accused. Thus the subversion of the law by the State agencies permits the use of extra-judicial violence on the part of the law enforcing agencies.

The guidelines issued by the Supreme Court in D.K. Basu's case[78] have been incorporated in the CrPC to prevent abuse of the powers of the police to arrest and to check illegal detention and custodial torture under Section 50A:

(1) Every police officer or other person making any arrest under this Code shall forthwith give the information regarding such arrest and place where the arrested person is being held to any of his friends, relatives or such other persons as may be disclosed or nominated by the arrested person for the purpose of giving such information.

(2) The police officer shall inform the arrested person of his rights under subsection (1) as soon as he is brought to the police station.

78 1997 Cri.L.J. 743

(3) An entry of the fact as to who has been informed of the arrest of such person shall be made in a book to be kept in the police station in such form as may be prescribed in this behalf by the State Government.

(4) It shall be the duty of the Magistrate before whom such arrested person is produced, to satisfy himself that the requirements of sub-section (2) and sub-section (3) have been complied with in respect of such arrested person.

An arrested person cannot be detained in custody by the police officer beyond a period of 24 hours. If the officer desires further custody, he has to produce the accused before the nearest Magistrate and obtain remand for a period upto fifteen days at a time after convincing the Magistrate that further custodial interrogation is required by producing the investigation papers, the police diary and making a written remand application (Sections 57 and 167(1). The CrPC does not allow a Magistrate to remand an accused to police custody beyond a period of 15 days and thereafter the person has to be sent to judicial custody. Police custody beyond this period has been held to be illegal.[79] All arrests without warrants have to be reported whether the accused have been released on bail or not (Section 58) and every person arrested without a warrant has to be forwarded before the Magistrate as soon as possible if not released on bail (Section 56). Where after arrest, upon investigation, the police officer believes that there is not sufficient evidence or reasonable ground of suspicion to justify his being forwarded to the Magistrate the officer may release him on his execution of bond, with or without sureties, and may also direct the person to appear before a Magistrate if required to do so (Section 169).

The person arrested shall not be subjected to more restraint than is necessary to prevent his escape (Section 49). Every police officer or other person arresting a person without a warrant shall tell him the full particulars of the offence for which he is arrested or other grounds for such arrest. When the offence is a bailable offence, the accused shall be informed by the police officer that he is entitled to be released on bail (Section 50). The accused can be sent for medical examination by the police officer when the offence alleged to have been committed is of such a nature and alleged to have been committed under such circumstances that there are reasonable grounds for believing that an examination of his person will afford evidence as to the commission of an offence. But a woman should be medically examined only by or under the supervision of a female registered medical practitioner. "Examination" includes the examination of blood, blood stains, semen, swabs in case of sexual offences, sputum and sweat, hair samples and finger nail clippings by the use of modern and scientific techniques including DNA profiling and such other tests which the registered medical practitioner thinks necessary in a particular case (Section 53). When a person is arrested on a charge of committing an offence of rape or an attempt to commit rape and there are reasonable grounds for believing that

79 CBI vs Anupam Kulkarni, 1992 CrLJ 2768

an examination of his person will afford evidence as to the commission of such offence, it shall be lawful for a registered medical practitioner employed in a hospital run by the Government or by a local authority and in the absence of such a practitioner within the radius of sixteen kilometers from the place where the offence has been committed, by any other registered medical practitioner, acting at the request of a police officer not below the rank of a sub-inspector, and for any person acting in good faith in his aid and under his direction, to make such an examination of the arrested person and to use such force as is reasonably necessary for that purpose. The registered medical practitioner conducting such examination shall, without delay, examine such person and prepare a report of his examination giving the following particulars, namely:

(i) The name and address of the accused and of the person by whom he was brought,

(ii) The age of the accused,

(iii) Marks of injury, if any, on the person of the accused,

(iv) The description of material taken from the person of the accused for DNA profiling, and

(v) Other material particulars in reasonable detail.

The report shall state precisely the reasons for each conclusion arrived at. The exact time of commencement and completion of the examination shall also be noted in the report. The registered medical practitioner shall, without delay, forward the report of the investigating officer, who shall forward it to the Magistrate referred to in section 173 as part of the chargesheet (Section 53A).

The arrested person also has the right to ask for medical examination when the same will afford evidence that he has not committed a particular offence or that an offence against his body has been committed. Copy of the medical report has to be furnished to the accused. (Section 54). An arrest or detention of a person in violation of the conditions mentioned above, especially the conditions mentioned in Sections 41, 50, 57 and 167 shall be considered to be illegal detentions. However, in most cases, where the accused has been held for some period in illegal detention, the courts do not vitiate the trial of the accused. But the police officers responsible for the illegal detention are liable to be prosecuted for wrongful confinement and wrongful restraint under Sections 341 to 348 of the Indian Penal Code. Under Section 358 also, if it appears to the Magistrate that there were no sufficient grounds for the arrest of a person, the Magistrate may award compensation not exceeding Rs.100 to be paid by the person so causing the arrest to the person so arrested for his loss of time and expenses in the matter. Apart from this the aggrieved person has his constitutional remedies.

In Joseph vs State of Kerala[80], where there was a delay of 10 days in arresting the accused though his name and address were given in the FIR and he was known to all, on the ground that it took this time to find his correct address, the Court acquitted the accused as the explanation was not convincing and the prosecution case appeared doubtful.

Conducting of Searches

After recording the FIR or upon receipt of the information of the offence, the investigating officer and his team are to proceed to the spot where the offence has been committed to verify the said information and investigate into the same. The police search the spot where the offence has been committed in order to discover any clues and in case any incriminating substance is found the police should seize the same. Any article recovered has to be sealed and packed with the details of the case written on it and the signatures of the witnesses to the search are obtained on these in order to be later used as evidence in the trial as the articles purported to be seized at the time of the search. An example of this is in a murder case, the police is expected to note down the position of the corpse, the wounds, the description of the body, the injuries, take charge of any footprints, fingerprints, blood stains, weapons and any other articles and also note down a description of the spot, including the places from where the articles and other evidence was seized. This evidence is crucial, as it is the earliest in point of time. The search can be conducted even before the police register the FIR where there is doubt as to whether the incident relates to the commission of an offence. The search can include the search of any person found in the place or suspected to have committed an offence or the search of a victim where the search would lead to evidence of the commission of an offence. The search of a place includes search of any particular object too. Searches are normally recorded as *Panchnamas* as they are records of events witnessed by an independent witness or *pancha*. Two *panchas* are to remain present during the entire conduct of the panchnama, though both need not be called to the court to prove the *panchnama*. *Panchnamas* are proved through the *panchas* though the *panchnama* may be scribed by a member of the police investigation team.

Under Section 165 of the CrPC, whenever an officer incharge of a police station or a Police officer making an investigation has reasonable grounds for believing that anything necessary for the purpose of an investigation into an offence which he is authorised to investigate may be found in any place within the limits of the police station of which he is incharge, or to which he is attached, and that such thing cannot in his opinion be otherwise obtained without undue delay, such officer may, after recording in writing the grounds of his belief and specifying in such writing, so far as possible the thing for which search is to be made, search, or cause search to be made for such thing in any place within the limits of such station. The officer can also search any

80 Joseph vs State of Kerala, 2003 CrLJ 2543

person present at the spot or otherwise if he considers such search necessary for the investigation of a case. The officer can also search any person or place after obtaining a search warrant under Section 100 of the CrPC. The principles and the manner of the Search under both the provisions are the same and are laid out in Section 100:

a) Whenever any place liable to search or inspection is closed, any person residing in, or being incharge of, such place shall on demand of the officer or other person executing the warrant and on production of the warrant, allow him free ingress into and afford all reasonable facilities for a search therein;

b) When the owner or occupier in disobedience of the lawful order refuses ingress, then the police officer has the right to enter into the premises by breaking into the same after giving notification of his authority and purpose and demand of admittance duly made and in case the place is occupied by a pardanashin woman after giving her reasonable facility for withdrawing provided she is not liable to be arrested for the said offence;

c) Where any person in or about such place is reasonably suspected of concealing about his person any article for which search should be made such person may be searched and if such person is a woman, the search shall be made by another woman with strict regard to decency;

d) Before making a search, the officer shall call upon two or more independent and respectable inhabitants of the locality in which the place to be searched is situated or of any other locality if not such inhabitant of the said locality is available or is willing to be a witness to the search, to attend and witness the search and may issue an order in writing to them or any of them to do so and such witnesses are known as panchas;

e) The search shall be made in their presence and a list of all things seized in the course of such search shall be prepared by such officer or other person and signed by such witnesses and this document is known as the panchnama;

f) The occupant of the place searched or some person on his behalf, shall be permitted to attend during the search and a copy of the list prepared under this search panchnama shall be delivered to such occupant or person;

g) When any person is searched, a list of all things taken possession of shall be prepared and a copy of the panchnama shall be delivered to such person;

h) Any person who without reasonable cause refuses or neglects to attend and witness a search when called upon to do so by an order in writing delivered or tendered to him shall be deemed to have committed an offence under Section 187 of the IPC (omission to assist public servant when bound by law to give such assistance and wilfully neglecting to aid a public servant who demands aid in the execution of process punishable with imprisonment upto six months or fine of Rs.500 or both).

Though the CrPC prescribes a clearly laid out procedure for the conduct of a search by the police, the courts have held that these provisions are not mandatory and their breach does not vitiate trial or the search or make the evidence of the search inadmissible. The Supreme Court has held that there can be no legal proposition that evidence of police officers unless supported by independent witnesses is unworthy of acceptance. Non-examination of independent witnesses or even the presence of such witness during police raid would cast an added duty on the court to adopt greater care while scrutinising the evidence of the police officers. If the evidence of the police officers were found acceptable it would be an erroneous proposition that the court must reject the prosecution version solely on the ground that no independent witness was examined.[81] It has been further held that even if the panchas were not local, this irregularity would not affect the legality of the proceedings.[82]

Discovery and Recovery Evidence

Under Section 27 of the Indian Evidence Act, facts recovered or discovered through the accused are admissible evidence and are not hit by the bar of confessions made to the police. The statement of the accused which leads to recovery of any material evidence, such as a weapon or clothes which are incriminating from a place which is known only to the accused or even if from a public place, if it is from a hidden place which is not known to anyone apart from the accused or discovery of any fact which would be only within the knowledge of the accused. Hence, for example clothes of the accused at the time of commission of the offence which give evidence of the commission of the same, have semen stains, blood or saliva, nail or other bites or hair of the victim or grass or mud similar to that of the scene of offence or body of the victim where the victim is dead or is missing or weapon hidden in any place by the accused would be admissible evidence. If any of the facts disclosed by the accused is already known to the police/investigating agencies, the same would not be admissible under Section 27 of the Indian Evidence Act, as only facts which are only within the knowledge of the accused and are discovered as a consequence of his disclosure are admissible against him.

The scope and ambit of Section 27 of the Evidence Act were illuminatingly stated in Pulukuri Kotayya v. Emperor[83] in the following words, "It is fallacious to treat the 'fact discovered' within the section as equivalent to the object produced; the fact discovered embraces the place from which the object is produced and the knowledge of the accused as to this and the information given must relate distinctly to this fact. Information as to past user or the past history, of the object produced is not related to its discovery in the setting in which it is discovered. Information supplied by a person in custody that 'I will produce

81 Kalpanath Rai vs. State (through CBI), (1997) 8 SCC 732

82 The State of Maharashtra vs. P.K. Pathak, AIR 1980 SC 1224

83 AIR 1947 PC 67

a knife concealed in the roof of my house' does not lead to the discovery of a knife; knives were discovered many years ago. It leads to the discovery of the fact that a knife is concealed in the house of the information to his knowledge, and if the knife is proved to have been used in the commission of the offence, the fact discovered is very relevant. But if to the statement the words be added 'with which stabbed A', these words are inadmissible since they do not relate to the discovery of the knife in the house of the informant." The Privy Council further held that it can seldom happen that information leading to the discovery of a fact forms the foundation of the prosecution case. It is one link in the chain of proof and the other links must be forged in manner allowed by law.

In Navjot Singh Sandhu's case[84], the Supreme Court was concerned with "whether pointing out a material object by the accused furnishing the information is a necessary concomitant of Section 27. We think that the answer should be in the negative. Though in most of the cases the person who makes the disclosure himself leads the Police Officer to the place where an object is concealed and points out the same to him, however, it is not essential that there should be such pointing out in order to make the information admissible under Section 27. It could very well be that on the basis of information furnished by the accused, the Investigating Officer may go to the spot in the company of other witnesses and recover the material object. By doing so, the Investigating Officer will be discovering a fact viz., the concealment of an incriminating article and the knowledge of the accused furnishing the information about it. In other words, where the information furnished by the person in custody is verified by the Police Officer by going to the spot mentioned by the informant and finds it to be correct, that amounts to discovery of fact within the meaning of Section 27. Of course, it is subject to the rider that the information so furnished was the immediate and proximate cause of discovery. If the Police Officer chooses not to take the informant -- accused to the spot, it will have no bearing on the point of admissibility under Section 27, though it may be one of the aspects that goes into evaluation of that particular piece of evidence."

The Supreme Court in State of Himachal Pradesh vs Jeet Singh[85] held that "There is nothing in Section 27of the Evidence Act which renders statement of the accused inadmissible if recovery of the articles was made from any place which is 'open and accessible to others. It is a fallacious notion that when recovery of any incriminating article is made from a place which is open or accessible to others, it would vitiate the evidence under Section 27 of the Evidence Act. Any object can be concealed in places which are open or accessible to others. For example, if the article is buried in the main roadside or if it is concealed beneath dry leaves lying on public places or kept hidden in a public office, the article would remain out of the visibility of others in normal circumstances. Until such article is disinterred, its hidden state would remain unhampered. The person

84 State (N.C.T. of Delhi) Vs. Navjot Sandhu @ Afsan Guru, (2005)11SCC600
85 (1999) 4 SCC 370)

who hid it alone knows where it is until he discloses that fact to any other person. Hence, the crucial question is not whether it was ordinarily visible to others. If it is not, then it is immaterial that the concealed place is accessible to others." In State of Maharashtra vs Bharat Fakira Dhiwar[86], the Supreme Court held that the clothes of the accused and the weapon that were recovered at the instance of the accused from an open field in tall grass were admissible under Section 27 of the Evidence Act.

In Amitsingh Bhikamsing Thakur vs State of Maharashtra[87] the Supreme Court reiterated the principles governing the discovery of facts and recovery of material evidence through the accused:

(1) The fact of which evidence is sought to be given must be relevant to the issue. It must be borne in mind that the provision has nothing to do with question of relevancy. The relevancy of the fact discovered must be established according to the prescriptions relating to relevancy of other evidence connecting it with the crime in order to make the fact discovered admissible.

(2) The fact must have been discovered.

(3) The discovery must have been in consequence of some information received from the accused and not by accused's own act.

(4) The persons giving the information must be accused of any offence.

(5) He must be in the custody of a police officer.

(6) The discovery of a fact in consequence of information received from an accused in custody must be deposed to.

(7) Thereupon only that portion of the information which relates distinctly or strictly to the fact discovered can be proved. The rest is inadmissible.

But where the independent witness to the recovery was not examined and the police officer stated to be accompanying the independent witness was shown in duty register to have departed from police station the day prior to the day the IO took up the investigation and reported at police station the next day evening, the recovery and seizure made were held to be doubtful.[88] Where the recovery was witnessed by thousands of people, the Supreme Court held that the recovery was doubtful as thousands of people cannot witness a recovery unless people had already come to know of the same.[89] The identification parade of the articles by the witness has to be done and identification in the court is not good as the articles were found to be of common use and can be found in any house.[90] In a case, the Supreme Court upon finding that the panchas were not

86 2000 Cri.LJ 218

87 MANU/SC/0004/2007: (2007) 1 BCR (Cr) SC 193

88 Lakhwinder Singh vs State of Punjab, 2003 CrLJ 3058

89 Babudas vs State of MP, 2003 CrLJ 2563

90 Pawan Kumar vs State of Haryana, 2003 CrLJ 2987

respectable inhabitants of the locality, it held that the circumstance would not invalidate the search. It would only affect the weights of evidence in support of the search and the recovery. The search and recovery will not become illegal even against the highest irregularity.[91] The Supreme Court has also held that the searching officer should give his personal search to the witness before entering the premises to be searched.[92] This precaution is meant to prevent planting of incriminating material in order to falsely implicate someone in a crime. In Salim Akhtar vs State of UP[93], the Supreme Court held that where the alleged recovery was made from an open place easily accessible to anyone and where the articles were not sealed, the recovery was doubtful and could not be relied upon.

Disposal of Seized Property

The property (which includes documents and articles) recovered during panchnama can be disposed of pending trial by the court. Any party who claims the property can apply to the court for return of the same under Seciton 451 of the CrPC and the concerned court after hearing all concerned may pass directions for safe custody of the said property. The court can pass orders directing for the proper custody pending conclusion of the inquiry or trial, order it to be sold or otherwise disposed of, after recording such evidence as it think necessary or if the property is subject to speedy and natural decay to dispose of the same. The Supreme Court in Sunderbhai Ambalal Desai Vs. State of Gujarat[94] held that the powers under Section 451 CrPC should be exercised expeditiously and judiciously. It would serve various purposes, namely:

1. Owner of the article would not suffer because of its remaining unused or by its misappropriation;
2. Court or the police would not be required to keep the article in safe custody;
3. If the proper panchnama before handing over possession of article is prepared, that can be used in evidence instead of its production before the Court during the trial. If necessary, evidence could also be recorded describing the nature of the property in detail; and
4. This jurisdiction of the Court to record evidence should be exercised promptly so that there may not be further chance of tampering with the articles.

The Court also laid laid down the guidelines for the exercise of powers under Section 541 CrPC for various types of property:

---

91 AIR 1956 SC 411; Radha Krishnan vs State of UP, AIR 1963 SC 822; State of MP vs Paltan Mallah, AIR 2005 SC 733

92 AIR 1969 SC 53

93 2003 CrLJ 2302; Also see Amarjit Singh vs State of Punjab, (1995) Supp 3 SCC 217; Sahib Singh vs State of Punjab, (1996) 11 SCC 685

94 (2002)10SCC283

With regard to valuable articles, such as, gold or silver ornaments or articles studded with precious stones, it is submitted that it is of no use to keep such articles in police custody for years till the trial is over. For this purpose, if material on record indicates that such articles belong to the complainant at whose house theft, robbery or dacoity has taken place, then seized articles be handed over to the complainant after:

(a) Preparing detailed proper panchnama of such articles;

(b) Taking photographs of such articles and a bond that such articles would be produced if required at the time of trial; and

(c) After taking proper security.

The bond and security should be taken so as to prevent the evidence being lost, altered or destroyed. The Court should see that photographs of such articles are attested or countersigned by the complainant, accused as well as by the person to whom the custody is handed over. Still however, it would be the function of the Court under Section 451 Cr.P.C. to impose any other appropriate condition.

In case, where such articles are not handed over either to the complainant or to the person from whom such articles are seized or to its claimant, then the Court may direct that such articles be kept in bank lockers. Similarly, if articles are required to be kept in police custody, it would be open to the SHO after preparing proper panchnama to keep such articles in a bank locker. In any case, such articles should be produced before the Magistrate within a week of their seizure. If required, the Court may direct that such articles be handed over back to the Investigating Officer for further investigation and identification. However, in no set of circumstances, the Investigating Officer should keep such articles in custody for a longer period for the purpose of investigation and identification. For currency notes, similar procedure can be followed.

In case where the vehicle is not claimed by the accused, owner, or the insurance company or by third person, then such vehicle may be ordered to be auctioned by the Court. If the said vehicle is insured with the insurance company then insurance company be informed by the Court to take possession of the vehicle which is not claimed by the owner or a third person. If Insurance company fails to take possession the vehicles may be sold as per the direction of the Court. The Court would pass such order within a period of six months from the date of production of the said vehicle before the Court. In any case, before handing over possession of such vehicles, appropriate photographs of the said vehicle should be taken and detailed panchnama should be prepared.

For articles such as seized liquor also, prompt action should be taken in disposing it of after preparing necessary panchnama. If sample is required to be taken, sample may kept properly after sending it to the chemical analyser, if required. But in no case, large quantity of liquor should be stored at the police station. No purpose is served by such storing.

Similarly for the Narcotic drugs also, for its identification, procedure under Section 451 CrPC should be followed of recording evidence and disposal. Its identity could be no the basis of evidence recorded by the Magistrate. Samples also should be sent immediately to the Chemical Analyser so that subsequently, a contention may not be raised that the article which was seized was not the same.

Magistrates should take immediate action for seeing that powers under Section 451 CrPC are properly and promptly exercised and articles are not kept for a long time at the police station, in any case, for not more than fifteen days to one month. This object can also be achieved if there is proper supervision by the Registry of the concerned High Court in seeing that the rules framed by the High Court with regard to such articles are implemented properly.

Recording of Statements of Witnesses

The police officer investigating the case can examine any person who is acquainted with the facts of the case. The oral examination is reduced into writing though the signature of the witness is not to be obtained in the said statement. The witness can be called to the police station for the examination, though a police officer cannot summon a woman or a child below 15 years of age to the police station for the purposes of interrogation. The police officer should go to the residence of the woman or child for interrogating them.[95] In case a person, for purposes of interrogation, attends any place apart from his place of residence, he is entitled to be reimbursed the expenses incurred for doing so. The witness is bound to answer truly all questions relating to such case put to him by the police officer investigating the case other than questions the answers to which would have a tendency to expose him to a criminal charge or to a penalty or forfeiture (Sections 160 and 161).

Ideally, the statements of the witnesses should be recorded at the earliest point of time. The Supreme Court has held that normally in a case where the commission of the crime is alleged to have been seen by witnesses who are easily available, a prudent investigator would give to the examination of such witnesses precedence over the evidence of other witnesses. It has also stated that delay of a few hours in recording the statements of eyewitnesses may not, by itself, amount to a serious infirmity in the prosecution case. But it may assume such a character if there are concomitant circumstances to suggest that the investigator was deliberately marking time with a view to decide about the shape to be given to the case and the eye-witnesses to be introduced. Thus, under the facts and circumstances of the case, the court looks if the delay in

95 Nandini Satpathy vs. P.L.Dani, AIR 1978 SC 1025

recording the statements of the material witnesses casts a cloud of suspicion on the credibility of the entire warp and woof of the prosecution story.[96] In Jagjit Singh vs State of Punjab[97], the Supreme Court held that a three day delay in recording the statement of the sole eye witness who was a child aged 7 years in a triple murder case by the police and six days in recording the same by the Magistrate on the ground that she was under shock was not convincing and her evidence was discarded in view of the medical evidence certifying her fitness. In the Best Bakery case, the Supreme Court held that it is not mandatory under the law that all statements made to the police ought to be recorded and reduced into writing.[98]

Thus, delay per se does not render the statements recorded by the police inadmissible. Joint statements of witnesses though is in violation of the law, it does not render the testimony of the witnesses in court inadmissible. The purpose of recording these statements is to know who are the witnesses of the case and their version of the event, though these statements cannot be a part of the substantive evidence in the case[99] and cannot be used to corroborate the evidence of the witness in the court[100]. The police have the power to call upon any person acquainted with the facts of the case to answer their questions and the Supreme Court has held in Nandini Satpathy's case[101] that this includes the accused. However, statements by the accused in the course of the investigation are not admissible being hit by the protection under Article 20(3) of the Constitution of India. The Constitutional Bench of the Supreme Court has discussed the scope of Article 20(3) in State of Bombay Vs. Kathi Kalu Oghad[102] and held that:

(1) An accused person cannot be said to have been compelled to be a witness against himself simply because he made a statement while in police custody, without anything more. In other words, the mere fact of being in police custody at the time when the statement in question was made would not, by itself, as a proposition of law, lend itself to the inference that the accused was compelled to make the statement, though that fact, in conjunction with other circumstances disclosed in evidence in a particular case, would be a relevant consideration in an enquiry whether or not the accused person had been compelled to make the impugned statement.

(2) The mere questioning of an accused person by a police officer, resulting in a voluntary statement, which may ultimately turn out to be incriminatory, is not 'compulsion'.

---

96 G.B. .Patel vs. State of Maharashtra, AIR 1979 SC 135

97 (2005)3 SCC 689

98 Zahira Habibulla H. Sheikh v. State of Gujarat, AIR 2004 SC 3114; Also see Alamgir vs State, 2003 CrLJ 456

99 Hazari Lal vs. State, AIR 1980 SC 873

100 Sat Paul vs. Delhi Administration, AIR 1976 SC 294

101 Nandini Satpathy vs. P.L.Dani, AIR 1978 SC 1025

102 AIR1961SC1808

(3) 'To be a witness' is not equivalent to 'furnishing evidence' in its widest significance; that is to say, as including not merely making of oral or written statements but also production of documents or giving materials which may be relevant at a trial to determine the guilt or innocence of the accused.

(4) Giving thumb impressions or impressions of foot or palm or fingers or specimen writings or showing parts of the body by way of identification are not included in the expression 'to be a witness'.

(5) 'To be a witness' means imparting knowledge in respect of relevant facts by an oral statement or a statement in writing, made or given in Court or otherwise.

(6) 'To be a witness' in its ordinary grammatical sense means giving oral testimony in Court. Case law has gone beyond this strict literal interpretation of the expression which may now bear a wider meaning, namely, bearing testimony in Court or out of Court by a person accused of an offence, orally or in writing.

(7) To bring the statement in question within the prohibition of Article 20(3), the person accused must have stood in the character of an accused person at the time he made the statement. It is not enough that he should become an accused, any time after the statement has been made.

The Bombay High Court has held that giving of voice samples by the accused does not amount to being a witness as envisaged under Article 20(3) of the Constitution of India.[103] A Division Bench of the Bombay High Court also held that administration of Brain Mapping and Lie Detector Tests, against the will of the person to whom it is sought to be administered does not violate any constitutional guarantee as it is not a statement and that it is not incriminatory in any manner.[104]

The deposition of the witnesses in the court will constitute the evidence, and the previous statements in writing can be used only for the purpose of contradicting the witness at the time of cross-examination of the witness in court by the accused or by the prosecution when the witness turns hostile, with the permission of the court. This is subject to the exception if the statement is by an accused person and leads to a discovery or recovery under Section 27 of the Evidence Act or is a statement admissible under Section 32(1) of the Evidence Act, which is a dying declaration. The statements can also be used in any other proceeding except the trial of the case relating to the offence. An omission to state a fact or circumstance in the statement may amount to contradiction if the same appears to be significant and otherwise relevant having regard to the context in which such omission occurs and whether any omission amounts to a contradiction in

103 CBI vs Adbul Karim Ladsab Telgi, 2005 CrLJ 2868

104 Ramchandra Ram Reddy and Ors. v. State of Maharashtra, reported in 2004 All MR (Cri) 1704

the particular context shall be a question of fact to be decided by the trial court. Inconsistencies between the statements made to the police and the evidence in court would render the evidence of the witness suspect. (Section 162).

However, the statement to the police need not be a detailed one. Hence, it is important that the statement be recorded as early as possible in order to prevent any fabrication of evidence. If a witness does not appear in court, his statement cannot be relied upon by the prosecution to prove its case. While no police officer can offer any threat, inducement or promise to obtain a statement, he is not duty bound to prevent, by any caution or otherwise, any person from making in the course of investigation, any statement which he may make on his own free will (Section 163).

Under Section 164A, when an offence of rape or attempt to commit rape is under investigation, and the victim is to be medically examined, such examination shall be conducted by a registered medical practitioner employed in a hospital run by the Government or a local authority and in the absence of such a practitioner, by any other registered medical practitioner, with the consent of such woman or of a person competent to give such consent on her behalf and such woman shall be sent to such registered medical practitioner within twenty-four hours from the time of receiving the information relating to the commission of such offence. The registered medical practitioner, to whom such woman is sent shall, without delay, examine her person and prepare a report of his examination giving the following particulars, namely:

(i) The name and address of the woman and of the person by whom she was brought;

(ii) The age of the woman;

(iii) The description of material taken from the person of the woman for DNA profiling;

(iv) Marks of injury, if any, on the person of the woman;

(v) general mental condition of the woman; and

(vi) other material particulars in reasonable detail,

The report shall state precisely the reasons for each conclusion arrived at. The report shall specifically record that the consent of the woman or of the person competent, to give such consent on her behalf to such examination had been obtained. The exact time of commencement and completion of the examination shall also be noted in the report. The registered medical practitioner shall, without delay forward the report to the investigating officer who shall forward it to the Magistrate as part of the chargesheet. But the medical examination of the victim without consent is unlawful.

Identification Parades

Identification parades are held in cases where the witness has seen the accused but does not know his identity. The police arrest a person on suspicion and then ask a Special Executive Officer to conduct an Identification Parade in order to identify the accused. Police officers are not meant to be associated with identification parades, as then the statements of the identifying witnesses would be hit by Section 162 of the CrPC and, hence,. be inadmissible.[105] Judges also do not associate themselves with the identification parades, which are known as test identification parades, as they test the ability of the witness to identify the accused. Under the amended Section 54A of the CrPC, the court can direct the police to conduct the identification parade for the identification of the accused by the witness.

The principles of the manner in which the identification parades should be conducted are the following:

a) The object of an identification parade is to make sure that the ability of the witness to recognise the suspect has been fairly and adequately tested;

b) It should be fair and seem to be fair and every precaution must be taken to exclude any suspicion of unfairness or risk of erroneous identification through the witness's attention being directed specially to the suspected persons instead of equally to all the persons to be paraded;

c) The parade should be arranged by an officer who is not a police officer;

d) After the commencement of the identification parade, every thing in respect of it should take place in the presence and hearing of the suspect, including any instruction to the witnesses attending it as to the procedure that is to be adopted;

e) All unauthorised persons should be strictly excluded from the place of identification parade;

f) The witnesses should be prevented from seeing the suspect before he is paraded with other persons, and witnesses who have previously seen a photograph or description of the suspect should not be led in identifying the suspect by reason of their recollection of the photograph or description, before the parade;

g) An Special Executive Officer, if called upon for the purpose of holding an Identification Parade, should remember that he is the person who conducts the parade; he will be in full and sole charge of the entire proceedings;

105 Ramkishan vs. Bombay State, AIR 1955 SC 104

h) The Special Executive Officer should first acquaint himself, very briefly, with the facts of the case and find out who is to be put in the parade for identification and who are the witnesses to be called up for identification;

i) Two independent respectable persons (not being persons connected with the Police) should be first called up. The police themselves will have normally arranged to call up such persons; but the Special Executive Officer will question them and satisfy himself that they are independent and fairly intelligent persons. In order that they may follow the proceedings intelligently, the Special Executive Officer should acquaint them, briefly, with the facts of the case and as to who is sought to be identified and who are to come for identification;

j) The parade should then be arranged in a room or a place which is such that the identifying witnesses, as well as the persons connected with the police, should not be able to look into it;

k) If there is only one accused person to be identified, there should be at least half a dozen persons placed in the parade. If two accused persons are to be identified, then there should be about 10 or 12 persons in the parade. Not more than two accused should be placed in any single identification parade. Normally, the police themselves will have called up the persons to be put in the parade; but the Special Executive Officer should see that they are persons of more or less the same physical appearance, and approximately of the same age, as the person to be identified. It is desirable that innocent persons to be mixed should be different for each such parade;

l) No person, other than the persons in the parade, and the two respectable persons, should be allowed to remain in the room where the identification proceedings are being held. In particular, all police officers and constables should be asked to withdraw themselves completely from the room. There is no objection to any of them remaining outside the room or otherwise at hand, ready to be called up in case the accused creates trouble, or in case of emergency. They should, however, not be visible from the room or the place where the parade is being held;

m) After the parade is arranged, one of the two respectable persons should be sent up to bring the accused from the lock-up. Care should be taken to see that when the accused is being brought from the lock up, the identifying witnesses do not have an opportunity of seeing him. They should be kept in quite a different room, out of sight of the lock up;

n) At this stage the, the Special Executive Officer should commence to write the memorandum of the identification parade. It should include:

i) The place at which and the date on which, parade is being held and the time at which it was commenced;

ii) The names, ages, occupations and the full addresses of the two respectable persons (panchas);

iii) The names and the approximate ages of the persons standing in the parade, mentioning clearly, one below the other, in numerical order their positions in the parade (which positions they should not be allowed afterwards to alter);

iv) The fact that no persons, other than those, in the parade and the two respectable persons, were allowed to remain in the room and that all police officers and constables were asked to withdraw; and

v) That respectable person so and so fetched the accused from the lock up and that the identifying witnesses were in a different room, so that they could not see him being brought from the lock up to the identification room.

o) When the accused is brought, the Special Executive Officer should ask him to take whatever place he likes in the parade. The place that he selects should be noted in the memorandum. The original numbering of the persons in the parade should not be altered simply because the accused has now joined in.

p) The accused should then be asked if he wants to make any alteration in his dress. He should be allowed to do so and that fact should be noted in the memorandum. If he does not wish to change his dress, then that fact should also be noted in the memorandum;

q) Then one of the panchas should be asked to fetch the first identifying witness from the room in which he may be sitting. When the witness arrives, the Special Executive Officer should question him and ascertain from him whether he had an opportunity to see the culprit at any time subsequent to the offence or after the arrest. He may either record the statement separately or make a reference to that statement in his memorandum. The witness should then be asked to view the parade carefully and see whether he would be able to identify the person, who, according to him committed the offence. The identifying witness will then goes up and look closely at the parade. If he identifies any person, he should be asked to go forward and touch that person, and not merely to point him out from a distance. This is necessary in order that there may be no doubt afterwards as to whom exactly he had identified. The fact that the identifying witness identified the accused, should be noted in the memorandum (along with the name of the accused) and also if he failed to identify him or identified a wrong person. It should further be noted whether the witness identified the accused straightway or after some hesitation or after first pointing out a wrong person and then correcting himself and pointing out the accused. When this is over, the identifying witness should be asked to go away into a different room and not to contact the remaining identifying witnesses. He may even be asked to go away;

r) After he leaves the room the accused should be asked once again, whether he desires to change his place in the parade. If he changes his place, it should be noted in the memorandum, and also if he declines to do so, he should be asked, again, if he wants to change his dress; and if he does so, or if he declines to do so, that fact should also be noted in the memorandum;

s) Then one of the panchas should be asked to fetch the second identifying witness. In regard to the identification by him also, the same procedure should be gone through as in the case of the first identifying witness, the memorandum being also written up side by side;

t) This procedure should be followed for each subsequent identifying witness;

u) After all the identifying witnesses have thus been exhausted one after the other, the memorandum should be wound up by stating the time at which it was concluded. Then the memorandum should be read over and explained to the panchas in a language, which they understand. If the panchas know English well, then they should be asked in addition to read over the memorandum for themselves;

v) After the memorandum is completed, the Special Executive Officer should make the following endorsement at the end:-

"Identification Parade was conducted by me personally with the help of the two respectable witnesses, namely Shri ....and Shri..... .... whose signatures have been obtained in token of what transpired in their presence", and shall sign below this endorsement and put the date below his signature. There shall be another endorsement to the following effect: -

"We read above memorandum (or it was explained to us) and it depicts the correct state of affairs as stated in the memorandum", and he shall obtain the signature of the two respectable persons with whose help he held the identification parade;

w) The Special Executive Officer himself should also sign every sheet of the memorandum;

x) All corrections and interlineations in the memorandum should be initialled by the Special Executive Officer;

y) The memorandum should be handed over to the police officer concerned;

z) Care should be taken to see that at no stage of the proceeding police officers or any police constables come into the room in which the parade is being held. The police should not be allowed to interfere with the proceedings, which are entirely to be conducted by the Special Executive Officer. It will be advisable to note in the memorandum itself that no police officer or constable was present at any time during the entire proceedings of the Identification Parade;

ai) The most important part of the memorandum will be the statements made by the identifying witnesses. These should be very carefully recorded, along with the questions asked to the identifying witnesses;

bii) If more than one accused are placed in parade, then in the memorandum they should not be referred as Accused No.1, Accused No.2, etc., but they should be referred to by their full names;

ciii) The memorandum should be written in the language of the Court;

div) At the hearing of the case, the Special Executive Officer who held the parade and wrote out the memorandum may be called upon to give evidence. In that case, he should state exactly what happened. He has a right to refresh his memory by referring to the memorandum, which he himself had prepared.[106]

Generally, the courts do not accept the first identification of an accused by the witness in the court without a test identification parade due to the lapse of time and the resultant changes in the physical appearance. Therefore, the identification parade should be held without any delay. The courts do not rely upon parades held after a long lapse of time irrespective of the reason for the delay due to this reason.[107] The Bombay High Court has held that all precautions are to be taken to obviate errors in conducting the identification and the requirements of the Criminal Manual should be substantially complied with.[108] Identification parade after showing the witness the photograph of the accused has been held to be bad.[109] Neither should the witness be shown the accused prior to the identification as this results in nullifying the purpose of the parade.[110] However, in cases where the accused are known to the witness, failure to hold the test identification parade and first identification in the court is not fatal to the case. Even in cases where there is evidence to show that the accused have been seen by the witness and the witness has had sufficient time and opportunity to get familiar with the accused, where the accused may not be previously known to the witness, the Supreme Court has held that failure to

106 A.K Gupte and S.D. Dighe, Criminal Manual, 4th Edition, 1999, Hind Law House, Pune, pages 23 to 29

107 See Soni vs State of UP, (1982) 3 SCC 368, Subhash vs State of UP, AIR 1987 SC 1222, State of Andhra Pradesh vs Dr. M.V. Ramana Reddy, AIR 1991 SC 1938; Suresh Chandra Bahri v. State of Bihar 1995 Supp (1) SCC 80 . However for a contra view see Bharat Singh vs State of UP (1973) 3 SCC 896; Daya Singh vs State of Haryana (2001) 3 SCC 468; Parasa Raja Manikyala Rao vs State of AP, 2004 CrLJ 378. Also see Amitsingh Bhikamsing Thakur vs State of MaharashtraMANU/SC/0004/2007: (2007) 1 BCR (Cr) SC 193

108 Pravin Kumar Kailashchandra Shukla vs. State of Maharashtra (1997) 2 Mh.L.J. 136)

109 AIR 1968 SC 938; D.Gopalakrishnan vs Sadanand Naik, 2004 CrLJ 4664

110 State of Maharashtra Vs Sukhdeo Singh, (1992)3SCC700

hold the Test Identification parade would not be fatal to the prosecution case and the evidence of identification in the court can be relied upon.[111]

In Lakhwinder Singh vs State of Punjab[112], the Supreme Court has held that when the witnesses do not know the accused, failure to hold the TI Parade would be fatal to the prosecution case.

In Munshi Singh Gautam vs State of M.P[113] the Supreme Court stated that, "the whole idea of a test identification parade is that witnesses who claim to have seen the culprits at the time of occurrence are to identify them from the midst of other persons without any aid or any other source. The test is done to check upon their veracity. In other words, the main object of holding an identification parade, during the investigation stage, is to test the memory of the witnesses based upon first impression and also to enable the prosecution to decide whether all or any of them could be cited as eyewitnesses of the crime. The identification proceedings are in the nature of tests and significantly, therefore, there is no provision for it in the Code and the Evidence Act. It is desirable that a test identification parade should be conducted as soon as after the arrest of the accused. This becomes necessary to eliminate the possibility of the accused being shown to the witnesses prior to the test identification parade. This is a very common plea of the accused and, therefore, the prosecution has to be cautious to ensure that there is no scope for making such allegation. If, however, circumstances are beyond control and there is some delay, it cannot be said to be fatal to the prosecution. It is trite to say that the substantive evidence is the evidence of identification in Court. Apart from the clear provisions of Section 9 of the Evidence Act, the position in law is well settled by a catena of decisions of this Court. The facts, which establish the identity of the accused persons, are relevant under Section 9 of the Evidence Act. As a general rule, the substantive evidence of a witness is the statement made in Court. The evidence of mere identification of the accused person at the trial for the first time is from its very nature inherently of a weak character. The purpose of a prior test identification, therefore, is to test and strengthen the trustworthiness of that evidence. It is accordingly considered a safe rule of prudence to generally look for corroboration of the sworn testimony of witnesses in Court as to the identity of the accused who are strangers to them, in the form of earlier identification proceedings. This rule of prudence, however, is subject to exceptions, when, for example, the Court is impressed by a particular witness on whose testimony it can safely rely, without such or other corroboration. The identification parades belong to the stage of investigation, and there is no provision in the Code which

111 Ronny alias Ronald James Alwaris vs. State of Maharashtra, 1998 All Mah R (Cri.) 898 (SC); R.N. Patel vs. State of Gujarat (2000)1 SCC 358; Rajesh Govind Jagesha vs State of Maharashtra, AIR 2000 SC 160; Sarwan Singh vs State of Punjab, 2003 CrLJ 21; Ashfaq vs State (Govt. of NCT of Delhi) AIR 2004 SC 1253.

112 2003 CrLJ 3058. Also see Kanan and Ors. v. State of Kerala (1979) SCC 621

113 (2005)9SCC631

obliges the investigating agency to hold or confers a right upon the accused to claim, a test identification parade. They do not constitute substantive evidence and these parades are essentially governed by Section 162 of the Code. Failure to hold a test identification parade would not make inadmissible the evidence of identification in Court. The weight to be attached to such identification should be a matter for the Courts of fact. In appropriate cases it may accept the evidence of identification even without insisting on corroboration."

The addition of 291A in the CrPC makes the Test Identification Parade Panchnama admissible as evidence without the examination of the Executive Magistrate preparing the same to prove the same. The section states that any document purporting to be a report of identification under the hand of an Executive Magistrate in respect of a person or property may be used as evidence in any inquiry, trial or other proceeding under this Code, although such Magistrate is not called as a witness: Provided that where such report contains a statement of any suspect or witness to which the provisions of section 21 (containing any admission), section 32 (where witness is deceased), section 33 (statement given in a previous proceeding), section 155 (where the accused wants to impeach the credit of witness) or section 157 (corroborative statement of the witness), as the case may be, of the Indian Evidence Act, apply, such statement shall not be used under this sub-section except in accordance with the provisions of those sections. The Court may, if it thinks fit, and shall, on the application of the prosecution or of the accused, summon and examine such Magistrate as to the subject matter of the said report.

Inquests

Under Section 174 of the CrPC, when the police officer receives information that a person has committed suicide, or has been killed by another or by an animal or by machinery or by an accident, or has died under circumstances raising a reasonable suspicion that some other person has committed an offence, he shall immediately give intimation thereof to the nearest Executive Magistrate empowered to hold inquests, and unless prohibited by any rule or order, shall proceed to the place where the body of such deceased person is, and there, in the presence of two or more respectable inhabitants of the neighborhood, shall make an investigation and draw up a report of the apparent cause of death, describing such wounds, fractures, bruises and other marks of injury as may be found on the body and stating in what manner or by what weapon or instrument such marks appear to have been inflicted. This report shall be signed by the police officer and the panchas and shall be forthwith forwarded to the District Magistrate or the Sub-divisional Magistrate. When the case involves suicide by a woman within seven years of her marriage, or the death of a woman within seven years of her marriage in any circumstances raising a reasonable suspicion that some other person committed an offence in relation to such woman, or when a woman within seven years of marriage dies and any relative of the woman makes a request in that behalf, or when there is any doubt regarding the cause of death, or the police officer for any other reason considers it expedient to do so, he shall forward the body to the nearest Civil Surgeon for its examination if the weather and the distance admit of its being so forwarded without risk of such putrefaction on the road as would render such examination useless.

The object of the proceedings under Section 174 is merely to ascertain whether a person has died under suspicious circumstances or an unnatural death and if so, what is the apparent cause of death. The question regarding the details as to how the deceased was assaulted or who assaulted him or under what circumstances he was assaulted appear to be foreign to the ambit and scope of the proceedings under Section 174.[114] Under Section 175, the police officer conducting an inquest panchanama may summon two or more persons to act as panchas and any other person who appears to be acquainted with the facts of the case, and every such person so summoned shall be bound to attend and to answer truly all questions other than those, the answers to which would have a tendency to expose him to a criminal charge or to a penalty or forfeiture. Provided that when the facts do not disclose the commission of a cognizable offence, such persons shall not be required by the police officer to attend a Magistrate's Court.

Under Section 176, in cases covered under Section 174, the nearest Magistrate empowered to hold inquests, may hold an inquiry into the cause of death either instead of, or in addition to, the investigation held by the police officer, and if he does so, he shall have all the powers in conducting it which he would have in holding an inquiry into an offence. And in cases where, any person dies or disappears, or rape is alleged to have been committed on any woman, while such person or woman is in the custody of the police or in any other custody authorised by the Magistrate or the Court, under this Code in addition to the inquiry or investigation held by the police, an inquiry shall be held by the Judicial Magistrate or the Metropolitan Magistrate, as the case may be, within whose local jurisdiction the offences has been committed. The Magistrate holding an inquiry under this section shall record the evidence taken by him in connection therewith in any manner according to the circumstances of the case and shall, wherever practicable, inform the relatives of the deceased whose names and addresses are known and shall allow them to remain present at the inquiry. Whenever such Magistrate considers it expedient to make an examination of the dead body of any person who has been already interred, in order to discover the cause of his death, the Magistrate may cause the body to be disinterred and examined. The Judicial Magistrate or the Metropolitan Magistrate or Executive Magistrate or

114 State of U.P vs. Abdul, (1997) 4 SCC 414; Pedda Narayana vs. State of A.P, AIR 1975 SC 1252

police officer holding an inquiry or investigation, as the case may be, under sub-section (1A) shall, within twenty-four hours of the death of a person, forward the body with a view to its being examined to the nearest Civil Surgeon or other qualified medical person (man) appointed in this behalf by the State Government, unless it is not possible to do so for reasons to be recorded in writing.

The Supreme Court has held that the scope of the inquiry under Section 174 is very limited and the non-mention of name of an eyewitness in the inquest report could not be a ground to reject his testimony. Similarly, the absence of the name of the accused in the inquest report cannot lead to an inference that he was not present at the time of commission of the offence as the inquest report is not the statement of a person wherein all the names (accused and also the eye-witnesses) ought to have been mentioned. The purpose of holding an inquest is very limited, viz., to ascertain as to whether a person has committed suicide or has been killed by another or by an animal or by machinery or by an accident or has died under circumstances raising a reasonable suspicion that some other person has committed an offence. There is absolutely no requirement in law of mentioning the details of the FIR, names of the accused or the names of the eye-witnesses or the gist of their statement nor it is required to be signed by any eye-witness. The details of the overt acts are not necessary to be recorded in the inquest report. The question regarding the details as to how the deceased was assaulted or who assaulted him or under what circumstances he was assaulted or who are the witnesses of the assault is foreign to the ambit and scope of proceedings under Section 174. Neither in practice nor in law it is necessary for the person holding the inquest to mention all these details.[115]

Filing of Chargesheet

Chargesheet is filed on completion of investigation and contains all the material gathered in the course of the investigation against the accused. Under Section 167(1) of the CrPC, whenever any person is arrested and detained in custody, and it appears that the investigation cannot be completed within the period of twenty-four hours, and there are grounds for believing that the accusation or information is well-founded, the officer in charge of the police station or the police officer making the investigation if he is not below the rank of sub-inspector, shall forthwith transmit to the nearest Judicial Magistrate a copy of the entries in the diary relating to the case, and shall at the same time forward the accused to such Magistrate. Under sub-section 2 of the above section, the Magistrate may authorise the detention of the accused in police custody after recording his reasons for doing so for purposes of facilitating the investigation for a period not exceeding 15 days. Thereafter if he deems fit, he may permit

115 Podda Narayana v. State of A.P. AIR 1975 SC 1252; Shakila Khader v. Nausher Gama AIR 1975 SC 1324 Eqbal Baig v. State of Andhra Pradesh AIR 1987 SC 923; Khujji @ Surendra Tiwari v. State of Madhya Pradesh AIR 1991 SC 1853; Amar Singh v. Balwinder Singh 2003 (2) SCC 518 Radha Mohan Singh vs State of U.P., (2006) 2 SCC 450

judicial or jail custody of the accused for a period not exceeding 90 days, where the investigation relates to an offence punishable with death, imprisonment for life or imprisonment for a term of not less than 10 years and in any other offence, for a period not exceeding 60 days. While computing the period of 15 days or 90 days of detention, the Supreme Court has held that the day of arrest of the accused or his surrender in court is to be excluded and the period commences from the date on which the Magistrate first remanded the accused into custody.[116] Failure to file chargesheet on completion of investigation within the stipulated period entitles the accused to be released on bail. This right can be claimed by the accused till the filing of the chargesheet and if the same were not claimed before the filing of the chargesheet, even if it is filed after the lapse of the stipulated period, the accused would not be entitled to bail.[117] However, the Supreme Court in Aslam Babulal Desai's case[118] has held that bail granted under the proviso to Section 167(2) of the CrPC cannot be cancelled on subsequent filing of the chargesheet.

Under sub-section 5, if in any case triable by a Magistrate as a summons-case and the investigation is not concluded within a period of six months from the date on which the accused was arrested, the Magistrate shall make an order stopping further investigation into the offence unless the officer making the investigation satisfies the Magistrate that for special reasons and in the interest of justice the continuation of the investigation beyond the period of six months is necessary.

The investigating officer has to maintain a dairy setting forth all the details of the investigation conducted by him such as the time at which the information reached him, the time at which he began and closed his investigation, the place or places visited by him and a statement of the circumstances ascertained through his investigation. Any court may send for the police diaries of a case under inquiry or trial in such Court and may use such diaries not as evidence in the case, but to aid it in such inquiry or trial. The accused is not entitled to call for these diaries nor see them merely because they are used by the court, but if a police officer uses these diaries to refresh his memory or if the court uses it to contradict the police officer, the accused will have a right to use the diary in his cross-examination in order to contradict the police officer's deposition in court (Section 172).

If upon an investigation, the police officer is of the opinion that there is sufficient evidence or reasonable ground to commit the accused for trial, then he shall forward the accused along with a police report to the concerned Magistrate to take cognizance of the case (Section 170). The police report comprises of the following:

116 Chaganti vs. State of A.P, AIR 1986 SC 2130
117 Abdul Wahid vs. State of Maharashtra, 1992 Mh.L.J. 595
118 AIR 1993 SC 1

a) The names of the parties;
b) The nature of the information;
c) The names of the persons who appear to be acquainted with the circumstances of the case;
d) Whether any offence appears to have been committed and, if so, by whom;
e) Whether the accused has been arrested;
f) Whether he has been released on his bond, and if so, whether with or without sureties;
g) Whether he has been forwarded in custody under section 170.

The Chargesheet filed at the conclusion of investigation contains the following:

a) The police report;
b) The First Information Report;
c) The statements of the prosecution witness recorded by the police;
d) The confessions and statements recorded by the Magistrate under Section 164 of the CrPC;
e) Any other document or relevant extracts thereof on which the prosecution proposes to rely such as reports of experts such as Post-mortem reports, Chemical Analysis reports, Inquest Panchanamas, Panchanamas relating to discovery and recovery of material evidence, other search and seizure panchanamas, etc.

The Supreme Court has held that the police report is an intimation to the magistrate that upon investigation into a cognizable offence the investigating officer has been able to procure sufficient evidence for the Court to inquire into the offence and the necessary information is being sent to the Court. In fact, the report under Section 173(2) purports to be an opinion of the investigating officer that as far as he is concerned he has been able to procure sufficient material for the trial of the accused by the Court. The report is complete if it is accompanied with all the documents and statements of witnesses as required by Section 175(5). Nothing more need be stated in the report of the Investigating Officer. It is also not necessary that all the details of the offence must be stated. The details of the offence are required to be proved to bring home the guilt to the accused at a later stage i.e. in the course of the trial of the case by adducing acceptable evidence[119].

119 Satya Narain Musadi and Ors. v. State of Bihar (1980 (3) SCC 152;

A copy of the Chargesheet has to be furnished to the accused free of cost. However, if the police officer is of opinion that any part of any such statement is not relevant to the subject-matter of the proceeding or that its disclosure to the accused is not essential in the interests of justice and is inexpedient in the public interest, he shall indicate that part of the statement and append a note requesting the Magistrate to exclude that part from the copies to be granted to the accused and stating his reasons for making such request. Even after filing a chargesheet, the police officer is entitled to continue further investigation into the offence and where upon subsequent investigation, he obtains further oral or documentary evidence, he shall forward the same to the Magistrate as a Supplementary Chargesheet. (Sections 173 and 207).

The purpose of the Chargesheet is to enable the trial court to know if there is sufficient case made out for proceeding with the trial of the case against the accused. In some cases where the Magistrate considers it proper, he may even direct further investigation into the case. It also enables the accused to know the material against him and enables him to prepare his defence. The accused has no right to have any say as regards the manner and method of investigation till the filing of the chargesheet.

Similarly, the complainant cannot be asked to augment the funds for the investigation on ground of financial crunch and a privately funded police investigation is vitiated. The Supreme Court cautioned that this was a precursor for miscarriage of justice. In constitutional scheme, the police and other statutory investigation agency cannot be allowed to be hackneyed by those who can afford it. All complaints shall be investigated with equal alacrity and with equal fairness irrespective of the financial capacity of the person lodging the complaint.[120]

The Supreme Court has held that manner and method of the investigation has to be left completely to the discretion of the police and the Magistrate should not interfere with the manner of investigation in exercise of its powers under Section 190. The Magistrate cannot direct the manner in which the chargesheet should be prepared but he has the right to refuse to accept the final report submitted by the police and may take cognizance of the offence and summon the accused even if the final report states that no case is made out.[121] Similarly, it has also held that the Public Prosecutor has no role to play in case prior to filing of the chargesheet and his role commences after the case is filed on completion of investigation. The Supreme Court in R Sarala vs T.S. Velu[122], held that investigation and prosecution are two different facets of administration of criminal justice. Involving the

120 Navinchandra N Majithia vs State of Meghalaya, 2000 CrLJ 4600

121 HS Bains vs State (UT of Chandigarh), AIR 1980 SC 1883; Jagdish Ram vs State of Rajasthan, (2004) 4 SCC 432; Union of India vs Prakash P. Hinduja, AIR 2003 SC 2612

122 2000 CrLJ 2453

PP in investigation is injudicious as well as pernicious in law. At any rate no investigation cannot be directed to consult the PP and submit the chargesheet in the court by the order of the court. Section 173 (3) casts an obligation upon the investigating officer to complete the investigation without unnecessary delay and sub section (2) enjoins on the officer in charge of the police station to forward the same to the Magistrate the police report on completion of the investigation. This power is subject only to supervision by the superior officer and the IO is not obliged to take the opinion of the PP or any authority.

However, in Vineet Narain's case[123] the Supreme Court gave several directions for the conduct of investigation in cases which involved influential persons and public officials to ensure impartial investigation and ensure rule of law in matters involving important issues of public interest. The case arose out of the scuttling of investigation in the Jain Dairies case involving graft by public officials and politicians. The Independent Review Committee (IRC) constituted by the Government gave several recommendations on the basis of which the Supreme Court gave directions under Article 32 read with Article 142 to implement the rule of law wherein the concept of equality enshrined in Article 14 is embedded,have the force of law under Article 141 and, by virtue of Article 144, it is the duty of all authorities, civil and judicial, in the territory of India to act in aid of the Court. The directions of the Court have been set forth hereunder:

I&II. Central Bureau of Investigation (CBI) and Central Vigilance Commission (CVC)

1. The Central Vigilance Commission (CVC) shall be given statutory status.
2. Selection for the post of Central Vigilance Commissioner shall be made by a Committee comprising the Prime Minister, Home Minister and the Leader of the Opposition from a panel of outstanding civil servants and others with impeccable integrity to be furnished by the Cabinet Secretary. The appointment shall be made by the President on the basis of the recommendations made by the Committee. This shall be done immediately.
3. The CVC shall be responsible for the efficient functioning of the CBI. While Government shall remain answerable for the CBI's functioning, to introduce visible objectivity in the mechanism to be established for over viewing the CBI's working, the CVC shall be entrusted with the responsibility of superintendence over the CBI's functioning. The CBI shall report to the CVC about cases taken up by it for investigation; progress of investigations; cases in which chargesheets are filed and their progress. The CVC shall review the progress of all cases moved by the CBI for sanction of prosecution of public servants which are pending with competent authorities, specially those in which sanction has been delayed or refused.

123 Vineet Narain Vs. Union Of India (1998)1 SCC226: AIR 1998 SC 889

4. The Central Government shall take all measures necessary to ensure that the CBI functions effectively and efficiently and is viewed as a non-partisan agency.
5. The CVC shall have a separate section in its Annual Report on the CBI's functioning after the supervisory function is transferred to it.
6. Recommendations for appointment of the Director, CBI shall be made by a Committee headed by the Central Vigilance Commissioner with the Home Secretary and Secretary (Personnel) as members. The views of the incumbent Director shall be considered by the Committee for making the best choice. The Committee shall draw up a panel of IPS officers on the basis of their seniority, integrity, experience in investigation and anti-corruption work. The final selection shall be made by Appointments Committee of the Cabinet (ACC) from the panel recommended by the Selection Committee. If none among the panel is found suitable, the reasons thereof shall be recorded and the Committee asked to draw up a fresh panel.
7. The Director, CBI shall have a minimum tenure of two years, regardless of the date of his superannuation. This would ensure that an officer suitable in all respects is not ignored merely because he has less than two years to superannuate from the date of his appointment.
8. The transfer of an incumbent Director, CBI in an extraordinary situation, including the need for him to take up a more important assignment, should have the approval of the Selection Committee.
9. The Director, CBI shall have full freedom for allocation of work within the agency as also for constituting teams for investigations. Any change made by the Director, CBI in the Head of an investigative team should be for cogent reasons and for improvement in investigation, the reasons being recorded.
10. Selection/extension of tenure of officers upto the level of Joint Director (JD) shall be decided by a Board comprising the central Vigilance Commissioner, Home Secretary and Secretary (Personnel) with the Director, CBI providing the necessary inputs. The extension of tenure or premature repatriation of officers upto the level of Joint Director shall be with final approval of the Board. Only cases pertaining to the appointment or extension of tenure of officers of the rank of Joint Director or above shall be referred to the Appointments Committee of the Cabinet (ACC) for decision.
11. Proposals for improvement of infrastructure, methods of investigation, etc. should be decided urgently. In order to strengthen CBI's in-house expertise, professionals from the revenue, banking and security sectors should be inducted into the CBI.
12. The CBI Manual based on statutory provisions of the CrPC provides essential guidelines for the CBI's functioning. It is imperative that the

CBI adheres scrupulously to the provisions in the Manual in relation to its investigative functions, like raids, seizure and arrests. Any deviation from the established procedure should be viewed seriously and severe disciplinary action taken against the concerned officials.

13. The Director, CBI shall be responsible for ensuring the filing of chargesheets in courts within the stipulated time limits, and the matter should be kept under constant review by the Director, CBI.

14. A document on CBI's functioning should be published within three months to provide the general public with a feedback on investigations and information for redress of genuine grievances in a manner which does not compromise with the operational requirements of the CBI.

15. Time limit of three months for grant of sanction for prosecution must be strictly adhered to. However, additional time of one month may be allowed where consultation is required with the Attorney General (AG) or any other law officer in the AG's office.

16. The Director, CBI should conduct regular appraisal of personnel to prevent corruption and/or inefficiency in the agency.

III. Enforcement Directorate

1. A Selection Committee headed by the Central Vigilance Commissioner and including the Home Secretary, Secretary (Personnel) and Revenue Secretary, shall prepare a panel for appointment of the Director, Enforcement Directorate. The appointment to the post of Director shall be made by the Appointments Committee of the Cabinet (ACC) from the panel recommended by the Selection Committee.

2. The Director, Enforcement Director like Director, CBI shall have a minimum tenure of two years. In his case also, premature transfer for any extraordinary reason should be approved by the aforesaid Selection Committee headed by the Central Vigilance Commissioner.

3. In view of the importance of the post of Director, Enforcement Directorate, it shall be upgraded to that of an Additional Secretary/Special Secretary to the Government.

4. Officers of the Enforcement Directorate handling sensitive assignments shall be provided adequate security to enable them to discharge their functions fearlessly.

5. Extensions of tenure upto the level of Joint Director in the Enforcement Directorate should be decided by the said Committee headed by the Central Vigilance Commissioner.

6. There shall be no premature media publicity by the CBI/Enforcement Directorate.
7. Adjudication/commencement of prosecution shall be made by the enforcement Directorate within a period of one year.
8. The Director, Enforcement Directorate shall monitor and ensure speedy completion of investigations/adjudications and launching of prosecutions. Revenue Secretary must review their progress regularly.
9. For speedy conduct of investigations abroad, the procedure to approve filing of applications for Letters Rogatory shall be streamlined and, if necessary, Revenue Secretary authorised to grant the approval.
10. A comprehensive circular shall be published by the Directorate to inform the public about the procedures/systems of its functioning for the sake of transparency.
11. In-house legal advice mechanism shall be strengthened by appointment of competent legal advisers in the CBI/Directorate of Enforcement.
12. The Annual Report of the Department of Revenue shall contain a detailed account on the working of the Enforcement Directorate.

IV. Nodal Agency

1. A Nodal Agency headed by the Home Secretary with Member (Investigation), Central Board of Direct Taxes, Director General, Revenue Intelligence, Director, Enforcement and Director, CBI as members, shall be constituted for coordinated action in cases having politico-bureaucrat-criminal nexus.
2. The Nodal Agency shall meet at least once every month.
3. Working and efficacy of the Nodal Agency should be watched for about one year so as to improve it upon the basis of the experience gained within this period.

V. Prosecution Agency

1. A panel of competent lawyers of experience and impeccable reputation shall be prepared with the advice of the Attorney General. Their services shall be utilised as Prosecuting Counsel in cases of significance. Even during the course of investigation of an offence, the advice of a lawyer chosen from the panel should be taken by the CBI/Enforcement Directorate.
2. Every prosecution which results in the discharge or acquittal of the accused must be reviewed by a lawyer on the panel and, on the basis of the opinion given, responsibility should be fixed for dereliction of duty, if any, of the

concerned officer. In such cases, strict action should be taken against the officer found guilty of dereliction of duty.

3. The preparation of the panel of lawyers with approval of the Attorney General shall be completed within three months.

4. Steps shall be taken immediately for the constitution of an able and impartial agency comprising persons of unimpeachable integrity to perform functions akin to those of the Director of Prosecutions in U.K. On the constitution of such a body, the task of supervising prosecutions launched by the CBI/Enforcement Directorate shall be entrusted to it.

5. Till the constitution of the aforesaid body, Special Counsel shall be appointed for the conduct of important trials on the recommendation of the Attorney General or any other law officer designated by him.

The learned amicus curiae had urged us to issue directions for the appointment of an authority akin to the Special or Independent Counsel in the United States of America for the investigation of charges in politically sensitive matters and for the prosecution of those cases and to ensure that appointments to sensitive posts in the CBI and other enforcement agencies and transfers therefrom were not made by the political executive. We are of the view that the time for these drastic steps has not come. It is our hope that it never will, for we entertain the belief that the investigative agencies shall function far better now, having regard to all that has happened since these writ petition were admitted and to the directions which are contained in this judgment. The personnel of the enforcement agencies should not now lack the courage and independence to go about their task as they should, even where those to be investigated are prominent and powerful persons.

In view of the problem in the States being even more acute, as elaborately discussed in the Report of the National Police Commission (1979), there is urgent need for the State Government also to set up credible mechanism for selection of the Police Chief in the States. The Central Government must pursue the matter within the State Governments and ensure that a similar mechanism, as indicated above, is set up in each State for the selection/appointment, tenure, transfer and posting of not merely the Chief of the State Police but also all police officers of the rank of Superintendent of Police and above. It is shocking to hear, a matter of common knowledge, that in some States the tenure of a Superintendent of Police is on an average only a few months and transfers are made for whimsical reasons. Apart from demoralising the police force, it has also the adverse effect of politicising the personnel. It is, therefore, essential that prompt measures are taken by the Central Government within the ambit of their constitutional powers in the federation to impress upon the State Governments that such a practice is alien to the envisaged constitutional machinery. The situation described in the National Police Commission's Report (1979) was alarming and it has become much worse by now. The desperation of the Union Home Minister in his letters to the state Governments, placed before us at the hearing, reveal a distressing situation which must be cured, if the rule of law is to prevail.

No action within the constitutional scheme found necessary to remedy the situations is too stringent in these circumstances. These directions require the strict compliance/adherence of the Union of India and all concerned.

In the Best Bakery case too, the Supreme Court ordered retrial and stated that "in the case of a defective investigation the Court has to be circumspect in evaluating the evidence and may have to adopt an active and analytical role to ensure that truth is found by having recourse to Section 311 or at a later stage also resorting to Section 391 instead or throwing hands in the air in despair. It would not be right in acquitting an accused person solely on account of the defect; to do so would tantamount to playing into the hands of the investigating officer if the investigation is designedly defective."[124] However, in a later decision in Satyajit Banerjee vs State of West Bengal[125] where the High Court had ordered retrial relying upon the Best Bakery case, the Supreme Court clarified that "The law laid down in the 'Best Bakery Case' in the aforesaid extraordinary circumstances, cannot be applied to all cases against the established principles of criminal jurisprudence. Direction for retrial should not be made in all or every case where acquittal of accused is for want of adequate or reliable evidence. In Best Bakery case, the first trial was found to be a farce and is described as 'mock trial.' Therefore, the direction for retrial was in fact, for a real trial. Such extraordinary situation alone can justify the directions as made by this Court in the Best Bakery Case (supra). So far as the position of law is concerned we are very clear that even if a retrial is directed in exercise of revisional powers by the High Court, the evidence already recorded at the initial trial cannot be erased or wiped out from the record of the case. The trial judge has to decide the case on the basis of the evidence already on record and the additional evidence which would be recorded on retrial."

The reading of the above chapter makes it apparent that the police have vast powers to investigate a case and deprive anyone of their liberty on suspicion

124 Zahira Habibulla H Sheikh v. State of Gujarat, AIR 2004 SC 3114. Also see Karnel Singh v. State of M.P. (1995(5) SCC 518)
125 (2005)1 SCC 115

that the person has committed an offence. Despite having such sweeping powers including practically an unlimited timeframe in investigating serious offences, there is a demand for grant of more powers by the police. If this demand is met, it will result in greater abuse of powers, in the absence of requisite checks and balances. The National Police Commission in its Third Report referring to the quality of arrests by the police in India mentioned power of arrest as one of the chief sources of corruption in the police. The report suggested that, by and large, nearly 60% of the arrests were either unnecessary or unjustified and that such unjustified police action accounted for 43.2% of the expenditure of the jails. The said Commission in its Third Report at page 31 observed thus:

"It is obvious hat a major portion of the arrests were connected with very minor prosecutions and cannot, therefore, be regarded as quite necessary from the point of view of crime prevention. Continued detention in jail of the persons so arrested has also meant avoidable expenditure on their maintenance. In the above period it was estimated that 43.2 per cent of the expenditure in the connected jails was over such prisoners only who in the ultimate analysis need not have been arrested at all."[126]

126 Quoted by the Supreme Court in Joginder Singh vs. State of U.P reported in 1994 Cri.L.J. 1981

CHAPTER 5

BASIC PRINCIPLES OF CRIMINAL LAW

Criminal law is divided into substantive law which explains basic concepts and to define what constitutes specific offences that are dealt with all phases of the criminal justice system and procedural law which encompasses such matters as rules of evidence, constitutional law and criminal procedure. Together they deal with means and methods necessary for making the criminal justice system operative, especially the functioning of judicial branch in a criminal proceeding.

Most crimes require the commission or omission of some act. In more serious offences malevolent state of mind (intent) that should have existed with/or without negligence for negligence too is a state of mind that leads to criminal liability when coupled with the prohibited act. Motive is irrelevant in assigning criminal liability though it can be of assistance in determining the presence of intention.

The main principles of criminal law in India are-

Individualisation of Offence

The offences in all the statutes seek to individualise the offence as the purpose of the law is to punish the offender and a necessary condition for that is that the liability of the act should be on a specific entity. Only individual human beings can be sentenced to imprisonment or death. This helps corporations escape criminal liability in cases where the victim or the prosecuting agency cannot fix criminal responsibility on any individual.

Motive is not Relevant

A natural corollary of the above factor is that generally the motive of the offender is immaterial. Law takes into consideration the intention of the individual to commit the offence and not his motive for doing so. This enables the legal system to overlook systemic causes such as poverty and oppression while trying an offender. However, motive can be seen as a mitigating factor or an extenuating circumstance in certain cases. The court while awarding the sentence takes this into consideration. Some of these circumstances are legally recognised as General Exceptions in Chapter IV of the Indian Penal Code (IPC).[127] Motive is also important in cases where there is no direct evidence but only circumstantial evidence, as in these cases motive for the commission of the

127 See Chapter 7 for a note on General Exceptions

offence would be held to be a circumstance against the accused. It has been held that where there is clear proof of motive for the crime, that lends additional support to the finding of the court that the accused was guilty but absence of clear proof of motive does not necessarily lead to the contrary conclusion. Hence, its presence or absence is generally used to corroborate the guilt of the accused and is generally not a material factor in a criminal trial.[128]

The only offence, which is punishable, based on the motive in the IPC is abduction. Section 362 of the IPC defines abduction as whoever by force compels, or by any deceitful means induces any person to go from any place is said to abduct the person. Though abduction per se is not an offence, it is an offence when done with the motive of committing murder (Section 364 IPC), for ransom (Section 364-A IPC), with intent to secretly and wrongfully confine person (Section 365 IPC), in order to compel a woman into marriage against her will or to force or seduce her to illicit intercourse (Section 366 IPC), in order to subject person to grievous hurt, slavery, or to unnatural lust of any person (Section 367 IPC) and with intent to steal from the person of a child below ten years (Section 369 IPC).

"Actus Reus" and "Mens Rea"

In criminal law, the essential ingredients of an offence are the act itself (actus reus) and the mental volition to commit the act (mens rea). The latter is the intention to commit the offence. In order to hold an individual responsible for an offence, he should have committed some act, which would be necessary for the commission of the offence, and these acts should be committed with the intention of committing the said offence. Thus, more than one individual may have performed the offence together or in part. An example of this is in the case of a murder of X, if A purchased the weapon knowing that it would be used for the murder of X, if B brought X to the place where C executed the act of murder of X in the presence of D who did nothing to prevent the offence but instigated C to commit the same and the entire plan was made by E, then all of them would be guilty of the murder of X and would be punishable for the same as if each of them had individually committed the act. Because of the requirement of the intention, criminal law sanctions do not apply to corporate entities and in order to launch a successful prosecution against criminal acts of corporations, the persons responsible for the same have to be named as accused and mens rea on their part proved. This leads to difficulty as the corporate veil makes it difficult to pin responsibility. In certain technical offences, however, mens rea is not an ingredient and prosecutions can be brought against the corporate bodies, but only the penalty of fine can be imposed in such cases as a corporation cannot be imprisoned.

128 Shivaji Sahabrao Bobade and Anr. v. State of Maharashtra. AIR 1973 SC 2622; AIR 1975 SC 12; AIR 1986 SC 1.899; (1997) 2 Crimes 111(SC)

Common Intention, Abetment and Criminal Conspiracy

Section 34 of the IPC states that when a criminal act is done by several persons, in furtherance of the common intention of all, each of such persons is liable for that act in the same manner as if it were done by him alone. A common intention can be formed on the spot and need not always be a pre-arranged plan. Though common intention may develop on the spot, it must, however, be anterior in point of time to the commission of offence showing a pre arranged plan and prior concert. The section has been held to mean that if two or more persons intentionally do a common thing jointly, it is the same as if each of them had done it individually and each and every one becomes responsible for the act of each and every other in execution and furtherance of their common purpose. As the purpose is common, so must be the responsibility.[129] Common intention has to be inferred from the totality of the circumstances and the prosecution has to prove the same. It cannot be inferred by mere presence of person at the time of commission of an offence by his confederates.[130] However, common intention is not the same as similar intention.

The abetment of an offence is also an offence. Section 107 of the IPC states that abetment is (i) instigating a person to do that offence, (ii) engaging with one or more other person or persons in any conspiracy for the doing that offence and (iii) intentionally aiding by any act or illegal omission, the doing of the offence. A person who by willful misrepresentation or by willful concealment of a material fact which he is bound to disclose, voluntarily causes or procures or attempts to cause or procure a thing to be done is said to instigate the doing of the offence. Whoever, either prior to or at the time of the commission of an offence, does anything in order to facilitate the commission of the offence is also liable for the aiding of the offence. To constitute the offence of abetment, it is not necessary that the act abetted should be committed or that the effect requisite to constitute the offence should be caused. Section 306 of the IPC makes abetment of suicide an offence punishable with imprisonment upto a term of ten years and fine. Even if the abettor does not know who the person committing the offence is, he would still be liable to be punished for abetment.

A criminal conspiracy is an agreement between two or more persons to commit or cause to commit an offence. Section 120B of the IPC provides for punishment for the conspiracy in the same manner as if the person has abetted such offence. In order to prove conspiracy; agreement and common design are necessary.

129 Krishna Govind Patil vs State of Maharashtra, AIR 1963 SC 1413; Amrik Singh vs State of Punjab, 1972 CrLJ 465; Ramaswamy Ayyanagar vs State of Tamil Nadu, AIR 1976 SC 2027; Parasa Raja Manikyala Rao vs State of AP, 2004 CrLJ 390

130 Malkhan vs State of UP, AIR 1975 SC 12; Bhaba Nanda Sarma vs State of Assam, AIR 1977 SC 2252; Maqsoodam vs State of UP, AIR 1983 SC 126

Under the law conspiracy is more difficult to prove than abetment or common intention as the evidence of the co-accused has limited value and there is little else to prove the agreement to commit an offence. This limitation in the law has encouraged the increasing use of contract killing by poor unemployed youth and given rise to the growing incidence of professionals depending on blue-collar crime for a living.

Whereas under Section 120A, the essence of the offence of criminal conspiracy is a bare agreement to commit the offence, the abetment under Section 107 requires the commission of some act or illegal omission pursuant to the conspiracy. A charge under Section 107/109 should, therefore, be in combination with a substantive offence, whereas the charge under Section 120A/120B could be an independent charge. Thus, Sections 120A & 120B made conspiracy a substantive offence and rendered the mere agreement to commit an offence punishable. Even if an overt act does not take place pursuant to the illegal agreement, the offence of conspiracy would still be attracted. In V C Shukla vs. State[131] the Supreme Court observed that in most cases it will be difficult to get direct evidence of the agreement, but a conspiracy can be inferred even from circumstances giving rise to a conclusive or irresistible inference of an agreement between two or more persons to commit an offence. The well known rule governing circumstantial evidence is that each and every incriminating circumstance must be clearly established by reliable evidence and "the circumstances proved must form a chain of events from which the only irresistible conclusion about the guilt of the accused can be safely drawn and no other hypothesis against the guilt is possible."

In the Parliament shoot out case[132], the Supreme Court held that a principle which deserves notice is that cumulative effect of the proved circumstances should be taken into account in determining the guilt of the accused rather than adopting an isolated approach to each of the circumstances. Of course, each one of the circumstances should be proved beyond reasonable doubt. Lastly, in regard to the appreciation of evidence relating to conspiracy, the Court must take care to see that the acts or conduct of the parties must be conscious and clear enough to infer their concurrence as to the common design and its execution. The Court further held that "We do not think that the theory of agency can be extended thus far, that is to say, to find all the conspirators guilty of the actual offences committed in execution of the common design even if such offences were ultimately committed by some of them, without the participation of others. We are of the view that those who committed the offences pursuant to the conspiracy by indulging in various overt acts will be individually liable for those offences in addition to being liable for criminal conspiracy; but, the non-participant conspirators cannot be found guilty of

131 AIR 1980 SC 962
132 State (N.C.T. of Delhi) Vs. Navjot Sandhu @ Afshan Guru, (2005)11SCC600

the offence or offences committed by the other conspirators. There is hardly any scope for the application of the principle of agency in order to find the conspirators guilty of a substantive offence not committed by them. Criminal offences and punishments therefor are governed by statute. The offender will be liable only if he comes within the plain terms of the penal statute. Criminal liability for an offence cannot be fastened by way of analogy or by extension of a common law principle." The Court held that while in the case of Section 34 IPC, the constructive liability for the crime is specifically fastened on each of those who participate in the crime in furtherance of the common intention. But Section 120B does not convey that idea.

In Kehar Singh's case[133] the Supreme Court held that, "the gist of the offence of conspiracy then lies, not in doing the act, or effecting the purpose for which the conspiracy is formed, nor in attempting to do them, nor in inciting others to do them, but in the forming of the scheme or agreement between the parties. Agreement is essential. Mere knowledge, or even discussion, of the plan is not, per se enough."

In the case of State v. Nalini[134], the Supreme Court observed that:

"In reaching the stage of meeting of minds, two or more persons share information about doing an illegal act or a legal act by illegal means. This is the first stage where each is said to have knowledge of a plan for committing an illegal act or a legal act by illegal means. Among those sharing the information some or all may form an intention to do an illegal act or a legal act by illegal means. Those who do form the requisite intention would be parties to the agreement and would be conspirators but those who drop out cannot be roped in as collaborators on the basis of mere knowledge unless they commit acts or omissions from which a guilty common intention can be inferred. It is not necessary that all the conspirators should participate from the inception to the end of the conspiracy; some may join the conspiracy after the time when such intention was first entertained by any one of them and some others may quit from the conspiracy. All of them cannot but be treated as conspirators. Where in pursuance of the agreement the conspirators commit offences individually or adopt illegal means to do a legal act which has a nexus to the object of conspiracy, all of them will be liable for such offences even if some of them have not actively participated in the commission of those offences."

Attempt and Preparation

Attempts to commit the offence are also punishable. In cases where the attempt to commit an offence is not an offence, Section 511 of the IPC prescribes

133 Kehar Singh vs State (Delhi Admn), AIR 1988 SC 1883
134 (1995) 5 SCC253

punishment for one-half of the longest term of imprisonment provided for that offence Attempts to commit certain offences are also specific offences with penalties prescribed. Section 307 of the IPC punishes attempts to murder with imprisonment upto ten years and if hurt is caused to any person by such act with maximum penalty of life imprisonment. Section 309 makes attempts to commit suicide an offence punishable with simple imprisonment upto one year.

Generally, preparations to commit an offence are not offences when no harm or offence of other nature occurs. But certain sections in the IPC make preparation to commit a certain offence also an offence. Section 399 of the IPC makes it an offence to make any preparation for committing dacoity and liable to be punished with rigorous imprisonment for a term upto ten years.

Burden of Proof

Section 101 of the Indian Evidence Act provides that whoever asserts a certain fact must prove it. This means that the burden of proof in criminal cases is on the prosecution. The prosecution has to prove two things -- that the accused committed the offence alleged and that the accused committed the same with the requisite mens rea. The prosecution must prove its case beyond reasonable doubt and the benefit of doubt goes to the accused, as one of the basic principles of modern criminal jurisprudence is that the innocent should in no case be punished. The doubt should be such as a reasonable person would honestly and conscientiously entertain as to the guilt of the accused. However, generally the court presumes that the act was done with the requisite intention and it is for the accused to prove lack of intention. The Indian Penal Code in its Chapter IV enumerates the various cases of general exceptions, which constitute the legal arena of lack of mens rea. Section 105 of the Indian Evidence Act states that when a person is accused of any offence, the burden of proving the existence of circumstance bringing the case within any of the exceptions is upon him and the court shall presume the absence of any such circumstance. In India, the accused does not have to give evidence or be examined under oath. The primary responsibility of proving the case lies on the prosecution and the burden shifts on the accused only after the prosecution has proved its case.

Presumptions Under Law

In certain cases the law may presume the existence of certain facts. Section 114 of the Indian Evidence Act states that the court may presume the existence of any fact which it thinks likely to have happened regard having been had to the common cause of natural events, human conduct and public and private business, in their relation to the facts of the particular case. The section proceeds to give nine illustrations of presumptions a court may make of which the following are relevant in criminal proceedings:

a) That a man who is in possession of stolen goods soon after the theft is either the thief or has received the goods knowing them to be stolen, unless he can account for his possession;

b) That an accomplice is unworthy of credit, unless he is corroborated in material particulars;

c) That judicial and official acts have been regularly performed;

d) That evidence which could be and is not produced, would, if produced, be unfavourable to the person who withholds it;

e) That if a man refuses to answer a question, which he is not compelled to, answer by law, the answer, if given, would be unfavourable to him.

That apart there are certain other presumptions which a court may have as in cases of suicide by married women within seven years of marriage where it is shown that the husband or his relatives had subjected her to cruelty, the court may presume, having regard to all other circumstances of the case, that such suicide had been abetted by her husband or by such relative of her husband (Section113A of the Indian Evidence Act).

In certain cases the court shall presume the existence of certain facts on the proof of other specified facts or circumstances. Under Section 113B of the said Act, when the question is whether a person has committed the dowry death of a woman and it is shown that soon before her death such woman had been subjected by such person to cruelty or harassment for, or in connection with, any demand for dowry, the court shall presume that such person had caused the dowry death. Under Section 114A of the said Act, in certain prosecutions for rape falling under Section 376(2) of the IPC where sexual intercourse by the accused is proved and the question is whether it was without the consent of the woman alleged to have been raped and she states in her evidence before the court that she did not consent, the court shall presume that she did not consent. Under Section 111A of the said Act, where a person is accused of having committed any offence of waging a war against the state in any area declared to be a disturbed area under any enactment for the time being in force, making provision for the suppression of disorder and restoration and maintenance of public order in any area in which there has been over a period of more than one month of extensive disturbance of the public peace, and it is shown that such person had been at a place in area at a time when firearms or explosives were used at or from that place to attack or resist the members of any armed forces or the forces charged with the maintenance of public order acting in the discharge of their duties, it shall be presumed unless the contrary is shown, that such person had committed such offence.

Oral Evidence

Evidence is that which is produced before the court at the time of trial through the witnesses. Evidence is substantive and corroborative. Substantive evidence is that which is conclusive on a fact in issue such as the eye witness account of the offence, a medical report proved by the concerned medical officer and which the court can rely upon to base a conviction. Corroborative evidence is that which the court cannot rely upon exclusively to come to any conclusion but which can be used to corroborate the substantive evidence. There are two types of evidence: oral and documentary. The type of oral evidence required proving a case is direct evidence and not hearsay evidence (Section 60 of the Indian Evidence Act). This means that the evidence should be of the person who is the witness to the event or is in any manner directly concerned with the subject of his deposition. All facts except the contents of documents may be proved by oral evidence. Hearsay evidence is inadmissible. Hearsay evidence has been defined by an English court as " a statement made otherwise than by a witness in giving evidence is called 'hearsay' when the object of such evidence is to establish the truth of what is contained in the statement and is generally deemed to be irrelevant and inadmissible". [135]

Evidence should be only with regards to the following:

1. Facts in issue, which means and includes any fact from which, either by itself or in connection with other facts, the existence, non-existence, nature of extent of any right, liability, or disability, asserted or denied in any proceeding (Section3). In short, facts in issue are those that are alleged by the prosecution and denied by the plea of not guilty of the accused.

   Section 5 of the Indian Evidence Act gives an illustration of this:

   A is tried for the murder of B by beating him with a club with the intention of causing his death.

   At A's trial, the following facts are in issue-
   A's beating B with the club;
   A's causing B's death by such beating;
   A's intention to cause B's death;
   The facts which are relevant to the facts in issue (Section 5)

2. Facts which form a part of the same transaction as the facts in issue (Section 6)

3. Facts which are the occasion, cause or effect (immediate or otherwise) of the facts in issue or which afforded an opportunity for their occurrence or transaction (Section 7)

4. Facts that show or constitute a motive or preparation for any fact in issue or relevant fact (Section 8)

135 R. vs. Harz, R. vs. Power, (1966) 3 All. E.R. 433, CCA

5. Facts showing the conduct of a person, for example if the accused absconded after the commission of the offence (Section 8)
6. Facts explaining or introducing a fact in issue (Section 9)
7. Facts supporting or rebutting an inference suggested by a fact in issue or relevant fact (Section 9)
8. Facts establishing identity where it is in issue, for example identification parades conducted where the identity of the accused was unknown (Section 9)
9. Facts fixing time and place of fact in issue or relevant fact happened (Section 9)
10. Facts showing the relationship of parties (Section 9)
11. Facts about things said or done by conspirator in reference to common design (Section 10)
12. Facts not otherwise relevant become relevant if they are inconsistent with any fact in issue or relevant fact or if by themselves or in connection with other facts they make the existence or non- existence of any fact in issue or relevant fact highly probable, that is, evidence of alibi (Section 11)
13. Facts showing the existence of any state of mind, such as intention, knowledge, good faith, negligence, rashness, ill-will or good-will or showing the existence of any state of body or bodily feeling when it is in issue or relevant (Section 14)
14. Facts bearing on question whether an act was accidental or intentional (Section15).

In criminal cases, previous good character of the accused is relevant but previous bad character of the accused is not relevant except in case where evidence has been given of the good character of the accused in order to disprove the same (Sections 53 and 54 of the Indian Evidence Act). The credit of a witness cannot be impeached except in the following cases:

1. By the evidence of persons who testify that they, from their knowledge of the witness, believe him to be unworthy of credit;
2. By proof that the witness has been bribed, or has accepted the offer of a bribe, or has received any other corrupt inducement to give his evidence;
3. By proof of former statements inconsistent with any part of his evidence which is liable to be contradicted. (Section 155 of Indian Evidence Act)

A witness is not excused from answering a relevant question on the ground that the answer would incriminate, however the witness will be protected from being prosecuted on the basis of such answers except in a prosecution for giving false evidence by such answer. Questions that impeach the credibility of the witness on the matter to which he testifies are permitted.

The Supreme Court has held that it would be erroneous to accord undue primacy to hypothetical answers of medical witnesses to exclude the eye witnesses account which had to be tested independently and not treated as the 'variable' keeping the medical evidence as the 'constant'. It is trite that where the eye witnesses account is found credible and trustworthy, medical opinion pointing to alternative possibilities is not accepted as conclusive. Eye witnesses account would require a careful independent assessment and evaluation for their credibility which should not be adversely prejudged making any other evidence including medical evidence as the sole touchstone for the test of such credibility.[136] In Alamgir vs State[137], the Supreme Court held that conviction cannot be based on the evidence of the handwriting expert and the same can be relied upon when supported by other items of evidence and simply corroborates circumstantial evidence.

Circumstantial Evidence

However, for a crime to be proved, it is not necessary that the crime must be seen to have been committed and must, in all circumstances, be proved by direct ocular evidence by examining before the Court those persons who had seen its commission, the offence can be proved by circumstantial evidence too. Circumstantial evidence is not direct to the point in issue but consists of evidence of various other facts that are so closely associated with the fact in issue that taken together, they form a chain of circumstances from which the existence of the principal fact can be legally inferred or presumed. When a case rests upon circumstantial evidence, such evidence must satisfy the following tests:

a) The circumstances from which an inference of guilt is sought to be drawn, must be cogently and firmly established;

b) Those circumstances should be of a definite tendency unerringly pointing towards the guilt of the accused;

c) The circumstances, taken cumulatively, should form a chain so complete that there is no escape from the conclusion that within all human probability the crime was committed by the accused and none else; and

d) The circumstantial evidence in order to sustain conviction must be complete and incapable of explanation of any other hypothesis than that of the guilt of the accused but should be inconsistent with his innocence.

In cases where the prosecution relies upon circumstantial evidence due to lack of direct or eyewitness, the evidence should be such that the chain of circumstances leads to no other conclusion except the guilt of the accused. In cases where

136 State of Madhya Pradesh vs Dahrkole, 2005 CrLJ 108. Also see State of UP vs Krishna Gopal, AIR 1988 SC 2154 ; Janak Singh vs State of UP, 2004 CrLJ 2533
137 2003 CrLJ 456

there is even one missing link in the entire chain of events, which could lead to the possibility of the innocence of the accused, the court should acquit the accused.[138] The Supreme Court has held in Babudas vs State of MP[139] that false plea of alibi on the part of the accused can be a link in chain of circumstances but it cannot be sole link or chain based on which a conviction can be based.

Types of Witnesses

All persons shall be competent to testify unless the court considers that they are prevented from understanding the questions put to them or from giving rational answers to those questions by tender years, extreme old age, disease, whether of body or mind, or any other cause of the same kind (Section 118 of the Indian Evidence Act). A speech-impaired person can give his evidence in writing or in sign language.

No particular number of witnesses is required in order to prove a case. The court can convict on the basis of the solitary evidence of one person who is the eyewitness provided the evidence is cogent and the court finds the witness trustworthy and inspiring confidence and an independent witness[140]as evidence has to weighed and not counted.[141] Generally, in cases where the witness is shown to be an interested witness, i.e. a person who has some direct interest in seeing that the accused is somehow or the other convicted, the court looks for corroboration and does not convict on the sole evidence of such a witness. Corroborative evidence must be independent testimony connecting the accused with the crime and can be direct or circumstantial, and not necessarily on every material circumstance. The sufficiency of corroboration depends on the facts and circumstances of each case and it need not be such that standing alone would sustain a conviction. An interested witness's evidence has to be subjected to scrutiny for any material contradictions and infirmities and for corroboration on material particulars. An accomplice who is a guilty associate or partner in crime is a competent witness. An accomplice by becoming an approver becomes a prosecution witness. An approver is an accomplice who is tendered a pardon in respect of offences, which are triable at Sessions level or punishable with imprisonment extending to seven years or more. The evidence of the approver must be subjected to the following tests:

(i) His evidence must be reliable, that is the court has to verify the probability of the truth, see whether the disclosure is full and complete and check whether the evidence is self-exculpatory;

(ii) His evidence should be sufficiently corroborated.[142]

138 Sharad Birdhichand Sarda vs. State of Maharashtra, (1984) 4 SCC 116; Dhananjoy Chatterjee vs. State of West Bengal, (1994) 2 SCC 220

139 2003 CrLJ 2563

140 Marwadi Kishor Parmanand vs. State of Gujarat, (1994) 4 SCC 549

141 Muluwa vs State of MP, AIR 1976 SC 989

142 Shankar vs. State of Tamil Nadu, (1994) 4 SCC 478

The victim or a relative of the victim is not considered an interested witness unless there are other reasons such as previous enmity, which make them interested. The Supreme Court has held that a relative is not likely to falsely implicate the accused unless enmity is alleged for which the foundation has to be laid and the court has to adopt a careful approach and analyse evidence to find out whether it is cogent and credible[143]. The evidence of a child witness can be relied upon for sustaining a conviction provided the court finds that the child is capable of understanding the nature of the facts deposed of by him.[144] But the child's testimony has to be evaluated carefully to see if he is able to understand the nature of the incident and because he is easy prey to tutoring, therefore the court looks for corroboration from other evidence to his testimony.[145] In rape cases the evidence of the victim should not be treated as that of the interested witness but that of the prosecutrix.[146] The Supreme Court has held that the conviction can be founded on the only evidence of victim of sexual assault if it inspires confidence unless there are compelling reasons for seeking corroboration. In case of sexual assault corroboration as condition for judicial reliance is not a requirement of law but guidance of prudence and statements of prosecutrix well corroborated by medical and other contemporaneous documents to prove charge against accused.[147] In cases where independent witnesses are available and not produced, the court could draw an adverse inference against the prosecution and the benefit of doubt would go to the accused.[148] In Banti vs State of MP[149], the Supreme Court held that there are two categories of witnesses to occurrences -- one who are close to the victim and the other who have no such relation. The Public Prosecutor's duty is to examine witnesses from latter category and limit their number. In the said case, the defence witness was found to have gone out of his way to help the accused and was found to be a compulsive liar and the court held that like any other witness his evidence has to be tested on the touchstone of reliability, credibility and trustworthiness particularly when he attempted to resile and speak against records and in derogation of his earlier conduct and behaviour. In doing so if the court finds it to be untruthful, there is no legal bar in discarding it.

---

143 Dalip Singh vs State of Punjab, AIR 1953 SC 364; Guli Chand vs State of Rajasthan, (1974) 3 SCC 698; Vadivelu Thevar vs State of Madras, AIR 1957 SC 614; Sucha Singh vs State of Punjab, (2003)7 SCC 643

144 AIR 1954 SC 54; AIR 1979 SC 1194,1347; (1981) 2 SCC 569; Ratansinh Dalsukhbhai Nayak vs State of Gujarat, AIR 2004 SC 23

145 State of Assam vs Mafizuddin Ahmed, (1983) 2 SCC 14; Bhagwan Singh vs State of MP, 2003 CrLJ 1262

146 Radha Bai vs. Union Territory of Pondicherry, (1995) 4 SCC 141; Kamalanantha vs State of Tamil Nadu (2005)5SCC194

147 Kamalanantha vs State of Tamil Nadu, (2005)5SCC194

148 1978 Cr. L.J. 177 (SC)

149 2004 CrLJ 372

In Kalpnath Rai's case, the Supreme Court held that there can be no legal provision that the evidence of police officers unless supported by independent witnesses is unworthy of acceptance. Non-examination of independent witness or even presence of such witness during police raid would cast an added duty on the court to adopt greater care while scrutinising the evidence of the police officers. If the evidence of the police officer is found acceptable, it would be an erroneous proposition that the court must reject the prosecution version solely on the ground that no independent witness has been examined.[150] However, they being interested in the result of the case, their testimony requires a more careful scrutiny[151]. But where the entire prosecution case depended on the testimony of the police officers and no effort was made to get independent respectable witnesses in whose presence seizure could be made, the Supreme Court held that the entire episode was shrouded in secrecy and sounded unnatural and acquitted the accused.[152]

Where the witness deposed on the facts on the first day and thereafter did a volte face and denied knowledge of the events, the Supreme Court held that the statement of the witness, as recorded on the first day including his cross-examination, was truthful and reliable. It is well settled that the evidence of a prosecution witness cannot be rejected in toto merely because the prosecution chose to treat him as hostile and cross-examined him. The evidence of such witness cannot be treated as effaced or washed off the record altogether but the same can be accepted to the extent his version is found to be dependable on a careful scrutiny thereof.[153]

The evidence of a prosecution witness not declared hostile can be relied upon by the defence.[154] The Supreme Court has held the witness's background ought to be kept in mind while assessing his evidence and in scanning the evidence of the various witnesses the court has to inform itself that variances on the fringes, discrepancies in details, contradictions in narrations and embellishments in inessential parts cannot militate against the veracity of the core of the testimony, provided there is impress of truth and conformity to probability in the substantial fabric of testimony delivered.[155]

150 Kalpnath Rai vs State (Through CBI), (1997) 8 SCC732; Also see Balbir Singh vs State, (1996) 11 SCC 139; Paras Ram vs State of Haryana, (1992) 4 SCC 662; Karamjit Singh vs State (Delhi Admn) 2003 CrLJ 2021

151 Tahir vs State (Delhi), (1996) 3 SCC 338

152 Bhagwan Singh vs State of Rajasthan, AIR 1978 SC 985

153 Radha Mohan Singh vs State of U.P., (2006) 2 SCC 450.Also see Bhagwan Singh v. State of Haryana AIR 1976 SC 202, Rabinder Kumar Dey v. State of Orissa AIR 1977 SC 170, Syed Akbar v. State of Karnataka AIR 1979 SC 1848 and Khujji @ Surendra Tiwari v. State of Madhya Pradesh AIR 1991 SC 1853

154 Raja Ram vs State of Rajasthan (2005) 5 SCC 272

155 Shivaji Sahabrao Bobade and Anr. v. State of Maharashtra (AIR 1973 SC 2622); Also see State of Punjab vs Hakam Singh, (2005) 7 SCC 498 where the witness was a rustic woman and the court held that her background had to be kept in view while evaluating her evidence.

In Sucha Singh vs State of Punjab[156], the Supreme Court held that the principle of "falsus in uno, falsus in omnibus" does not apply in India and is merely a rule of caution. Thus, even if a major portion of evidence of witness is found to be deficient, in case the residue is sufficient to prove the guilt of the accused, then notwithstanding the acquittal of the co-accused, his conviction can be maitnaiend. The court has to separate grain from chaff and appraise in each case as to what extent the evidence is acceptable. If this separation cannot be done, then the evidence has to be rejected in toto. Minor variations in the evidence would not affect its reliability if the evidence appears trustworthy.[157] But material improvements in the form of contradictions, exaggerations, embellishments and inconsistencies in the testimony over the police statement would make the evidence doubtful and the witness's evidence would have to be discarded.[158] In Tahsildar Singh's case[159], the Supreme Court held that a statement made to the police but not reduced to writing, could not be used for any purpose, not even for contradiction. It was incorrect to say that all omissions in regard to important features of the incident which were expected to be included in the statement made before the police, should be treated as contradictions. It was for the trial judge to decide in each case, after comparing the part or parts of the statement. Relevant and material omissions amount to vital contradictions which can be established by cross-examination and confronting the witness with his previous statement to the police recorded by the police with that made in the witness-box, whether the recital intended to be used for contradiction was one of the nature indicated above. The Court concluded that the following propositions emerge:

(1) A. statement in writing made by a witness before a police officer in the course of investigation can be used only to contradict his statement in the witness-box and for no other purpose;

(2) Statements not reduced to writing by the police officer cannot be used for contradiction;

(3) Though a particular statement is not expressly recorded, a statement that can be deemed to be part of that expressly recorded can be used for contradiction, not because it is an omission strictly so-called but because it is deemed to form part of the recorded statement;

(4) Such a fiction is permissible by construction only in the following three cases:

156 (2003)7 SCC 643
157 Sukhdeo Yadav vs State of Bihar, (2001)8 SCC 86
158 Hasan Murtza vs State of Haryana, (2002)3 SCC 1
159 Tahsildar Singh vs State of UP, 1959 AIR 1012

(i) When a recital is necessarily implied from the recital or recitals found in the statement ; illustration: in the recorded statement before the police the witness states that he saw A stabbing B at a particular point of time, but in the witness-box he says that he saw A and C stabbing B at the same point of time; in the statement before the police the word " only " can be implied, i.e., the witness saw only A stabbing B;

(ii) A negative aspect of a positive recital in a statement; illustration: in the recorded statement before the police the witness says that a dark man stabbed B, but in the witness-box he says that a fair man stabbed B; the earlier statement must be deemed to contain the recital not only that the culprit was a dark complexioned man but also that he was not of fair complexion; and

(iii) When the statement before the police and that before the Court cannot stand together; illustration: the witness says in the recorded statement before the police that A after stabbing B ran away by a northern lane, but in the Court he says that immediately after stabbing he ran away towards the southern lane; as he could not have run away immediately after the stabbing, i.e., at the same point of time, towards the northern lane as well as towards the southern lane, if one statement is true, the other must necessarily be false. The aforesaid examples are not intended to be exhaustive but only illustrative. The same instance may fall under one or more heads. It is for the trial Judge to decide in each case' after comparing the part or parts of the statement recorded by the police with that made in the witness-box, to give a ruling, having regard to the aforesaid principles, whether the recital intended to be used for contradiction satisfies the requirements of law.

Admissions and Confessions

An admission in a criminal trial would be incriminating evidence by the accused based on a statement made by him, whether written or oral. Though in a criminal trial an accused is not bound to give evidence, certain statements made by him regarding a fact in issue or a relevant fact would be admissible against him. The difference between a confession and an admission is that if the statement by itself is sufficient to prove the guilt of the accused it is a confession, but if on the other hand, the statement falls short of it, it amounts to an admission. The acid test is that where a conviction can be based upon that statement alone it is a confession and that where supplementary evidence is needed to authorise a conviction, it is an admission.[160]

Sections 24 to 30 of the Indian Evidence Act deal with confessions. A confession made by an accused is irrelevant in a criminal proceeding if it appears to the

160 AIR 1959 All. 518; AIR 1942 Mad. 654

court that the confession was caused by any inducement, threat or promise made by a person in authority and sufficient to give the accused grounds to reasonably suppose that by making it he would gain any advantage or avoid any evil of a temporal nature in reference to the proceedings against him (Section 24). However, if such a confession is made after the impression caused by any such inducement, threat or promise is in the opinion of the court fully removed, it becomes relevant. Thus, the basic principle is that the confession should be voluntary and genuine, even if it is subsequently retracted, and wherever possible, should be corroborated in order to base the conviction on it. Confessions are judicial or extra- judicial. Judicial confessions are those made before a judicial authority under Section 164 of the Code of Criminal Procedure, 1973, while extra- judicial confessions are made before any person. Extra judicial confessions can be relied upon and their acceptability depends upon the reliability of the person to whom such confession is supposed to have been made by the accused and requires material corroboration.

The Supreme Court of India has explained the law with regards confessions in the Auto Shankar case based on its earlier decisions in Paragraph 33

> "The confession is a form of admission consisting of direct acknowledgement of guilt in a criminal charge. It must be in express words by the accused in a criminal case of the truth of the guilt fact charged or some essential part of it and a statement that contains a self-exculpatory matter cannot amount to a confession. The confession should be a voluntary one that means not caused by inducement, threat or promise. Whether a confession is voluntary or not is essentially a question of fact. The judicial confessions are those that are made before a Magistrate or in court in due course of legal proceedings and when such a confession is retracted, the courts have held that apart from the statement being voluntary it should be true and should receive sufficient corroboration in material particulars by independent evidence. The rule of prudence namely requiring corroboration does not mean that each and every circumstance mentioned in the confession with regard to the participation of the accused in the crime must be separately and independently corroborated. It is sufficient if there is general corroboration of the important incidents, just like in the case of an approver's evidence and it is not necessary that the corroborative evidence itself should be sufficient for conviction... it is not illegal to base a conviction on an uncorroborated confession of an accused person but as a rule of prudence which has sanctified itself to the rule of law, the courts do look for corroboration before acting upon and accepting the retracted confession and what amount of corroboration would be necessary in a case would be a question of fact to be determined in the light of the circumstances of the case".[161]

161 (Shankar alias Gauri Shankar and others Vs. State of Tamil Nadu, (1999) 4 SCC 478

A confession made to a police officer shall not be proved against a person accused of an offence (Section 25). A confession made by any person whilst he is in the custody of a police officer shall also not be proved as against such person unless it is made in the immediate presence of a Magistrate (Section 26). However, when any fact is deposed to as discovered in consequence of information received from a person accused of an offence, in the custody of a police officer, so much of such information, whether it amounts to a confession or not, as related distinctly to the fact thereby discovered, may be proved (Section 27). This statement should lead to fresh discovery of a fact related to the case including the recovery of any incriminating object within the exclusive knowledge of the accused. If a confession is otherwise relevant, it does not become irrelevant because it was made under a promise of secrecy or in consequence of a deception practiced on the accused for the purpose of obtaining it or when he was drunk or because it was made in answer to questions which he need not have answered whatever may have been the form of those questions or because he was not warned that he was not bound to make such confession and that evidence of it might be given against him (Section 29 of the Indian Evidence Act). When more than one person are being tried jointly for the same offence, and a confession made by one of such persons affecting himself and some other of such persons is proved, the court may take into consideration such confession as against such other person as well as against the person who makes the confession (Section 30).

As earlier stated in order to be admissible confession should be true and voluntary. The court has to take certain precautions and look into the surrounding circumstances in order to judge whether the statement was voluntary, and if it passes the test, then it is admissible even if subsequently retracted.

Principles Governing Confessions

Some of the principles in order make confessions admissible are:

1. Accused persons willing to make a confession should be taken for the purpose before a Judicial Magistrate and, whenever possible, before the Magistrate who will not eventually try the case. Any Metropolitan Magistrate or Judicial Magistrate may, whether or not he has jurisdiction in the case, record any confession or statement made to him in the course of an investigation under the Code of Criminal Procedure, 1973 or any other law for the time being in force, or at any time afterwards before the commencement of the inquiry or trial, as required by Section 164 of the Code of Criminal Procedure, 1973.
2. In the absence of exceptional reasons, confessions should ordinarily be recorded in open court and during court hours.

3. The examination of the accused person immediately after the police bring him into court, is deprecated. When the accused is produced before the Magistrate, the Police Officers should be removed from the courtroom unless, in the opinion of the Magistrate, the duty of ensuring their safe custody cannot safely be left to other attendants. In that case, only the minimum number of police officers necessary to secure the safe custody of the accused person should be allowed to remain in the courtroom.
4. It should be impressed upon the accused that he is no longer in police custody.
5. The Magistrate should then question the accused whether he has any complaint to make of ill-treatment against the police or others responsible for his arrest or custody, and shall place on record the questions put and the answers given.
6. If the prisoner makes an allegation of ill-treatment, the Magistrate shall take judicial note of the complaint and follow due process (explained in Chapter IV).
7. If the accused does not complain of any ill-treatment or improper conduct or inducement on the part of the police, or if in spite of the alleged ill-treatment, misconduct or inducement, he adheres to his intention of making a confessional statement, the Magistrate should give the accused a warning that he is not bound to make the confession and that, if he does so, it will be taken down and may thereafter be used as evidence against him. A note of the warning given to accused should be kept on record.
8. Thereafter, the Magistrate should give the accused a reasonable time, which should ordinarily not be less than 24 hours, for reflection on circumstances in which he would be free from the influence and any other person interested in having the confession recorded.
9. After the accused is produced before the Magistrate again, it should be ascertained from him whether he is willing to make a confession. If he expresses his desire to confess, all police officers should be removed from the courtroom, unless in the opinion of the Magistrate, the duty of ensuring his safe custody cannot safely be entrusted to other attendants. In that case, only the minimum number of police officers necessary to secure the safe custody of the accused person should be allowed to remain in the courtroom. In any case, it is not desirable that the police officer making the investigation should be present.
10. The Magistrate should then question the accused as to the length of time during which he has been in the custody of the police. It is not sufficient to note the date and hour recited in the police papers, at which the accused is said to have been formally arrested.

11. The provisions of Sections 163 and 164 of the Code of Criminal Procedure, 1973, should be carefully attended to. The first clause of Section 163, taken with Section 24 of the Indian Evidence Act, provides that if a confession is caused by any inducement, threat or promise, offered or made, or caused to be offered or made by any police officer or person in authority in reference to the charge against the accused person, then if in the opinion of the court, the inducement, threat or promise was sufficient to give the accused person grounds, which would appear to him reasonable, for supposing that by making the confession he would gain any advantage or avoid any evil of a temporal nature in reference to the proceedings against him, and unless in the opinion of the court the impression caused by any such inducement, threat or promise, has been fully removed, such confession is irrelevant, that is, it cannot be used as evidence in any criminal proceeding.

12. Under clause (2) of Section 163, for a confession of an accused person made in the course of a police investigation to have any value, it must be one that the accused person was disposed to make of his own free will. Before recording any such confession, the Magistrate is bound to question the accused person, and unless upon that questioning he has reason to believe that the confession is voluntary, he cannot make the memorandum at the foot of the record. He cannot say "I believe that this confession was voluntarily made" unless he has questioned the accused person, and from that questioning has formed the belief not a doubtful attitude of mind, but a positive belief that the confession is a statement which the accused person was disposed to make of his own free will.

13. Before recording a confession, the Magistrate should question the accused with a view to ascertaining the exact circumstances in which his confession is being made and the connection of the police with it under clauses 5,7 and10 above. In particular, where more than one accused is involved in the case, he should question the accused whether he has been induced to make a confession by promise to make him an approver in the case. Anything in the nature of cross-examination of the accused is to be deprecated. It should, however, be the endeavour of the Magistrate, without having recourse to checking or attempts to entrap the accused, to record the statement with as much detail as possible regarding the circumstances under which the confession was being made, the extent to which the police had anything to do with the accused prior to his offer to make a confession, as well as the fullest possible particulars of the incidents to which the confession relates. These details are important as they furnish the material on which the value of the confession is to be estimated; and the greater the detail, the greater the chances of a correct estimate. Every question and every answer should be recorded in full.

14. The Magistrate should add to the certificate required by Section 164 of the Code of Criminal Procedure, 1973 a statement in his own hand, of the grounds on which he believes that the confession is genuine, the precautions which he took to remove the accused from the influence of the police, and the time, if any, given to the accused for reflection.

15. The Magistrate should scrupulously follow the provisions of Section 164(3) of the Code of Criminal Procedure, 1973, which lays down that if the person appearing before the Magistrate refused to make a confession, the Magistrate shall not authorise the detention of such person in police custody.

16. As far as possible, the statement should be recorded in the language of the accused and if that is not practicable, then in the language of the court or in English; and such record shall be shown or read out to the accused or, if he does not understand the language in which it is written, shall be interpreted to him in the language which he understands, and he shall be at liberty to explain or add to his answers. Every question put to the accused and every answer given by him shall be recorded in full. In order to obtain clarification, the Magistrate may put him relevant questions but such questions shall not be in the nature of cross-examination. When the record is complete, it shall be signed by the accused and the Magistrate who shall certify under his own hand that the examination was taken in his own hand that the examination was taken in his presence and hearing and that record contains a full and true account of the statements made by the accused. At the foot of such statement, the Magistrate shall make a memorandum to the following effect:

    "I have explained to.... that he is not bound to make a confession and that, if he does so, any confession he may make be used as evidence against him and I believe that this confession was voluntarily made. It was taken in my presence and hearing and was read over to the person making it and admitted by him to be correct, and it contains a full true account of the statement made by him."

17. After a prisoner has made a confession, he should ordinarily be committed to jail, and the Magistrate should not be on the warrant for the information of the Superintendent of the Jail concerned, that the prisoner has made a confession.

18. A remand to police custody should not be made unless the officer making the application is able to show good an satisfactory grounds for it; a general statement that the accused may be able to give further information should not be accepted as being in itself a sufficient reason for remand. If the object of the remand is the verification of the prisoner's statement, he should ordinarily be remanded to magisterial custody. The period of remand should always be as short as possible. A prisoner who has been produced for the purpose of making a confession and has made a statement, which

from the point of view of the prosecution is unsatisfactory, should in no circumstances be remanded to police custody.

19. The police may be permitted to take copies of confessions recorded by Magistrates.

20. Any instance of misconduct or abuse of authority by a police officer, which may come to the notice of a Magistrate, shall be reported to the Sessions Judge to whom the Magistrate is subordinate. The Sessions Judge, on receipt of such a report, should bring the matter to the notice of the District Magistrate for such action, as he may deem fit. In cases of gross misconduct, if the Sessions Judge finds that appropriate action has not been taken against the officer concerned, he may bring the matter to the notice of the High Court. [162]

The Supreme Court has held that all the requirements of Section 164 of the CrPC should be complied with and the Magistrate recording the confessional statement should besides also ensure that the confession is voluntary and without pressure. Non-compliance thereof renders the confession not admissible or reliable. If a part of the confession is excluded under any provision of law, the entire confessional statement in all its parts, including the admission of minor incriminating facts must be excluded unless proof of it is permitted by some other section, such as Section 27 of the Indian Evidence Act.[163] In Bhagwan Singh vs State of MP[164], the accused was produced before the Magistrate in handcuffs and the Magistrate did not ascertain whether any physical or mental pressure was put on him, the Supreme Court held that the retracted confessional statement could not be relied upon. In Chandran vs State of Tamil Nadu.[165], the Supreme Court held that the law peremptorily requires that after recording the confession of the accused, the Magistrate must append at the foot of the record a memorandum certifying that he believes that the confession was voluntarily made. It was further held that the reason for requiring compliance with this mandatory requirement at the close of the recording of confession, appears to be that it is only after hearing the confession and observing the demeanor of the person making it, that the Magistrate is in the best position to append the requisite memorandum certifying the voluntary nature of the confession made before him. If the Magistrate recording a confession of an accused person produced before him in the course of police investigation, does not, on the face of the record, certify

162A.K Gupte and S.D. Dighe, Criminal Manual, 4th Edition, 1999, Hind Law House, Pune, pages 35 to 45

163 Dhananjaya Reddy vs. State of Karnataka (2001) 4 SCC 9; Kehar Singh vs. State (Delhi Admn.) (1988) 3 SCC 609.

164 2003 CrLJ 1262

165 (1978) 4 SCC 90. Also see Bharatbhai vs State of Gujarat, (2002)8SCC447

in clear, categorical terms his satisfaction or belief as to the voluntary nature of the confession recorded by him, nor testifies orally, as to such satisfaction or belief, the defect would be fatal to the admissibility and use of the confession against the accused at the trial.

The Supreme Court has held that conviction cannot be based on the confession of the co-accused but if there is other corroborating evidence, they can be referred to as lending assurance to that conclusion and for fortifying it.[166] In Shankar Guha Niyogi's murder case, the Supreme Court acquitted the accused as apart from the extra judicial confession of the co-accused, there was no other evidence of conspiracy and involvement of the accused.[167]

Dying Declarations

The general rule regarding evidence is that the person giving the evidence should be directly concerned with the subject matter of his evidence and should not testify as to the experience of a third- party. Section32 of the Indian Evidence Act provides an exception to the rule of hearsay evidence and permits use of statements made by persons who cannot testify under certain circumstances.

Section 32 (1) of the Indian Evidence Act, 1872, lays down the proposition for the admissibility of dying declarations. It provides that when a statement, written or verbal, is made by a person as to the cause of his death or as to any of the circumstances of the transaction, which resulted in his death, is relevant in cases in which the cause of that person's death comes into question. The section further states that such statements are relevant whether the person who made them was or was not, at the time when they were made, under expectation of death, and whatever may be the nature of the proceeding in which the cause of his death comes into question. Section 32, thus, provides that the statements of persons as to the cause or any circumstances relating to his/her death are relevant in proceedings that are concerned with the same. Though Section 32 is silent as to when and how the statements should be made and the evidentiary value of a dying declaration in the absence of any other evidence or the evidentiary value an exculpatory dying declaration when there is other evidence and the mental and physical fitness of the maker of the statement, the judiciary has in a series of judgments both enlarged and narrowed the scope of dying declarations. One of the earlier cases decided by the Supreme Court on the evidentiary value of dying declarations was Ram Nath vs. State of Madhya Pradesh[168] where the Court stated that it was not safe to convict only on the basis of a dying declaration. In another earlier decision, the Supreme Court discarded the dying declaration as the doctor stated that it was unlikely that the

166 Nathu vs State of UP, AIR 1956 SC 56
167 State of MP vs Paltan Mallah, AIR 2005 SC 733
168 AIR 1953 SC 420: 1953 Cr. L.J. 1772

deceased was fit to make the statement.[169] The Supreme Court also laid down that the dying declarations should not be in a narrative form with many details as it is likely to give impression that it is not genuine[170]. In Khushal Rao vs State of Bombay[171], for the first time the Supreme Court held that dying declarations can be the sole basis of conviction. The Court held that:

> "...(1) that it cannot be laid down as an absolute rule of law that a dying declaration cannot form the sole basis of conviction unless it is corroborated; (2) that each case must be determined on its own facts keeping in view the circumstances in which the dying declaration was made; (3) that it can not be laid down as a general proposition that a dying declaration is a weaker kind of evidence than other pieces of evidence; (4) that a dying declaration stands on the same footing as another piece of evidence and has to be judged in the light of surrounding circumstances and with reference to the principles governing the weighing of evidence; (5) that a dying declaration which has been recorded by a competent Magistrate in the proper manner, that is to say, in the form of questions and answers, and as far as practicable, in the words of the maker of the declaration, stands on a much higher footing than a dying declaration which depends upon oral testimony which may suffer from all the infirmities of human memory and human character, and (6) that in order to test the reliability of a dying declaration, the Court has to keep in view the circumstances like the opportunity of the dying man for observation, for example, whether there was sufficient light if the crime was committed at night; whether the capacity of the man to remember the facts stated had not been impaired at the time he was making the statement, by circumstances beyond his control; that the statement has been consistent throughout if he had several opportunities of making a dying declaration apart from the official record of it; and that the statement had been made at the earliest opportunity and was not the result of tutoring by interested parties."

This principle has been reiterated in various judgments of the Court[172].

---

169 Bhagwan Dass vs. State of Rajasthan, AIR 1957 SC 589: 1957 Cr. L.J. 889

170 Bakhshish Singh vs State of Punjab, AIR 1957 SC 904: 1958 SCR 409

171 AIR 1958 SC 22: 1958 Cr. L.J 106

172 See Tarachand Damu Sutar vs State of Maharashtra, AIR 1962 SC 130: (1962) 1 Cr. L.J 196; Lallubhai Devchand vs. State of Gujarat, AIR 1972 SC 1776: 1972 Cr. L.J 828; K. Ramachandra Reddy vs Public Prosecutor, AIR 1976 SC 1994: 1976 Cr. L.J 1548; State of Assam vs. Mafizuddin Ahmed, AIR 1983 SC 274; Laxman vs State of Maharashtra, AIR 2002 SC 2973; State of Karnataka vs Shariff, 2003 CrLJ 1254; PV Radhakrishnan vs State of Karnataka, 2003 CrLJ 3717;

Over the years the Court has evolved the various principles relating to dying declarations:

a) Dying declarations are relevant where the cause or circumstance of the death is subject of a proceeding such as in cases of culpable homicide, suicide and its abetment and death caused due to rash and negligent acts;[173]

b) Dying declarations are relevant where the same relates to the cause or circumstances of the maker's death. Hence, evidence of harassment or any circumstances relating to the death such as abetment, are relevant. For example in Kans Raj vs State of Punjab and Haryana, where the Apex Court in a case of dowry death, has held that dying declarations must relate to circumstances which have a proximity to the death, but the test of proximity should not be literally construed as the "Distance of time would depend or vary with the circumstances of each case. For instance, where death is a logical culmination of a continuous drama long in process and is, as it were, a finale of the story, the statement regarding each step directly connected with the end of the drama would be admissible because the entire statement would have to be read as an organic whole and not torn out of context. Sometimes statements relevant to or furnishing an immediate motive may also be admissible as being a part of the transaction of death. It is manifest that all these statements come to light only after the death of the deceased who speaks from death. For instance, where the death takes place within a very short time of the marriage or the distance of time is not spread over more than 3-4 months the statement may be admissible under Section 32";[174]

c) The statement need not be made in anticipation or expectation of death. Thus, letters written prior to the death or statements made regarding threats and harassment are relevant;[175]

d) The statement should be made earliest in point of time when the declarant had the opportunity to make the same. Delay in making the statement has to be seen in the light of the opportunity the person had for making the statement.[176]

e) The statement may be oral or written. In the case of a written dying declaration, they have to be proved by proof that (i) it was made by the

173 Sharad Birdhichand Sarda vs State of Maharashtra, AIR 1984 SC 1622 where the letters written by the deceased to her sister and friend about her strained relations were held to be relevant under Section 32 to prove her suicidal state of mind. In another recent case, Ramesh Kumar vs State of Chhattisgarh, 2001 Cr. L.J 4724, the Supreme Court acquitted the husband on the basis of the letters of the deceased wife that blamed herself for the ill- treatment by the husband and proclaimed the husbands love towards her.

174 AIR 2000 SC 2324. Quotation is from para 11(2) at page 2332

175 AIR 2000 SC 2324; Sharad Birdhichand Sarda vs State of Maharashtra, AIR 1984 SC 1622; Ramesh Kumar vs State of Chhattisgarh, 2001 Cr. L.J 4724

176 See Khushal Rao, AIR 1958 SC 22: 1958 Cr. L.J 106

person fulfilling the criteria of Section 32 (1) and (ii) that the person making it was capable, both physically and mentally, of making the same. Section 32 is silent on mental or physical fitness of the witness making the statement. However, Section 118 of the Indian Evidence Act excludes incompetent witnesses from deposing in Court. One of the conditions of incompetence is lunacy. This is the reason for the exclusion of evidence of a mentally unfit person by the Courts. Thus, the courts have held in a series of cases that there should be a medical certification as to the fitness of the declarant to make the declaration in order for the court to rely upon the same.[177]

Dying declarations recorded on the bases of nods and gestures is not only admissible but possesses evidentiary value, the extent of which shall depend upon who recorded the statement, what is his educational attainment, what gestures or nods were made, what were the questions asked, whether they were simple or complicated and how effective or understandable the nods and gestures were.[178]

Additionally the courts have held there should have been no coercion, threat or influence on the person making it, such as the presence of family members in cases of women who are seen as being interested in implicating husband or his family[179]. The court has to be convinced that the statement was voluntary and truthful. Further the person who is the writer of the statement has to prove the statement by proving facts (i) and (ii) in paragraph (e) above. While it is not mandatory that a Magistrate should record the statement, and anyone including police officers can record statements, the same should be recorded by the person to whom made unless for some reason stated in the record itself, the person is not the scribe of the statement.[180] In case of oral statements they have to be proved through the witness to whom the dying declarations were made and they are subjected to cross examination and have to prove the statement as any other witness in the court.

The Supreme Court in Sunder Lal Vs. State of Rajasthan[181] summed up the the principles governing dying declaration:

(i) There is neither rule of law nor of prudence that dying declaration cannot be acted upon without corroboration.

---

177 Laxmi vs Om Prakash (2001) 6 SCC 118

178 Meesala Ramakrishnan Vs. State of Andhra Pradesh (1994) 4 SCC 182

179 However in State (Delhi Administration) vs Laxman Kumar, AIR 1986 SC 250, the Supreme Court disbelieved the exculpatory dying declaration of the deceased wife recorded by the Police on several grounds including the fact that none of her relatives were present while the same was recorded in the presence of the doctor who was examined by the defense as their witness to prove the dying declaration.

180 Ghulam Hussain vs State of Delhi, 2000 Cr.L.J. 3949

181 MANU/SC/2007/559

(ii) If the Court is satisfied that the dying declaration is true and voluntary it can base conviction on it, without corroboration.

(iii) The Court has to scrutinize the dying declaration carefully and must ensure that the declaration is not the result of tutoring, prompting or imagination. The deceased had an opportunity to observe and identify the assailants and was in a fit state to make the declaration.

(iv) Where dying declaration is suspicious, it should not be acted upon without corroborative evidence.

(v) Where the deceased was unconscious and could never make any dying declaration the evidence with regard to it is to be rejected.

(vi) A dying declaration which suffers from infirmity cannot form the basis of conviction.

(vii) Merely because a dying declaration does contain the details as to the occurrence, it is not to be rejected.

(viii) Equally, merely because it is a brief statement, it is not to be discarded. On the contrary, the shortness of the statement itself guarantees truth.

(ix) Normally, the Court in order to satisfy whether deceased was in a fit mental condition to make the dying declaration look up to the medical opinion. But where the eyewitness said that the deceased was in a fit and conscious state to make the dying declaration, the medical opinion cannot prevail.

(x) Where the prosecution version differs from the version as given in the dying declaration, the said declaration cannot be acted upon.

(xi) Where there are more than one statement in the nature of dying declaration, one first in point of time must be preferred. Of course, if the plurality of dying declaration could be held to be trustworthy and reliable, it has to be accepted.

While dying declarations are an important piece of evidence and the courts have repeatedly held that a conviction can be based on the sole evidence of the dying declaration, it has to pass the test of reliability, which effectively means that it has to be scrutinised in the light of the other evidence available. Further, dying declarations are possible only in cases of unnatural death where death is not instantaneous and the victim is capable of making a statement as to the cause of the death. Moreover, these have to be balanced with the other requirements of criminal jurisprudence, which include procedural rules and the rights of the accused. One of the foremost principles of criminal law is that the burden of proof is on the prosecution. The second principle is that the prosecution has to prove its case beyond reasonable doubt and the benefit of doubt goes to the accused. A fact is said to be proved under Section 3 of the Indian Evidence Act when "after considering the matter before it, the Court either believes it to exist, or considers its existence so probable that a prudent man ought under the circumstances of the particular case, to act upon the supposition that it exists".

Documentary Evidence

The contents of any document relied upon by the parties has to be proved generally by the production of the original document for the inspection of the court. This is known as Primary evidence. In case of photographs, the negative is considered the primary evidence. Carbon copies are primary evidence. If a document is required to be attested, then the attesting witness should testify to that effect except in cases where the document is registered. Secondary evidence includes:

1. Certified copies;
2. Copies made from the original by mechanical processes which in themselves insure the accuracy of the copy and copies compared with such copies;
3. Copies made from or compared with the original;
4. Counterparts of the documents as against the parties who did not execute them;
5. Oral accounts of the contents of a document given by some person who has himself seen it (Section 63 of the Indian Evidence Act).

Secondary evidence includes photographs, photocopies, films and tape recording.

Secondary evidence is permissible only in certain circumstances. Certified copies of documents are permitted in case where the original is a public document or permissible under law. Secondary evidence is also allowed in case where the original is in the possession or power of the person against whom the document is sought to be proved or of any person out of reach of or not subject to the process of the court, or of any person legally bound to produce it who after notice to produce the same does not produce it; where the original has been lose or destroyed or when the party offering it as evidence cannot for any other reason not due to his own default or neglect produce it in reasonable time (Section 65).

The principles of law governing the conduct of criminal legal system enunciated in this chapter pertain to the rules of evidence. The law of evidence is common to both civil and criminal cases, but the rules with regard to sufficiency of evidence and degree of proof required differ. These by no means are the only principles of law governing crime prevention, detection and correction in India. The Constitution of India gives the humane face to criminal jurisprudence and so do some of the provisions of the Code of Criminal Procedure, 1973.

CHAPTER 6

TRIAL OF CASES

Criminal and civil trials differ as in a criminal trial the onus is on the prosecution to prove its case except in certain stipulated cases. The burden of proof required is also to prove that it is beyond reasonable doubt. The other difference is that while only the aggrieved party can institute civil action, ordinarily criminal law can be set into motion by anyone, including a stranger. This is also subject to exceptions. Matrimonial offences and defamation cases can be instituted by the aggrieved parties or a close relative and criminal cases under the labour laws can be instituted only by the worker with the permission of the Inspector appointed under the concerned Act or by the said Inspector himself. Thus, though criminal law is said to be uniformly applicable to all, the most vulnerable groups are discriminated against by being denied access to the remedies available.

Limitation

Another point of difference between civil and criminal law is regarding limitation of period in bringing forth action against the accused. Chapter XXXVI of the CrPC deals with limitation for taking cognizance of certain offences. The period of limitation for launching prosecution is as follows:

Table 1

Nature of the Offence	Period of Limitation for Taking Cognizance
Offence punishable with fine	Six months
Offence punishable with imprisonment for a period not exceeding one year	One year
Offence punishable with imprisonment for a period of more than one year but not exceeding three years	Three years

The period of limitation for offences, which may be tried together, shall be determined with reference to the offence, which is punishable with the more severe punishment. For offences, which are punishable with imprisonment for more than three years, no limitation is fixed (Section 468). While computing the period of limitation, it shall commence:

1. On the date of offence; or
2. From the date of knowledge of the commission to any person or police officer whichever is earlier; or
3. Where the offender is not known, from the day the identity of the offender is known to the aggrieved or police officer, whichever is earlier;
4. The date from which such period is to be computed shall be excluded;
5. In case of a continuing offence, a fresh period of limitation shall begin to run at every moment of the time during which the offence continues.

   (Sections 469 and 472)

Exclusion of time in computing limitation:

1. Time in which any person has been prosecuting with due diligence another prosecution on the same facts;
2. Time intervening due to injunction, stay or order of any court;
3. Time intervening for obtaining sanction for prosecution, inclusive of both days;
4. Time during which the offender is outside India or absconding;
5. Days on which the Court remained closed.

   (Sections 470 and 471)

The court can take cognizance even after expiry of time in the following cases:

1. It is satisfied that the delay has been properly explained;
2. It is necessary to take cognizance in the interest of justice.
   (Section 473)

Jurisdiction

Chapter XIII of the CrPC deals with the jurisdiction of the Criminal Courts to conduct inquiries and trials. The same can be summarised as follows:

1. Every offence shall ordinarily be inquired into or tried by a court within whose local jurisdiction it was committed (Section 177);
2. When it is uncertain in which of several local areas an offence was committed, maybe inquired into or tried by a court having jurisdiction over any of the local areas (Section 178(a);
3. Where an offence is committed partly in one local area and partly in another, maybe inquired into or tried by a court having jurisdiction over any of the local areas (Section 178(b);

4. Where an offence is a continuing one, and continues to be committed in more local areas than one, maybe inquired into or tried by a court having jurisdiction over any of the local areas (Section 178(c);

5. Where an offence consists of several acts done in different local areas, it may be inquired into or tried by a court jurisdiction over any of the local areas (Section 178(d);

6. When an act is an offence by reason of anything that has been done and of a consequence that has ensued, the offence may be inquired into or tried by any court within whose local jurisdiction such thing has been done or such consequence has ensued (Section 179). An example is that the manufacturer of a defective good can be prosecuted not only where the said article was manufactured, but also where it was purchased;

7. When an act is an offence by reason of its relation to any other act which is also an offence or which would be an offence if the doer was capable of committing an offence, the first mentioned offence may be inquired into or tried by a court within whose local jurisdiction either act was done (Section 180).this means that the court having jurisdiction to try the criminal conspiracy can also try the offences committed in pursuance of the conspiracy even if those offences were committed outside the jurisdiction of that court;

8. Any offence of being a thug, or murder committed by a thug, of dacoity, of dacoity with murder, or belonging to a gang of dacoits, or of escaping from custody, may be inquired into or tried by a Court within whose local jurisdiction the offence was committed or the accused is found (Section 181(1);

9. Any offence of kidnapping or abduction of a person may be inquired into or tried by a Court within whose local jurisdiction the person was kidnapped or abducted or was conveyed or concealed or detained(Section 181(2);

10. Any offence of theft, extortion or robbery may be inquired into or tried by a Court within whose local jurisdiction the offence was committed or the stolen property which is the subject of the offence was possessed by any person committing the offence, or by any person who received or retained such property knowing or having reason to believe it to be stolen property (Section 181(3);

11. Any offence of criminal misappropriation or of criminal breach of trust may be inquired into or tried by a Court within whose local jurisdiction the offence was committed or any part of the property which is the subject matter of the offence was received or retained, or was required to be returned or accounted for by the accused person (Section 181(4). Hence a woman can file a criminal case for return of *streedhana* either at the place where she resided with her husband or her residence after leaving her husband;

12. Any offence which includes the possession of stolen property may be inquired into or tried by a Court within whose local jurisdiction the offence

was committed or the stolen property was possessed by any person who received or retained it knowing or having reason to believe it to be stolen property (Section 181(5);

13. Any offence which includes cheating may, if the deception is practiced by means of letters or telecommunication messages, be inquired into or tried by any Court within whose local jurisdiction such letters or messages were sent or were received (Section 182(1);

14. Any offence of cheating and dishonestly inducing delivery of property may be inquired into or tried by a Court within whose local jurisdiction the property was delivered by the person deceived or was received by the accused person (Section 182(1);

15. An offence bigamy may be inquired into or tried by the court within whose local jurisdiction the offence was committed or the offender last resided with his or her spouse by the first marriage, or the wife by the first marriage has taken up permanent residence after the commission of the offence(Section 182(2);

16. When an offence is committed while the person by or against whom, or the thing in respect of which, the offence is committed is in the course of performing a journey or voyage, the offence may be inquired into or tried by a court through or into whose local jurisdiction that person or thing passed in the course of that journey or voyage (Section 183)

17. Where offences committed or accused are being tried jointly, they may be inquired into or tried by any Court competent to inquire into or try any of the offences (Section 184);

18. When an offence is committed outside India by a citizen of India, whether on the high seas or elsewhere, or by a person, not being an Indian citizen, on any ship or aircraft registered in India, he may be dealt with in respect of such offence as if it had been committed at any place within India at which he may be found, with the previous sanction of the Central Government (Section 188);

19. Notwithstanding any of the above provisions, the State Government may direct that any cases or class of cases committed for trial in any district may be tried in any sessions division, provided that such direction is not repugnant to any direction previously issued by the High Court or the Supreme Court, under the Constitution, under the CrPC or any other law (Section 185);

20. Where two or more Courts have taken cognizance of the same offence, and a question arises as to which of them ought to inquire into or try that offence, the question shall be decided by that High Court, if the Courts are subordinate to the same High Court, and if they are not subordinate to same High Court, by the High Court within the local limits of whose

appellate criminal jurisdiction, the proceedings were first commenced, and thereupon, all other proceedings in respect of that offence shall be discontinued (Section 186).

Sanction for Prosecution of Public Servants

Certain offences need the sanction of the Government in order to launch prosecution. Generally sanction for prosecution of public servants in certain cases is required in order to grant them protection from vexatious litigation for acts performed in the discharge of their official duties. Section 197 of the CrPC stipulates that sanction is required in order to prosecute Judges and public servants which was committed in either his official capacity or under colour of office. These cases are of two categories:

1. The act complained of is one authorized by a Statute or law, but became questionable on account of the fact that it was done with fraudulent or dishonest intention, and
2. The act complained of though not authorized by Statute or law, is ultimately and internally connected with his official or statutory duty and has thus a reasonable nexus to the discharge of duty.[182]

The designated officer of the concerned government grants the sanction. Sanction for prosecution is required only in cases of persons who are not removable from office save by or with the sanction of the Government. Under Section 21 of the Indian Penal Code, the definition of public servant includes police, jail staff, members of the Armed forces and para-military forces, court staff and every officer of the Government whose duty it is to prevent offences, to give information of offences, to bring offenders to justice or to protect public health, safety or convenience. Even retired public servants or judges cannot be prosecuted for offences covered under this section. Grant of sanction is not an empty formality but requires application of mind and the superior officer is required to scan, scrutinize and carefully examine the material against the concerned accused and evaluation of the fact whether or not there are sufficient grounds to proceed against the accused.[183] Where the prosecution is launched against a public servant for an offence that is entirely personal and unconnected with the discharge of his official duties as a public servant, then no sanction is necessary for prosecution.[184]

The Supreme Court has held that the words 'any offence alleged to have been committed by him while acting or purporting to act in the discharge of his official duty' employed in Section 197(1) of the Code, are capable of a narrow as well as a wide interpretation. If these words are construed too narrowly, the

---

182 1991 Cr. L.J. 498 ; State of Maharashtra vs. Dr.B.K.Subbarao, 1993 Cr.L.J. 2984 ; Manohar Nath vs. State of Jammu and Kashmir, AIR 1983 SC 610

183 AIR 1958 SC 287;

184 Yoal vs. State of Maharashtra, (1991) 2 BCR 485

section will be rendered altogether sterile, for, 'it is no part of an official duty to commit an offence, and never can be'. In the wider sense, these words will take under their umbrella every act constituting an offence, committed in the course of the same transaction in which the official duty is performed or purports to be performed. The right approach to the import of these words lies between two extremes. While on the one hand, it is not every offence committed by a public servant while engaged in the performance of his official duty, which is entitled to the protection of Section 197 (1), an act constituting an offence, directly and reasonably connected with his official duty will require sanction for prosecution under the said provision. Use of the expression, 'official duty' implies that the act or omission must have been done by the public servant in the course of his service and that it should have been in discharge of his duty. The Section does not extend its protective cover to every act or omission done by a public servant in service but restricts its scope of operation to only those acts or omissions which are done by a public servant in discharge of official duty. It has been widened further by extending protection to even those acts or omissions which are done in purported exercise of official duty. That is under the colour of office. Official duty therefore implies that the act or omission must have been done by the public servant in course of his service and such act or omission must have been performed as part of duty which further must have been official in nature. The Section has, thus, to be construed strictly, while determining its applicability to any act or omission in course of service. Its operation has to be limited to those duties which are discharged in course of duty. But once any act or omission has been found to have been committed by a public servant in discharge of his duty then it must be given liberal and wide construction so far its official nature is concerned. For instance a public servant is not entitled to indulge in criminal activities. To that extent the Section has to be construed narrowly and in a restricted manner. But once it is established that act or omission was done by the public servant while discharging his duty then the scope of its being official should be construed so as to advance the objective of the Section in favour of the public servant. Otherwise the entire purpose of affording protection to a public servant without sanction shall stand frustrated. For instance a police officer in discharge of duty may have to use force which may be an offence for the prosecution of which the sanction may be necessary. But if the same officer commits an act in course of service but not in discharge of his duty and without any justification therefor then the bar under Section 197 of the Code is not attracted. Before Section 197 can be invoked, it must be shown that the official concerned was accused of an offence alleged to have been committed by him while acting or purporting to act in the discharge of his official duties. It is not the duty which requires examination so much as the act, because the official act can be performed both in the discharge of duty as well as in dereliction of it. This act must fall within the scope and range of the official duties of the public servant concerned. It is the quality of the act which is important and the protection of this section is available if the act falls within the scope and range of official duties of the public official concerned. It is the quality of the act which is important and the protection of this section is available if .the act falls within the scope and range of his official duty. There cannot be a universal rule to determine whether there is a reasonable connection between the act done and the official duty, nor is it possible to lay down any such rule. One safe and sure test in this regard would be to consider if the omission or neglect on the part of the public servant to commit the act complained of could have made answerable for a charge of dereliction of his official duty, if the answer to this question is in the affirmative, it may be said that such act was committed by the public servant while acting in the discharge of his official duty and there was every connection with the act complained of and the official duty of the public servant. This aspect makes it clear that the concept of Section 197 does not get immediately attracted on institution of compliant case.[185]

Matajog Dobey v. H. C. Bhari[186] the Constitutional Bench of the Supreme stated that the offence alleged to have been committed (by the accused) must have something to do, or must be related in some manner with the discharge of official duty ... there must be a reasonable connection between the act and the discharge of official duty; the act must bear such relation to the duty that the accused could lay a reasonable (claim) but not a pretended or fanciful claim, that he did it in the course of the performance of his duty. In the said case, the Supreme Court held that the question of sanction can be considered at any stage of the trial and not necessarily as soon as the compliant is lodged. The Supreme Court has in a litany of judgments held that the question whether sanction is necessary or not may have to be determined from stage to stage. It has been held that torture during investigation is not carried out in the discharge of official duty and hence no sanction is required for the same. [187]

Plea Bargaining

Plea Bargaining was not allowed in India under the law. However it has been introduced through the insertion of Chapter XXIA through The Criminal Law (Amendment) Act, 2005. This chapter does not apply to juveniles covered under the Care and Protection of Children) Act, 2000(56 of 2000) (Section 265L). The No Appeal lies against the order passed under this chapter except for appeals under Article 136 of the Constitution to the Supreme Court and writ petition to the High Court under articles 226 and 227 of the Constitution (Section

---

185 B. Saha. v. M. S. Kochar (1979 (4) SCC 177); State of H.P. v. M.P. Gupta (2004 (2) SCC 349), State of orissa through Kumar Raghvendra Singh & Ors. v. Ganesh Chandra Jew (JT 2004(4) SC 52), Shri S.K. Zutshi and Anr. v. Shri Bimal Debnath and Anr. (JT 2004(6) SC 323), K. Kalimuthu v. State by DSP (2005 (4) SCC 512) and Rakesh Kumar Mishra v. The State of Bihar and Anr. (2006 (1) SCC 557).; Parkash Singh Badal vs State of Punjab, (2007)1SCC1. For a contra view see Sankaran Moitra vs Sadhna Das, (2006) 4 SCC 584

186 AIR 1956 SC 44

187 (1984) 2 Crimes 772

265G). Section 265 H empowers the court, for the purposes of discharging its functions under this Chapter, all the powers vested in respect of bail, trial of offences and other matters relating to the disposal of a cast in such Court under this Code.

It is applicable to offences other than an offence for which the punishment of death or of imprisonment for life or of imprisonment for a term exceeding seven years has been provided under the law for the time being in force but which is not an offence that affects the socio-economic condition of the country[188] or has been committed against a woman, or a child below the age of fourteen years after the chargesheet has been filed or process has been issued in case of a private complaint [189] and is applicable to first time offenders[190]. The accused may make an application for plea bargaining in the Court in which such offence is pending for trial[191] This application shall contain a brief description of the case including the offence to which the case relates and shall be accompanied by an affidavit sworn by the accused stating therein that he has voluntarily preferred, after understanding the nature and extent of punishment provided under the law for the offence, the plea bargaining in his case and that he has not previously been convicted by a Court in a case in which he had been charged with the same offence. Upon receipt of the application the court shall issue notice to the PP or the Complainant as the case maybe and after examining the accused in camera in the absence of the other party satisfy itself that the application has been filed voluntarily, Upon being so satisfied the court shall provide time to the Public Prosecutor or the complainant, as the case may be, and the accused to work out a mutually satisfactory disposition of the case which may include giving to the victim by the accused the compensation and other expenses during the case and thereafter fix the date for further hearing of the case. If the Court finds that the application has been filed involuntarily by the accused or he has previously been convicted by a Court in a case in which he had been charged with the same offence, it shall proceed further in accordance with the provisions of this Code from the stage such application has been filed.[192]

In cases of plea bargaining under Section 265C, in working out a mutually satisfactory disposition, the Court shall follow the following procedure, namely:

---

188 Under Section 265A (2) of the CrPC, the Central Government shall, by notification, determine the offences under the law for the time being in force which shall be the offences affecting the socio-economic condition of the country.

189 Section 265A of the CrPC

190 Section 265B

191 Section 265B

192 Section 265B

(a) In a case instituted on a police report, the Court shall issue notice to the Public Prosecutor, the police officer who has investigated the case, the accused and the victim of the case to participate in the meeting to work out a satisfactory disposition of the case;

(b) In a case instituted otherwise than on police report, the Court shall issue notice to the accused and the victim of the case to participate in a meeting to work out a satisfactory disposition of the case;

(c) Provided that it shall be the duty of the Court to ensure, throughout such process of working out a satisfactory disposition of the case, that it is completed voluntarily by the parties participating in the meeting;

(d) Provided further that if the victim of the case or the accused, as the case may be, so desires, he may participate in such meeting with his pleader engaged in the case.

Where a satisfactory disposition of the case has been worked out, the Court shall prepare a report of such disposition which shall be signed by the presiding officer of the Court and all other persons who participated in the meeting and if no such disposition has been worked out, the Court shall record such observation and proceed further in accordance with the provisions of this Code from the stage the application[193].

Under Section 265E, where a satisfactory disposition of the case has been worked out, the Court shall dispose of the case in the following manner, namely:

(a) The Court shall award the compensation to the victim in accordance with the disposition under section 265D and hear the parties on the quantum of the punishment, releasing of the accused on probation of good conduct or after admonition under section 360 or for dealing with the accused under the provisions of the Probation of Offenders Act, 1958(20 of 1958) or any other law for the time being in force and follow the procedure specified in the succeeding clauses for imposing the punishment on the accused;

(b) After hearing the parties under clause (a), if the Court is of the view that section 360 or the provisions of the Probation of Offenders Act, 1958(20 of 1958) or any other law for the time being in force are attracted in the case of the accused, it may release the accused on probation or provide the benefit of any such law, as the case may be;

(c) After hearing the parties under clause (b), if the Court finds that minimum punishment has been provided under the law for the offence committed by the accused, it may sentence the accused to half of such minimum punishment;

(d) In case after hearing the parties under clause (b), the Court finds that the offence committed by the accused is not covered under clause (b) or clause

193 Section 265D

(c), then, it may sentence the accused to one-fourth of the punishment provided or extendable, as the case may be, for such offence.

The Court shall deliver its judgment in the open Court and the same shall be signed by the presiding officer of the Court (Section 265F). The provisions of section 428 shall apply, for setting off the period of detention undergone by the accused against the sentence of imprisonment imposed under this Chapter, in the same manner as they apply in respect of the imprisonment under other provisions of this Code. The provisions of this Chapter shall have effect notwithstanding anything inconsistent therewith contained in any other provisions of this Code and nothing in such other provisions shall be construed to constrain the meaning of any provision of this Chapter (Section 265J). Under Section 265K, notwithstanding anything contained in any law for the time being in force, the statements or facts stated by an accused in an application for plea bargaining filed under section 265B shall not be used for any other purpose except for the purpose of this Chapter.

Trial of Police Cases

The trial procedure of cases instituted by the State, whether tried in the Magistrates or the Sessions Courts is similar. Cases tried by the High Court also follow the same procedure. The Public Prosecutor or the Assistant Public Prosecutor on behalf of the State conducts the prosecution in all these cases and the victim is a witness for the prosecution. If the victim wants so, he can instruct another lawyer to participate in the proceedings and assist the public prosecutor, and with the permission of the Court, submit written arguments after the evidence is closed in the case (Sections 225 and 301of the CrPC).

In Johri Mal's case[194], the Supreme Court held that the appointment of the public prosecutor has to be made in accordance with the CrPC. Section 25A. of the CrPC inserted by the Code of Criminal Procedure (Amendment) Act, 2005, established the Directorate of Prosecution. The section empowers the State Government to establish a Directorate of Prosecution consisting of a Director of Prosecution and as many Deputy Directors of Prosecution as it thinks fit who will be advocates with not less than ten years practice and such appointment shall be made with the concurrence of the Chief Justice of the High Court. The Head of the Directorate of Prosecution shall be the Director of Prosecution, who shall function under the administrative control of the Head of the Home Department in the State with Deputy Directors of Prosecution subordinate to the Director. All Public Prosecutors, Additional Public Prosecutors and Special Public Prosecutors appointed to conduct cases in the High Court shall be subordinate to the Director of Prosecution and to the Deputy Director of

194 State of UP vs Johri Mal, (2004) 4 SCC 714

Prosecution. The powers and functions of the Director of Prosecution and the Deputy Directors of Prosecution and the areas for which each of the Deputy Directors of Prosecution have been appointed shall be notified by the State Government. The provisions of this section shall not apply to the Advocate General for the State while performing the functions of a Public Prosecutor.

In J K International vs State, Govt of NCT of Delhi[195], the Supreme Court has held that the private party can seek the permission of the Magistrate to conduct trial. The Court opined that, "The private person who is permitted to conduct prosecution in the magistrate's court can engage a counsel to do the needful in the Court in his behalf. It further amplifies the position that if a private person is aggrieved by the offence committed against him or against any one in whom he is interested he can approach the magistrate and seek permission to conduct the prosecution by himself. It is open to the Court to consider his request. If the court thinks that the cause of justice would be served better by granting such permission the courts would generally grant such permission. Of course, this wider amplitude is limited to Magistrates' courts, as the right of such private individual to participate in the conduct of prosecution in the sessions court is very much restricted and is made subject to the control of the Public Prosecutor. The limited role which a private person can be permitted to play for prosecution in the Sessions Court has been adverted to above. All these would show that an aggrieved private person is not altogether to be eclipsed from the scenario when the criminal court takes cognizance of the offences based on the report submitted by the police. The reality cannot be overlooked that the genesis in almost all such cases is the grievance of one or more individual that they were wronged by the accused by committing offences against them."

Trial of all cases except rape cases, is held in an open court to which the public generally may have access, provided that if the presiding Judge shall if he thinks fit, ask all or any person to leave the court at any stage of the trial. Rape trials are held in camera and their proceedings cannot be printed or published except with the previous permission of the court (Section 327).

Under Section 319 of the CrPC, the trial court has jurisdiction to add any person not being the accused before it to face the trial along with other accused persons, if the Court is satisfied at any stage of the proceedings on the evidence adduced that the persons who have not been arrayed as accused should face the trial. Such person even though had initially been named in the F.I.R. as an accused, but not charge sheeted, can also be added to face the trial. The trial court can take such a step to add such persons as accused only on the basis of evidence adduced before it and not on the basis of materials available in the

195 (2001)3SCC462

charge-sheet or the case diary, because such materials contained in the charge sheet or the case diary do not constitute evidence.[196] In Sohan Lal and Ors. v. State of Rajasthan[197] it was held that the position of an accused who has been discharged stands on a different footing.

Procedure where the Accused is of Unsound Mind

Chapter XXV of the CrPC deals with the procedure to be followed where the accused is of unsound mind. Where the court believes that the accused before it is of unsound mind, and consequently incapable of making his defense, it shall postpone further proceedings in the case after having the accused medically examined and recording a finding to that effect. Thereafter the court shall either release the accused person on security being furnished that he shall be properly taken care of and shall be prevented from doing injury to himself or to any other person and for his appearance when required before the court or such officer as the court appoints in this behalf. If the court is of the opinion that bail should not be granted or if sufficient security is not given, then the court may order that the accused be detained I safe custody in such place and manner as it thinks fit. Provided that if the accused is committed to a mental asylum, the court should follow the procedure laid down in the Mental Health Act. Only after the accused has been certified fit and capable of making his defense, then the trial would commence.

Processes to Compel Appearance

If the accused is on bail, then he is issued summons upon the chargesheet being filed and has to attend court unless his personal appearance in court has been dispensed with (Section 205). If the accused refuses to answer the summons for appearance issued to him, the court can issue a warrant of arrest for his appearance. Upon production on execution of warrant, the court may release the accused on his personal bond or on furnishing of fresh security or cancel his bail and commit him to custody until completion of trial, even in a bailable offence. In case the accused has been released on bail upon furnishing of surety, the warrant may be addressed to the surety to produce the accused. The court may cancel the warrant if the accused appears before it before its execution. (Sections 70 to 81)

If the accused does not appear and the warrant cannot be executed because the accused has absconded or concealed himself, then the court may publish a written proclamation requiring him to appear at a specified place and at a specified time not less than thirty days from the date of publishing such proclamation. The proclamation shall be published by being publicly read in some conspicuous place of the village or town, by being affixed to some conspicuous part of the

196 MANU/ SC-2007-558

197 MANU/SC/0379/1990

house where the accused person resides or a conspicuous part of his village or town and by affixing a copy to some conspicuous part of the court house. The court may also direct that a copy be published in a daily newspaper circulating in the place where the accused normally resides (Section 82). The court may along with the proclamation, also order the attachment of movable or immovable property belonging to the accused after recording his reasons for doing so in writing. This should be done in cases where the court is satisfied that the accused is about to dispose of the whole or any part of his property, or is about to remove the whole or any part of his property from the jurisdiction of the court. The attachment may be made through the appointment of a Court Receiver, by seizure, taking possession, by order in writing prohibiting the delivery of such property or rent thereof to the accused or anyone on his behalf or all or any two of such methods as the court thinks fit. The court may order sale of the property if it is perishable in nature and the proceeds of the sale shall abide by the order of the court. This attachment can be challenged by any person other than the accused claiming interest in the property within six months of the order. The court shall release the property attached if the accused appears within the time specified in the proclamation. The court may also set aside the order of attachment or direct the sale proceeds, if any, be handed over to the accused, if the accused within two years, appears before the court and satisfies the court that he did not abscond or conceal himself for the purpose of avoiding the execution of the warrant and had no notice of the proclamation (Sections 83 to 85).

If the accused is in custody, then the trial court sends a production warrant to the prison where he is lodged asking him to be produced before the court on the date fixed for hearing. The prison officials send the accused unless there is an order of the State Government to the contrary or when he is sick or in case of other specified contingencies (Sections 267 to 270).

Discharge of the Accused

The court has the power to discharge the accused if after perusing the records of the case and hearing the parties it comes to the conclusion that there is not sufficient ground for proceeding against the accused, after recording its reasons for the same (Sections 227 and 239).

The Supreme Court has laid down the following principles governed the power to discharge on the part of the Sessions Court under Section 227 of the CrPC:

1. That the Judge while considering the question of framing the charges under Section 227 of the Code has the undoubted power to sift and weigh the evidence for the limited purpose of finding out whether or not a prima facie case against the accused has been made out;

2. Where the materials placed before the Court disclose grave suspicion against the accused which has not been properly explained, the Court will be fully justified in framing a charge and proceeding with the trial;
3. The test to determine a prima facie case would naturally depend upon the facts of each case and it is difficult to lay down a rule of universal application. By and large however if two views are equally possible and the Judge is satisfied that the evidence produced before him while giving rise to some suspicion but not grave suspicion against the accused, he will be fully within his right to discharge the accused;
4. That in exercising his jurisdiction under Section 227 of the Code, the Judge which under the present Code is a senior and experienced court, cannot act merely as a post office or a mouthpiece of the prosecution, but has to consider the broad probabilities of the case, the total effect of the evidence and the documents produced before the Court, any basic infirmities appearing in the case and so on. This however does not mean that the judge should make a roving inquiry into the pros and cons of the matter and weigh the evidence as if he was conducting a trial.[198]

Framing of Charge

If the trial court is of the opinion that there is sufficient ground for presuming that the accused has committed the offence, it may frame charge against the accused. Charge serve the purpose of notice or intimation to the accused, drawn up according to the precise language of law, giving clear and unambiguous notice of the nature of accusation that the accused is called upon to meet in the course of trial. The object of a charge is to warn the accused person of the case he is to answer. The particulars including time, place and person as also the particulars of law should be spelt out in the charge. In a criminal trial, the charge is the foundation of the accusation and every care must be taken to see that it is not only properly framed but evidence is only tendered with respect to the matters put in the charge and not other matters. However the court has the power to alter or add to any charge at any time before judgment is pronounced. A defect in framing of the charge or failure to frame charge does not by itself vitiate trial, unless it results in failure of justice by misleading an accused and prejudicing him (Sections 211 to 216, 228 and 240).

198 State of Bihar vs Ramesh Singh, AIR 1977 SC 2018; Union of India vs. Prafulla Kumar Samal (1979) 3 SCC 4; Superintendant and Remembrancer of legal Affairs, West Bengal v. Anil Kumar Bhunja and Others (1980) 1 SCR 323; State of Delhi v. Gyan Devi and Others, (2000) 8 SCC 239; State of Madhya Pradesh v. S.B.Johari and Others (2000) 2 SCC 57; State of Orissa vs Debendra Nath Padhi, (2005)1 SCC 568

In State of Maharashtra vs Salman Salim Khan[199], the Supreme Court held that the law governing the trial of criminal offences provides for alteration of charges at any stage of the proceedings depending upon the evidence adduced in the case. If the trial is being held before a court of Magistrate, it is open to that court at any stage of trial if it comes to the conclusion that the material on record indicates the commission of an offence which requires to be tried by a superior court, it can always do so by committing such case for further trial to a superior court as contemplated in the CrPC. On the contrary if the trial is being conducted in a superior court like the Sessions Court and if that court comes to a conclusion that the evidence produced in the said trial makes out a lesser offence than the one with which the accused is changed, it is always open to that court based on evidence to convict the accused for such lesser offence.

The Supreme Court has held that if joinder of charges is in contravention of procedure prescribed under Section 218, it would be misjoinder of charges and curable under Section 464 and Section 465 Cr.P.C., provided no failure of justice has in fact been occasioned thereby.[200]

Conviction on Plea of Guilty

Under Sections 229 and 241, the Sessions and the Magistrates courts respectively, have the discretion to convict the accused if the accused pleads guilty, after recording his plea. However if the accused is not legally represented and the court fails to ask him if he desires legal aid, then the trial will be vitiated.[201]

Evidence for the Prosecution

1. Issue of Summons to Witnesses

If the accused does not plead guilty and if the accused is entitled to legal aid, after providing legal aid, the trial proceeds, with the prosecution examining its witnesses. All indigent or illiterate persons and those otherwise unable to engage a lawyer are entitled to legal aid except those involved in economic offences, offences against prostitution or child abuse where social justice requires that free legal services may not be provided by the State.[202] The assistance offered must be effective for meaningful defence. Assigning an inexperienced lawyer will not discharge the obligation of the State.[203] The court sends summons to the witnesses the prosecution seeks to examine, on its application. The court can also issue summons for the production of any documents or other articles that form a part of the material evidence in the case (Section 91). Prior to the commencement of the trial, the court may

199 2004 CrLJ 920
200 Kamalanantha vs State of Tamil Nadu, (2005)5SCC194
201 Khatri vs. State of Bihar, (1981) 1 SCC 627
202 Suk Das vs. Union Territory, AIR 1986 SC 991
203 Kishore vs. State of HP, (1991) 1 SCC 286

pass order directing return of the property seized during the investigation of a case upon application by the person who claims to be the owner of the said property on the undertaking that the applicant will produce the property whenever directed by the court and comply with any order of the court with regards the disposal of property. (Section 451). Examples of this is return of stolen property recovered to the victim and return of streedhana seized to the wife during the pendency of the trial. . If the witness who has been summoned fails to do so or produce the article or thing he has been summoned to do so without just excuse, the court can issue warrant against him and sentence him upto Rs.100 for failure to appear and upto seven days imprisonment for his failure to produce the article or document (Sections 349 and350).

2. **Trial to be in Presence of Accused**

The evidence has to be recorded in the presence of the accused or when his personal attendance is dispensed with, in the presence of his advocate (Section 273). However under Section 317, at any stage of an inquiry or trial, if the Judge is satisfied for reasons to be recorded, that the personal attendance of the accused before the Court is not necessary in the interests of justice, or that the accused persistently disturbs the proceedings in Court, the Judge may, if the accused is represented by an advocate, dispense with his attendance and proceed with such inquiry or trial in his absence and may at any subsequent stage of the proceedings direct the personal attendance of the accused. If the accused is not represented by an advocate or if the Judge thinks that his personal attendance is necessary, he may either adjourn the proceedings or order that the case of such accused be taken up or tried separately. In State of Maharashtra vs Praful B. Desai[204], the Supreme Court allowed video conferencing for recording of evidence of witness whose presence could not be procured through a Commission appointed by the court. The Court held that this would not offend the principle of Section 273 as presence does not mean the actual physical presence in the court. The court held that when the accused and his advocate are present when the evidence is being recorded by video conferencing, that evidence would be deemed to be recorded in his presence. In Kalyan Chandra Sarkar vs Rajesh Ranjan @ Pappu Yadav[205], where the undertrial prisoner whose case was pending in Bihar was transferred to Delhi, the Supreme Court directed that the trial be held through video conferencing facility.

3. **Manner of Recording of Evidence**

The evidence shall be recorded as it is being deposed and it shall either be in the language of the witness, or where not possible, a true translation in the language of the Court. The evidence shall be taken down in the

---

204 2003 CrLJ 2033
205 (2005) 3 SCC 284

narrative form under the direction of the Presiding Judge or under his supervision and direction. However if the court desires, it may take down any part of the evidence in question and answer form. While recording the evidence, the court may also record any remarks about the demeanour of the witness while under examination. The evidence taken down shall be signed by the Magistrate or the Judge and form a part of the record. After the evidence of each witness is recorded, the notes of the evidence shall be read over to him and interpreted, if he does not know the language in which it is recorded, and if necessary is corrected, or his objections over the record noted. This should also be done in the presence of the accused or his advocate. (Sections 275 to280). Where the accused does not understand the language of the court or the language in which the evidence is given, it shall be interpreted to him and if he is represented by an advocate who does not understand the language in which the evidence is given, if it is other than the language of the court, it shall be interpreted to the advocate (Section 279). If the accused cannot be made to understand the proceedings, the court may continue with the trial, and if the trial ends in a conviction, then the proceedings shall be forwarded to the High Court with a report of the circumstances of the case, and the High Court shall pass such order as it deems fit (Section 318).

The witness concerned should tender the requisite documents as evidence and they should be marked as exhibits. The witness, who is not deposing on official matters or technical matters, should not be allowed to refresh memory. The deposition of the witness in the court would form substantive evidence and the same is given on oath. Giving false evidence in court amounts to an offence. The witness initially deposes his version in the examination-in-chief. No leading questions are allowed in the examination-in-chief. Leading questions are those questions that contain the answer in them and hence the required response is a yes or no. Thereafter the cross-examination by the accused or his advocate takes place. Leading questions are allowed during cross-examination. The court may allow the cross-examination of a witness to be deferred until any other witness or witnesses have been examined or recall any witness for further cross-examination.

The court may direct payment on the part of the Government of the reasonable expenses of any complainant or witness attending the court (Section 312). Though session's trials should be held on a day to day basis, the court has the power to adjourn the trial from time to time for reasons to be recorded in writing (Section 309). When a judge is transferred or the case is transferred after the evidence has been recorded in part or entirely, then the successor judge can act on the evidence recorded by his predecessor (Section 326).

Generally when one witness is giving evidence, the other witnesses in the case who have not yet given their evidence, should not be present in the court as it would enable the witness to depose in conformity to that of the other witnesses and also cover up the omissions and contradictions in the evidence of the previous witness by giving reasonable explanations for the same. If the witness is present in the court, the court on its own or on the request of the other side can ask the witness to leave the courtroom. However after the witness has finished giving his evidence, it is permissible for him to remain in court. Contradictions between the evidence of the different witnesses also damage the case of the party. However even if the accused is appearing as a witness, he is still entitled to remain present during the deposition of the other witnesses.

4. Issue of Commissions

Whenever in the course of any inquiry, trial or other proceeding, it appears to a Court that the examination of a witness is necessary for the ends of justice, and that the attendance of such witness cannot be procured without an unreasonable amount of delay, expense or inconvenience, the Court may dispense with such attendance and may issue a Commission for the examination of the witness. If the witness is in India the commission shall be directed to the Chief Judicial Magistrate or the Chief Metropolitan Magistrate of the place, and if it is outside India, to the Court or officer with whom arrangements have been made by the Central Government with the Government of such country or place for taking the evidence of witnesses in relation to criminal matters. Upon receipt of the commission, the Commissioner shall summon the witness before him or proceed to the place where the witness is and take down his evidence in the same manner that the trial court does. The Court while issuing a commission for the examination of a prosecution witness, direct payment to the accused for meeting the expenses incurred by the accused including the advocate's fees. The parties to the proceeding may respectively forward any interrogatories in writing that the Court directing the Commission may think relevant to the issue and it shall be lawful for the commissioner to examine the witness upon such interrogatories. Any party may appear before the commissioner and examine, cross-examine or re-examine the witness. The commission shall be returned after its execution along with the deposition of the witness and it shall form a part of the record of the proceedings. The trial shall be adjourned during the period of the execution of the commission. Evidence of the President or the Vice-President of India, or the Governor of any state or the Administrator of a Union Territory shall be obtained only by issuing a commission. (Sections 284 to 289) The court may also issue a commission in order to obtain evidence of any witness or any person who is confined or detained in a prison (Section 271).

5. **No Formal Proof of Certain Documents**

Under Section 294, where any document is filed before any court by the prosecution or the accused, the particulars of every such document shall be included in a list and the prosecution or the accused, may call upon the other side to admit or deny the genuineness of each document. Though the court may require the signature appearing on the document to be proved even of those documents admitted by the opposite party. These documents that are admitted need not be proved. Other documents that need not be proved through their maker are reports of certain Government scientific experts upon any matter or thing duly submitted to him for examination or analysis (Section 293). It is not necessary that the entire article seized be sent for analysis. A sample is sufficient. What is important is that there should not be any tampering with the evidence. The Supreme Court has held that the fingerprint expert's report can be used in evidence without examining the expert.[206] However the Karnataka High Court has held that the opinion of handwriting expert does not fall in the categories of experts contemplated under Section 293. Opinion of handwriting expert cannot be admitted in evidence without examining the handwriting expert unless the genuineness of such document is admitted by the accused when called upon to do so by the Court.[207]

6. **Affidavits**

Only evidence of formal nature can be tendered by way of affidavits in a criminal trial and all material witnesses should either depose in court or before a commission.

7. **Power to Summon and Examine Persons**

Under Section 311, any court may, at any stage of any inquiry, trial or other proceeding, summon any person as a witness, or examine any person in attendance, though not summoned as a witness, or recall and re-examine any person already examined, if his evidence appears to it to be essential to the just decision of the case. This provision is there to prevent any danger of miscarriage of justice owing due to any particular witness not being called. The object of this section is to do justice not only from the point of view of the accused or the prosecution, but from the point of discovering relevant facts or obtaining proper proof of such facts for a just decision of the case. The powers are wide and cannot be curtailed in any way. Under Section 311A, the Magistrate of the first class can if satisfied that it is expedient for the investigation or trial, direct any person, including an accused person, to give specimen signatures or handwriting and the person to whom the order relates shall be produced or shall attend at the time and place specified in such order and shall give his specimen signatures

206 AIR 1972 SC 1975

207 State of Karnataka vs. Mutha Nayak, (1995) 1 ALT (Crl.)93

or handwriting. Provided that no order shall be made under this section unless the person has at some time been arrested in connection with such investigation or proceeding.

8. **Local Inspection**

   Under Section 310, any Judge or Magistrate may, at any stage of any inquiry, trial or other proceeding, after due notice to the parties, visit and inspect any place in which an offence is alleged to have been committed, or any other place which it is in his opinion necessary to view for the purpose of properly appreciating the evidence given at such inquiry or trial and shall without unnecessary delay record a memorandum of any relevant facts observed at such inspection. This memorandum shall form a part of the record and if any party so desires, a copy of the same shall be furnished to them free of cost.

Entering Upon the Defence

In a session's triable case, if after taking the evidence for the prosecution, examining the accused and hearing the prosecution and the defence on the point, the judge considers that there is no evidence that the accused committed the offence, it may acquit the accused (Section 232). In a case triable by a Magistrate or where the accused is not acquitted under Section 232, the accused shall be called upon to enter on his defence and adduce any evidence he may have in support thereof. The accused may file his written statement or apply for the issue of summons to any witness, and the court shall issue the same unless it is of the opinion that the application is made for the purpose of vexation or delay or for defeating the ends of justice. The court may also refuse to summon any witness, whom the accused has cross-examined or had the opportunity of cross-examining any witness before entering on his defence, unless the court is satisfied that it is necessary for the ends of justice. The judge may direct that the payment of reasonable expenses of any witness so summoned be made by the accused (Sections 233 and 243).

No accused can be compelled to be a witness, though he is entitled to give evidence if he so desires, and any failure on his part to volunteer to be a witness, should not give rise to any presumption against him or be made the subject of any comment by any of the parties or the Court (Section 315).

But under Section 313, in every inquiry or trial, for the purpose of enabling the accused to personally explain any circumstances appearing in the evidence against him, the court may at any stage without warning the accused put such questions to him as it considers necessary and shall, after the witnesses for the prosecution have been examined and before he is called on for his defense, question him generally on the case. This examination shall not be on oath and the accused shall not render him liable to punishment by refusing to answer such questions or by giving false answers to them. The answers given by the accused may be taken into consideration in such inquiry or trial, and put in evidence for or against him in any other inquiry into or trial for any other offence that such answers may tend to show he has committed. Irregularity as regards compliance of the provisions of Section 313 of putting every adverse circumstance against the accused to him in order to enable him to explain it, if it results in prejudice to the accused renders the trial vitiated.[208] The falsity of the defense cannot take the place of proof of facts, which the prosecution has to establish I order to succeed. A false plea maybe considered as an additional circumstance if other circumstances prove and establish the guilt of the accused.[209] Thus the answers given by the accused in response to his examination under Section. 313 can be taken into consideration for proving his guilt.[210]

The Supreme Court has held that Section 313 of the Code is a statutory provision and embodies the fundamental principle of fairness based on the maxim audi alterant partem. It is trite law that the attention of the accused must be specifically invited to inculpatory pieces of evidence or circumstances laid on record with a view to giving him an opportunity to offer an explanation if he chooses to do so. The section imposes a heavy duty on the court to take great care to ensure that the incriminating circumstances are put to the accused and his response solicited. The words 'shall question him' clearly bring out the mandatory character of the clause and cast an imperative duty on the court and confer a corresponding right on the accused to an opportunity to offer his explanation for such incriminating material appearing against him. It is, therefore, true that the purpose of the examination of the accused under Section 313 is to give the accused an opportunity to explain the incriminating material which has surfaced on record. The stage of examination of the accused under Clause (b) of Sub-section (1) of Section 313 reaches only after the witnesses for the prosecution have been examined and before the accused is called on to enter upon his defence. At the stage of closure of the prosecution evidence and before recording of statement under Section 313, the learned judge is not expected to evaluate the evidence for the purpose of deciding whether or not he should question the accused. After the Section 313 stage is over he has to hear the oral submissions, of counsel on the evidence adduced before pronouncing on the evidence. The trial judge is not expected before he examines the accused under Section 313 of the Code, to sift the evidence and pronounce on whether or not he would accept the evidence regarding any incriminating material to determine whether or not to examine the accused on that material. To do so would be to pre-judge the evidence without hearing the prosecution under Section 314 of the

208 AIR 1973 SC 2622

209 Shankarlal Gyarasilal Dixit vs. State of Maharashtra, (1981) 2 SCC 35; Tanviben Pankajkumar Devetia vs. State of Gujarat, (1997) 7 SCC 156

210 State of Maharashtra Vs Sukhdeo Singh, (1992)3SCC700; Hate Singh v. State of Madhya Bharat 1953 Crl. L.J. 1933

Code. Therefore, no matter how weak or scanty the prosecution evidence is in regard to a certain incriminating material, it is the duty of the court to examine the accused and seek his explanation thereon. It is only after that stage is over that the oral arguments have to be heard before the judgment is rendered. It is only where the court finds that no incriminating material has surfaced that the accused may not be examined under Section 313 of the Code. If there is material against the accused he must be examined.[211] But circumstances not appearing in evidence cannot be put to the accused.[212] It is not necessary to put each and every circumstance against the accused to him in his statement under Section 313. the purpose is to give the accused an opportunity to explain the circumstance adverse to him in the prosecution evidence. The nature of the questions to be asked should be such that any reasonable person in the position of the accused may be in a position ot give an rational explanation to the questions as had been asked. Composite questions should not be asked bundling many facts together.[213] A statement under Section 313 cannot be the sole basis of conviction of the accused.[214]

In Basavaraj R.Patil's case[215] the Supreme Court held that where the accused was exempted and was out of the country, his advocate could answer the questions raised under Section 313. For this the accused has to file an application before the trial court accompanied by an affidavit sworn to by the accused himself containing the following matters: (a) A narration of facts to satisfy the court of his real difficulties to be physically present in court for giving such answers. (b) An assurance that no prejudice would be caused to him, in any manner, by dispensing with his personal presence during such questioning. (c) An undertaking that he would not raise any grievance on that score at any stage of the case. If the court is satisfied of the genuineness of the statements made by the accused in the said application and affidavit it is open to the court to supply the questionnaire to his advocate (containing the questions which the court might put to him under Section 313 of the Code) and fix the time within which the same has to be returned duly answered by the accused together with a properly authenticated affidavit that those answers were given by the accused himself. He should affix his signature on all the sheets of the answered questionnaire. However, if he does not wish to give any answer to any of the questions he is free to indicate that fact at the appropriate place in the questionnaire as a matter of precaution the Court may keep photocopy or carbon copy of the questionnaire before it is supplied to the accused for

211 Jit Bahadur Chetri v. State of Arunachal Pradesh 1977 Crl. L.J. 1833; Asokan v. State of Kerala 1982 Crl. L.J. 173; State of Maharashtra Vs Sukhdeo Singh, (1992)3SCC700

212 Kalpnath Rai vs State (through CBI), (1997) 8 SCC 732

213 State of Punjab vs Swaran Singh, (2005)6 SCC 101

214 Mohan Singh vs Prem Singh, 2003 CrLJ 11

215 Basavaraj R Patil vs. State Of Karnataka, (2000) 8 SCC 740

answers. If the accused fails to return the questionnaire duly answered as aforesaid within the time or extended time granted by the court, he shall forfeit his right to seek personal exemption from court during such questioning.The above course if adopted in exceptional exigency it would not violate the legislative intent envisaged in Section 313 of the Code.

Arguments

After the defense evidence is complete, the prosecutor shall sum up his case and the accused or his advocate shall be entitled to reply. Provided that where any point of law is raised by the accused, the prosecution may, with the permission of the court, make his submissions with regard to such point of law (Section 234). The parties may submit written arguments before the completion of their oral arguments and furnish a copy of the same to the other side (Section 314).

Judgment of Acquittal or Conviction

After hearing arguments and points of law, if any, the Judge shall give a judgment in the case. If the accused is convicted, the Judge shall hear the accused on the question of sentence and then pass sentence on him in accordance with law, unless he releases the accused on probation. This is a mandatory requirement and its basis is humane sentencing taking into account all the extenuating circumstances. Another reason for this requirement being mandatory is that all offences prescribe a maximum penalty even in cases where a minimum penalty has been prescribed, which gives the trial court discretion to award sentence. Here the court looks into circumstances other than the guilt or innocence of the accused, such as the circumstances in which the offence was committed, the profile of the accused, circumstances peculiar to the accused, the relationship between the parties and the type and quantum of punishment that would suit the ends of justice. Examples of this are seen where the parties are related to each other, the courts generally order compensation to the victims as also in sexual offences and matrimonial offences where the parties have reconciled, the court may not sentence the accused to imprisonment.

If the accused is convicted and has been previously convicted and hence liable to enhanced penalty, then if the accused does not admit to previous conviction, the court shall take evidence of the previous conviction and shall record a finding thereof. If the court finds the accused not guilty, he shall record an order of acquittal. (Sections 235,236 and 248) If the court while acquitting is of the opinion that there was no reasonable ground for making the accusation against the accused, the court may, in his order of discharge or acquittal, call upon the complainant to pay compensation to such accused (Section 250).

Wherever the accused is entitled to probation under the Probation of Offenders

Act, such as cases where the accused is below 21 years of age, is a first time offender and is convicted for offences which are covered by the ambit of the Probation of Offenders Act, the court is duty bound to release the accused on probation except if it deems fit not to do so, for reasons to be recorded in writing.[216]

When cross cases are instituted between the parties, it would be just and fair that both be decided together by the same court. The fair procedure to adopt would be that after completion of recording evidence in one case, he must hear the arguments, but reserve the judgment. Thereafter he must hear the cross case and after recording of evidence, he must hear the arguments and reserve judgment. Then he must deliver separate judgments in both cases relying only on the evidence recorded in that particular case and both judgments pronounced one after the other.[217]

Kamalanantha vs State of Tamil Nadu,[218] the Trial Court resorted to Section 31 Cr.P.C. and ordered the sentence to run consecutively, subject to proviso (a) of the said Section. The Supreme Court held that the term 'imprisonment; is not defined under the Code of Criminal Procedure. Section 31 of the Code tails under Chapter III of the Code which deals with power of Courts. Section 28 of the Code empowers the High Court to pass any sentence authorised by law. Similarly, Sessions Judge and Additional Sessions Judge may pass any sentence authorised by law, except the sentence of death which shall be subject to confirmation by High Court. In our opinion the term "imprisonment" would include the sentence of imprisonment for life.

The accused and the prosecution can file appeals against the judgment, and in cases where no appeal lies, they can file for revision of the order. The procedure for these has been set out in Chapter 2. The appeal and revision proceedings are considered to be a continuation of the trial.

Compensation to the Victim

Under Section 357 of the CrPC, upon passing sentence of conviction, the Court (which includes the Appellate Court) has the power to direct the payment of part of the fine amount imposed as compensation to the victim. The Court can order payment of compensation to the victim even where fine is not part of the sentence. The Court can also direct the compensation to any bona fide purchaser of any stolen property from the fine amount. The Court ought to give opportunity to the accused so that the relevant aspects like the need to award compensation, capacity of the accused to pay and several other relevant facts can be taken note of .[219] In Delhi Domestic Workers Forum vs Union of India[220] the Supreme Court held that compensation for victims shall be

216 Bhupesh Ramchandra More vs. State of Maharashtra, 1993 Mh.L.J 1425
217 Nathilal vs State of UP, (1990) Supp SCC 145; State of MP vs Mishrilal, 2003 CrLJ 2312
218 (2005)5SCC194
219 Mangilal vs State of MP, AIR 2004 SC 1280
220 (1995) 1 SCC 14)

awarded by the court on conviction of the offender and by the Criminal Injuries Compensation Board whether or not a conviction has taken place. The Board will take into account pain, suffering and shock as well as loss of earnings due to pregnancy and the expenses of childbirth if this occurred as a result of the rape. In Bodhisatwa vs Subhra Chakraborty[221], the Supreme Court held that rape was a violation of fundamental right under Article 21 which includes the right to live with dignity. In this case, interim compensation was awarded to the victim by the Court pending the trial. In a later case, Chairman, Railway Board vs Chandrima Das[222], relying on the earlier decision, the Supreme Court held that for the offence of rape by public officials, the State was laible to pay compensation for its failure to protect the individual from the violation of the fundamental rights by the State authorities and the state is vicariously liable for the act of tort of its employees and hence liable to pay damages to the victim.

Under Section 358 of the CrPC, the Magistrate can award compensation not exceeding Rs. 100 to any person wrongly arrested.

Trial of Private Complaints

"Complaint" means any allegation made orally or in writing to a Magistrate, with a view to his taking action under the CrPC, that some person, whether known or unknown, has committed an offence, but does not include a police report. However a police report that discloses after investigation, the commission of a non-cognizable offence shall be deemed to be a complaint and the police officer by whom such report is made shall be deemed to be the complainant (Section 2(d).

The trial procedure for private complaints varies from that of cases instituted on a police complaint in certain respects. The trial also varies as per the type of case being tried. The CrPC defines two types of cases:

Warrant case, which means a case relating to an offence punishable with imprisonment for a term exceeding two years;

Summons case, which means a case relating to an offence, not being a warrant case. A private complaint would normally come to an end on the death of the complainant but the heirs can apply to the court to continue with the prosecution.[223]

221 AIR 1996 SC 922
222 2000 Cri.L.J 1473
223 Jimmy Jahangir Madan vs Bolly Cariyappa Hindley, AIR 2005 SC 48

Trial of Warrant Cases

1. Examination of Complainant

The Magistrate takes cognizance of an offence under Section 190(1) in three cases:

a) Upon receiving a compliant of facts which constitute such offence;

b) Upon a police report of such facts;

c) Upon information received from any person other than a police officer, or upon his won knowledge that such an offence has been committed.

Upon taking cognizance of a case upon receiving a complaint the magistrate examines upon oath the complainant and any witness, and the substance of such examination shall be reduced into writing and signed by its maker and the Magistrate. This is known as the verification of the complaint and its purpose is to see whether the ingredients of the offence are made out. However the Magistrate need not verify the complaint if it is filed by a public servant in the discharge of his duty or if he transfers the case over to another Magistrate who has the jurisdiction to try the case. (Section 200) it is not necessary to examine all the witnesses. Generally only the Complainant is examined. If upon verification, the Magistrate is convinced that the complaint discloses an offence, he issues process against the accused. If no offence is disclosed, the Magistrate can dismiss the complaint (Section 203). The Supreme Court has held that where the complaint has been dismissed under Section 203 CrPC, there is no statutory bar in filing a second complaint on the same facts in exceptional circumstances namely, where the previous order was passed on an incomplete or on a misunderstanding of the nature of complaint or it was manifestly absurd or where new facts which could not have been brought on record with due diligence in the previous proceedings, have been adduced.[224]

Where the Magistrate deems fit, he may postpone the issue of process against the accused and either inquire into the case himself or direct an investigation by a police officer or any other person in order to ascertain whether there are sufficient grounds for proceeding (Section 202). The inquiry under Section 202 is not in the nature of a trial and the scope of the inquiry is extremely limited and is only to ascertain the truth or falsehood of the allegations made in the complaint:

a) On the material placed by the complainant before the court;

b) For the limited purpose of finding out whether a prima facie case for issue of process has been made out; and

224Pramatha Nath Talukdar vs Saroj Ranjan Sarkar, AIR 1962 SC 876; Mahesh Chand vs B.Janardhan Reddy, (2003)1 SCC 734; Poonam Chand Jain vs Fazru, 2005 CrLJ 100

c) For deciding the question purely from the point of view of the complainant without at all adverting to any defense that the accused may have.

The accused has no locus standi and is not entitled to be heard on the question whether or the process should be issued against him.[225] The Magistrate can issue process even if the police report is against the complainant.[226]

The Magistrate, if upon receiving a complaint, which discloses the commission of a cognizable offence, may instead of proceeding with the complaint, may issue an order under Section 156(3) direct any officer in charge of a police station to investigate into the case and upon this direction, the police would have to file a chargesheet and the case would proceed as a police case.[227]

2. Issue of Process

If in the opinion of the Magistrate taking cognizance of the case, there is sufficient ground for proceeding against the accused, he shall either issue summons or a warrant against the accused for his appearance. A copy of the complaint should accompany this. (Section 204) the order of issue of process need not be a speaking order, but should be supported by the facts as revealed by the complaint, any documents filed in support of the case, the verification statement, any inquiry report and should reveal an application of mind on the part of the judge. However what is important is that a prima facie case should be made out, and it is not necessary that the facts as revealed should be sufficient to result in the conviction of the accused.

3. Evidence for the Prosecution

In a warrant case instituted other than in a police report, after the accused enters appearance, the Magistrate shall proceed to hear the prosecution and take all such evidence as may be produced in support of the prosecution. The Magistrate may issue summons to any of the prosecution witnesses upon an application on that behalf, directing them to appear or produce any document or any other thing (Section 244). Non -production of material witness in any trial, whether instituted on a police report or other wise, not only warrants an adverse inference against the prosecution, but also vitiates the trial.[228]

4. Discharge

If upon taking evidence for the prosecution, the Magistrate considers, for reasons to be recorded that no case has been made out against the accused,

225Smt. Nagawwa vs. Veeranna, AIR 1976 SC 1947, Laxmi Kishor vs. State of Maharashtra, 1993 Mah.L.J 609

226 Abhinandan Jha vs. Dinesh Mishra, AIR 1968 SC 117

227 Madhu Bala vs. Suresh Kumar, AIR 1997 SC 3104

228 AIR 1954 SC 51

which if unrebutted, would warrant his conviction, the Magistrate shall discharge him. However even before taking the same, if the Magistrate feels that the charge is groundless, then for reasons to be recorded, he may discharge the accused. (Section 245). The principles relating to discharge of the accused are the same as that in police cases.

5. **Procedure Where the Accused is Not Discharged**

If after taking evidence, or at any previous stage of the case, the Magistrate is of the opinion that there is ground for presuming that the accused has committed an offence, which the court is competent to try, then he may frame charge against the accused. If the accused pleads guilty, the Magistrate may convict him, and if does not do so, he may be tried. Here the evidence recorded prior to charge being framed also forms a part of the record, and the accused has the right to recall any witness already examined and cross-examine him, with the permission of the court. Thereafter the evidence of any other witness may be recorded. (Section 246) The complainant conducts prosecution and he has to appoint a private advocate to conduct the same. The procedure is the same as in trials for the cases instituted on a police report.

7. **Absence of the Complainant**

When the proceedings have been instituted upon complaint and on any day fixed for the hearing of the case, the complainant is absent, and the offence may be lawfully compounded and is not a cognizable offence, the Magistrate may in his discretion, at any time before the charge is framed, discharge the accused (Section 249).

Trial of Summons Case

The procedure for trial of summons cases is the same as that of warrants triable cases till the stage of issue of process. At the time of issuing process, in a summons triable case, the Magistrate issues summons against the accused and only on his failure to appear then or at any subsequent stage of the proceedings can the court exercise its powers to issue warrant or even a proclamation in case the accused absconds. Chapter XX governs the procedure for a summons triable case.

The Supreme Court has held that if the accused is aggrieved by the order of issue of process, in the absence of the provision for discharge, the trial court cannot review or reconsider its earlier order and the accused would have to take recourse to filing a revision or getting the order quashed by the High Court in the exercise of its jurisdiction under Section 482 CrPC.[229]The

229Adalat Prasad vs. Rooplal Jindal & Ors. (2004) 7 Scale 137; Subramanium Sethuraman vs State of Maharashtra (2004) AIR SCW 5326; Poonam Chand Jain vs Fazru, 2005 CrLJ 100

procedure for trial of summons cases is briefer than that of warrants triable cases, due to the relative non-seriousness of charge. However in any case which is punishable with imprisonment for a term exceeding six months, if during the course of the trial it appears to the Magistrate that in the interests of justice, the offence should be tried in accordance with the trial procedure for warrants cases, the Magistrate may proceed to rehear the case in the manner provided for warrants case, and may recall any witness who may have been examined (Section 259).

The procedure is as follows:

1. **Substance of Accusation to be Stated**

   Charge is not framed and only the substance of the accusation is stated to the accused and he is asked whether he pleads guilty or not. This is known as recording the plea of the accused. Upon his pleading guilty, the Magistrate shall record the plea as nearly as possible in words of the accused and may convict him. (Sections 251 and 252)

2. **Conviction on Plea of Guilty in absence of Accused in Petty Cases**

   Where the summons has been issued for a petty offence which is punishable only with fine not exceeding Rs.1000, or offences specified by the State Government which are not punishable for a period exceeding three months, and the summons issued to the accused specifies that the accused can send the plea in writing along with the fine in case he pleads guilty, without actual appearance, upon his doing so, the Magistrate may convict the accused in his absence. (Sections 206 and 253)

3. **Procedure When Not Convicted**

   Where the accused is not convicted, the Magistrate shall hear the evidence for the prosecution and summon all witnesses for the prosecution on its application. The accused shall also have the right to cross-examine the prosecution witnesses and thereafter also produce any witness on its behalf. (Section 254) The rules of evidence shall be the same as in all criminal trial and the proceedings shall also be similar except for the differences stated here. In any summons case instituted otherwise than upon a complaint, a Magistrate of the First Class, or with the previous sanction of the Chief Judicial Magistrate, any Judicial Magistrate, may stop the proceedings at any stage, after recording his reasons for the same, and without pronouncing the judgment. In case the evidence of any principle witness has been recorded, it shall amount to an acquittal and in other cases, to a discharge (Section 258). After completion of evidence, the Magistrate shall either acquit or convict the accused following the same procedure as in all criminal trials (Section 255).

4. Dispension of Personal Attendance of the Accused

Under Section 205(2) of the CrPC, the Magistrate has the powers to dispense with the presence of the accused at any stage of the proceedings. This dispension is discretionary and should be exercised in rare cases due to distance or any physical disability or enormous hardship or cost or other good reason, in the interests of justice. This dispension could be continued even during the recording of evidence, provided his counsel is present and the accused gives an undertaking that he will not dispute his identity in the case, and that he has no objection in taking evidence in his absence. The Supreme Court has held that the main concern of the court is administration of criminal justice and for that purpose the court proceedings should register progress. Presence of the accused is not for marking attendance just for the sake of seeing him in the court but to enable the court to proceed with the trial.[230]

5. Non-Appearance or Death of Complainant

Where the complainant does not appear on the date of hearing of the case, the Magistrate may acquit the accused, unless he thinks it proper to adjourn the proceedings to some other day. The Magistrate may exempt the appearance of the complainant where he is represented by an advocate, when he does not deem the personal appearance of the complainant necessary for the trial to proceed. The Magistrate may dismiss the complaint and acquit the accused on the death of the complainant during the pendency of the complaint (Section 256).

6. Withdrawal of Complaint

If the complainant at any time before a final order is passed in a case, satisfies the Magistrate that there are sufficient grounds for permitting him to withdraw his complaint against any or all the accused, the Magistrate may permit him to do so and shall thereupon acquit the accused against whom the complaint is so withdrawn (Section 257).

Summary Trials

Chapter XXI of the CrPC deals with the procedure for summary trials. Section 262 states that the procedure for this shall be the same as that followed in summons cases except that no sentence of imprisonment for a term exceeding three months shall be passed in the case of conviction for a trial held summarily. Section 264 also specifies that in every case tried summarily, in which the accused does not plead guilty; the Magistrate shall record the substance of the evidence and a judgment containing a brief statement of the reason for the finding.

230 Bhaskar Industries Ltd. vs. Bhiwani Denim & Apparels Ltd. (2001) 7 SCC 401

Any Magistrate can hold summary trials in the following cases:

a) Offences not punishable with imprisonment for a period exceeding two years;

b) Theft (Sections 379 to 381 of the IPC), where the value of the property stolen does not exceed Rs.2000;

c) Receiving or retaining stolen property (Section 411 of the IPC) where the value of the property does not exceed Rs.2000;

d) Assisting in the concealment or disposal of stolen property (Section 414 of the IPC) where the value of the property does not exceed Rs.2000;

e) Lurking house trespass or house-breaking under Sections 454 and 456 of the IPC;

f) Insult with intent to provoke a breach of the peace (Section 504 IPC) and criminal intimidation punishable with imprisonment for a term which may extend to two years, or with fine, or with both (Section 506 IPC);

g) abetment or attempt to commit any of the above offences; and

h) Any offence for which a complaint may be made under Section 20 of the Cattle Trespass Act, 1871.

During the course of summary trial, if the Magistrate is of the opinion that the nature of the case is such that it is undesirable to try it summarily, the Magistrate shall recall any witnesses who may have been examined and proceed to re-hear the case in the manner provided in the CrPC (Section 260)

Every case tried summarily, shall have the record containing the following particulars:

a) the serial number of the case;

b) the date of the commission of the case;

c) the date of the report or complaint;

d) the name of the complainant, if any;

e) the name, parentage and residence of the accused;

f) the offence complained of and the offence, if any, proved, and in cases involving stolen property, the value of the property in respect of which the offence has been committed;

g) the plea of the accused and his examination, if any;

h) the finding;

i) the sentence or other final order;

j) The date on which proceedings terminated.(Section 263).

Chapter Cases

Chapter cases are proceedings conducted under Chapter VIII of the CrPC, which ask for Security for keeping the peace and good behaviour. Except for the proceedings under Section 106, Executive Magistrates conduct the rest. They are not considered trials for offences and action under this chapter is meant to be preventive in nature and is either held in addition to the criminal case or in cases where the respondent commits no cognizable offence.

Under Section 106, whenever a person is convicted for committing an offence which involves breach of peace, is an offence against public tranquility under Chapter VIII of the Indian Penal Code, or an offence which includes assault, use of criminal force, mischief or criminal intimidation, the trial court, while passing sentence against the accused, may order him to execute bond, with or without sureties, for keeping peace, for such period not exceeding three years as it deems fit.

Chapter proceedings can be conducted by the Executive Magistrate, who is a police officer of the rank of the Assistant Commissioner of Police:

Table 2

SECTION	DEFINITION	PERIOD
107	Any person who is likely to commit breach of peace or disturb the public tranquility or to do any wrongful act that may occasion the same within local jurisdiction or by person within local jurisdiction	Bond for keeping peace upto one year with or without surety
108	Any person who, within local jurisdiction, orally or in writing, intentionally disseminates or attempts or abets the same, of any matter the publication of which: is punishable as sedition, creating enmity between classes, imputations, assertions which are prejudicial to national integration and which maliciously insult the religion or religious beliefs of any class; any matter concerning a Judge acting in the discharge of his official duty which amounts to defamation or criminal intimidation; makes, sells, distributes or publicly exhibits any obscene matter.	Bond for keeping good behaviour for a period upto one year with or without surety

SECTION	DEFINITION	PERIOD
110	Person, within local jurisdiction who is a habitual offender of the following categories: Robber, house-breaker ,thief or forger; Receiver of stolen property; Protector or harbourer of thieves or aids in the concealment or disposal of stolen property.	Bond with or without sureties for good behaviour for upto three years
	Commits, abets or attempts to commit offence of kidnapping, abduction, extortion, cheating or mischief, or any offence under chapter XII of the IPC (offences relating to coins and government stamps, or offence of forgery under Sections 489 A to D of the IPC: Commits, abets or attempts to commit offences relating to breach of peace; Commits, abets or attempts to commit the offence under the the Foreigners Act, 1946(31 of 1946), Drugs and Cosmetics Act, the Foreign Exchange regulation Act, Employees Provident Funds and Family Pension Fund Act, Prevention of Food Adulteration Act, Untouchability (Offences) Act, Customs Act and any offence punishable under any other law providing for the prevention of hoarding or profiteering or of adulteration of food or drugs or of corruption; Is so desperate and dangerous as to render his being at large without security hazardous to the community.	

When the magistrate decides to commence chapter proceedings against any person, he shall issue a show cause notice under Section111, with an order in writing setting forth the substance of information received, the amount of bond to be executed, the term for which it is to be in force and the number, character and class of sureties, if any, required. This show cause notice would be sent along with summons or warrant, where the Magistrate has reason to fear the commission of a breach of the peace which cannot be prevented except by the immediate arrest of the person. When the person appears before the Magistrate, he shall proceed to inquire into the truth of the information received under Section 116, and take such evidence as may be necessary. The copies of all the material against the respondent should be furnished to him. Where there are two or more persons associated together in the matter under inquiry, they may be dealt with in the same or separate inquiries. The inquiry should be completed within six months from the date of its commencement, and if it is incomplete, it shall stand terminated unless, for special reasons to be recorded in writing, the Magistrate otherwise directs. However in case the respondent is kept under detention, the inquiry cannot be extended. The Magistrate, after commencement of the inquiry and before its completion, if he considers that immediate measures are necessary for the prevention of a breach of peace or disturbance of the public tranquility or the commission of any offence or for public safety, may for reasons to be recorded in writing, direct the respondent to execute a bond with or without sureties, for keeping the peace or maintaining good behaviour until the conclusion of the inquiry and may detain him in custody until such bond is executed or, in default of execution, until the inquiry is completed. It is illegal to ask for interim bond along with the show cause notice or without holding any inquiry into the truth of the allegations. The interim bond should not be more onerous than that required in the original show cause notice.

Chapter proceedings should not be started against anyone who has only one case against him and there should be sufficient grounds to believe that a person's liberty would threaten greater pubic good. Under the Habitual Offenders Act, a habitual offender is one who has been convicted thrice within a period of five years. After the conclusion of the inquiry, the person shall either be discharged, or asked to execute bond which should not be more severe than that specified in the show cause notice. The aggrieved person can approach either the Sessions Court or the High Court against the order of the Magistrate. If the person fails to furnish the bond, or if the Magistrate holds that the person after executing bond, has committed breach of the bond, he may be arrested and detained in prison for the period of the bond.

Irregular proceedings

Chapter XXXV of the CrPC deals with irregular proceedings. There are certain irregularities, which are held to lead to failure of justice and are incurable, and vitiate the trial while others are curable and do not affect the legality of the trial.

The following acts of the Magistrate who is not empowered to do them, would make his proceedings void, according to Section 461 of the CrPC:

a) Attachment and sale of property of person against whom a proclamation is issued;

b) Issues a search warrant for a document, parcel or other thing in the custody of a postal or telegraph authority;

c) Demands security to keep the peace or good behaviour;

d) Discharges a person lawfully bound to be of good behaviour;

e) Cancels a bond to keep the peace;

f) Makes an order for maintenance;

g) Makes an order under Section 133 of the CrPC as to a local nuisance;

h) Prohibits, under Section 143, the repetition or continuance of a public nuisance;

i) Makes and order under Part C (Urgent cases of nuisance or apprehended danger under Section 144) and Part D (Disputes as to immovable property under Sections 145 to 148) of Chapter X;

j) Takes cognizance of an offence under Section 190 (1(c) of the CrPC;

k) Tries an offender;

l) Tries an offender summarily;

m) Passes a sentence under Section 325, on proceedings recorded by another Magistrate;

n) Decides an appeal;

o) Calls for proceedings under revisional powers;

p) Revises an order passed on forfeiture of bail bond.

No finding, sentence or order of any criminal court shall be set aside merely on ground that the inquiry, trial or other proceedings in the course of which it was arrived at or passed, took place in a wrong sessions division, district, sub-division or other local area unless it appears that such error has in fact occasioned a failure of justice (Section 462). Similar is the case where there is an error, omission or irregularity in the charge including any misjoinder of charge, or in the complaint, summons, warrant, proclamation, order, judgment or other proceedings before or during trial or in any inquiry or other proceedings subject to Section 461 (Sections 464 and 465).

Release Under Certain Conditions

Furlough

Furlough and Parole are release of convicted prisoners of certain categories while they are undergoing their sentences. This is a periodic release after which the prisoner returns to the prison and the period of furlough and parole is included in computing the period of sentence undergone. It is a part of the sentence and is not excluded.

Furlough has been held by the Bombay High Court to be a legal right, though the Rules state that it is a discretionary power given to the Sanctioning Authority through the Superintendent of Jail. Furlough is granted for a period of two weeks per year to those convicted to serve sentence of less than five years but over a year and for two weeks every two years for those serving sentences of over five years. The release on furlough can be refused on the report of the Police of the area, and the Superintendent being negative. The convict has to furnish surety and follow the conditions that may be imposed in the furlough order and overstaying will lead to penalty and the period so overstayed is not counted towards the sentence.

Habituals and certain categories of prisoners specified by the Rules may be denied furlough.

Parole

Unlike furlough parole is not for a fixed period and not granted as of right. Parole is granted in special circumstances such as death, serious illness of any family member or close relative or for any other just cause. The period of parole may be extended if necessary. The terms may be imposed on grant of parole.

Remission

Remission is granted to convicts. It is a deduction of the sentence of the convict given periodically. The period of remission is counted in the computing of the sentence undergone. However Section 433A of the Cr. P.C. states that in case of a life sentence, the period of sentence undergone even after computing the remissions should not be less than 14 years. It is of various kinds such as ordinary remission, annual remission for good conduct, special remission and state remission. The Remission Rules state the period of ordinary remission different categories of prisoners are entitled to. Ordinary Remission can be withheld and prisoners who are undergoing sentence of imprisonment in lieu of fine or simpliciter are not eligible for ordinary remission. Ordinary Remission can be withheld on disciplinary grounds too. Special remission is granted under specific circumstances for exemplary behavior and is granted in addition to ordinary remission. State remission is granted on such occasions of national importance or public rejoicing as the State Government may determine grant to such prisoners for such period as may be specified. The total period of ordinary and special remissions should not exceed one-third of the total period of sentence. In Kamalanantha vs State of Tamil Nadu,[231] the Supreme Court upheld the order of the trial court that any remission of sentence or amnesty on any special occasions announced or to be announced be either by the Central or the State Government shall not apply to the sentence

231 (2005)5SCC194

Suspension

The appropriate government has the power to suspend or remit the entire sentence of the convict with or without conditions. The Government may take into account the opinion of the convicting judge in making its decision.

Commuting

The appropriate government may also commute the sentence, i.e. reduce the sentence of a person. Under Section 433 of the Cr. P.C the sentence of death may be commuted to any other punishment provided in the IPC, a sentence of life imprisonment for imprisonment for a term not exceeding 14 years or for fine, a sentence for rigorous imprisonment for simple imprisonment or for fine and a sentence of simple imprisonment for fine subject to the qualification of Section 433 A mentioned above.

Set Off

Set off is granted for the period undergone in prison prior to conviction as an undertrial except where the sentence is in default of payment of fine.

CHAPTER 7

RIGHTS OF ACCUSED PERSONS

The rights of accused persons are elucidated in the Code of Criminal Procedure (CrPC for short) and the Constitution of India. These include the fundamental rights, especially Articles 20 to 22(2). These articles form the bulwark of the human rights jurisprudence in India. Initially the fundamental rights were interpreted in isolation and not in consonance with the principles laid down in the entire part and that in Part IV that lists the Directive Principles of State Policy, but in the Bank Nationalisation case,[232] the Supreme Court held that all the fundamental rights had to be read together. Taking this stand further, the Supreme Court in Maneka Gandhi's case[233] held that any procedure established by law which deprives a person of his life or personal liberty under Article 21 should be fair and just and stand the test of non-arbitrariness as envisaged by Article 14. This broadened the scope for interpretation of Article 21, which is today considered the edifice of the basic structure of our Constitution. Earlier in Keshavananda Bharati's case,[234] the Supreme Court had held that the fundamental rights should read the Directive Principles into them while interpreting them. These judgments gave rise to a series of judgments that developed human rights jurisprudence and were based on the principles of social justice. The arena of prisoners' rights saw a whole series of judgments from 1978 onwards when many educated inmates wrote letters to the Supreme Court highlighting the pathetic conditions of prisoners. The swift action and receptiveness of the court encouraged many people to come out with more horrific stories and paved the way for development and understanding of prisoners rights, until then an unknown concept and changed the way the country and its courts looked at prisoners, accused, imprisonment and punishment. It also led to several interventionist projects in the prison and ultimately the famous Tihar experiment.

While there is no denying that one of the most dynamic roles played by the Judiciary, especially the Supreme Court, in developing prisoners rights and human rights jurisprudence, through its affirmative action, one has to understand this stand of the Court in its proper historical perspective. Several factors played a part in the Supreme Court's willingness to respond to the call of the people and use its power to take the Government head on in many of these encounters. Some of the important factors were:

232 AIR 1970 SC 564
233 Maneka Gandhi vs. Union of India AIR 1978 SC 597
234(1973) 4 SCC 225

- The Emergency and the suspension of the fundamental rights;
- The judgment of the Supreme Court in the Habeas Corpus case,[235] where four judges of the Supreme Court held that no person had any locus standi to move any petition or to enforce any right to personal liberty as the proclamation of emergency was perfectly valid and that Article 21 was the sole repository of the right to life or personal liberty, so that when Article 21 was suspended, as during Emergency, no petition would lie in respect of the illegal detention;
- The large scale detention and arrest of persons during Emergency, including political dissidents and white collar offenders, all a part of the middle class intelligentsia;
- The formation of the Janata Government in 1977 and the debate on constitutionality of the 42nd Amendment which abrogated the supremacy of the fundamental rights, the detentions during Emergency and their validity, the oppression by the Executive and the need to check the same, the denial of rights to the detenus and the role of the Court in upholding the democratic principles and people's rights instead of upholding State action and in this case, excesses.

This criticism of the role of the judiciary in failing to rise to the occasion and act as an independent entity answerable only to the people, also pushed the Supreme Court to make amends by shaping Public Interest Litigation and developing it to respond to what it considered social justice issues. This has led to a whole series of judgments where the court has intervened including cases already referred to such as the Hussainara Khatoon cases where it ordered release of indigent undertrials who could not afford bail to setting out the broad framework of procedure in case of arrest as in D.K.Basu's case.[236] All these judgments have been based on the 3 principle fundamental rights along with Article 32, which has led to the innovative and radical class action. Before dealing with the judgments of the Apex Court, it is important to look at the protection accorded under Articles 20 to 22(2):

1. No person shall be convicted of any offence except for violation of a law in force at the time of the commission of the act charged as an offence (Criminal law to be prospective in application and not retrospective);
2. No person shall be subjected to a penalty greater than that which might have been inflicted under the law in force at the time of the commission of the offence;
3. No person shall be prosecuted and punished for the same offence more than once (Rule of Double Jeopardy);

235 Additional District Magistrate, Jabalpur vs S.S.Shukla, 1976 Sup. SCR 172
236 1997 Cri.L.J. 743

4. No person accused of any offence shall be compelled to be a witness against himself;
5. No person shall be deprived of his life or personal liberty except according to procedure established by law;
6. No person who is arrested shall be detained in custody without being informed, as soon as maybe, of the grounds for such arrest;
7. No person who is arrested shall be denied the right to consult and to be defended by, a legal practitioner of his choice;
8. Every person who is arrested and detained in custody shall be produced before the nearest magistrate within a period of twenty-four hours of such arrest excluding the time necessary from the place of arrest to the court of the magistrate and no such person shall be detained in custody beyond the said period without the authority of a magistrate.

Over the last decade there has been a growing concern with the rights of the victim as opposed to that of the accused and there has been a roll back in the judgments of the court regarding humane treatment and sentencing. While many of the procedural rights enunciated by the Supreme Court in its landmark judgments have today made their way into the Code of Criminal Procedure, there has also been a narrowing of the right to grant of bail in non bailable offences. The recommendations of the Supreme Court in Joginder Kumar's case and the National Police Commission's findings regarding the misuse of the power to arrest and suggestion that arrests should not be made in all offences has been ignored. The Courts have also reversed many hitherto well settled principle of criminal jurisprudence regarding benefit of doubt and standard of proof. Though it should be mentioned here that many of these judgments have been passed in cases where IPC provisions were used along with provisions of other special acts, which reduced the standard of proof to that permissible in civil law and reversed the onus on the accused. Confessional statements which were earlier seen as suspect were given sacrosanct status in the new laws and these have found their way in the interpretation of judgments pertaining to the regular penal offences. It is to be remembered that the changes in the law regarding burden of proof was a demand of progressive groups following the rape of Mathura, a 15 year old girl in a police lock up and the shameful acquittal of the policemen by the court believing the men in khaki and not the lower caste lower class girl. Nothing much seems to have changed except the law. Despite the shift of the onus, custodial rapes still go unpunished. Custodial torture continues unabated. The oppressed masses fighting for their rights and activists who take up their cases are routinely targeted and picked up under draconian laws with little due process rights. There has been an erosion of democratic right to dissent. In Kamalananthan's case, the Supreme Court held that it was okay for the police to use third degree on the victim girls in order to make them speak the truth! In the current scenario where legal activism is the hobby of the 'haves', it is pertinent to note that it is the hand of the state that is being strengthened at the cost of the rights of the citizens whether they be arraigned as victims or accused. Rights of accused is the basis of a civilized society -- we are after all judged by how we treat our last citizens.

The broad principles of rights of accused persons, which emerges from this whole series of judgments spanning over twenty years is summarised below:

Rights on Arrest

1. No arrest can be made because it is lawful for the police officer to do so. The existence of the power of arrest is one thing. The justification for the exercise of it is quite another. The police officer must be able to justify the arrest apart from his power to do so. Arrest and detention in police lockup of a person can cause incalculable harm to the reputation and self-esteem of the person. No arrest can be made in a routine manner on a mere allegation of commission of an offence made against the person. It would be prudent for a police officer in the interest of protection of constitutional rights of a citizen and perhaps in his own interest that no arrest should be made without a reasonable satisfaction reached after some investigation as to the genuineness and bonafides of a complaint and a reasonable belief both as to the person's complicity and even so as to the need to effect arrest;[237]
2. The police personnel carrying out the arrest and handling the interrogation of the arrest should bear accurate, visible and clear identification and name tags with their designations. The particulars of all such police personnel who handle interrogation of the arrestee must be recorded in a register;
3. The Police Officer carrying out the arrest of the arrestee shall prepare a memo of arrest at the time of arrest and such memo shall be attested by at least one witness, who may either be a member of the family of the accused or a respectable person of the locality from where the arrest is made. It shall also be countersigned by the arrestee and shall contain the time and date of arrest;
4. A person who has been arrested or detained and is being held in custody in a police station or interrogation centre or other lock up, shall be entitled to have one friend or relative or other person known to him or having interest in his welfare being informed, as soon as practicable, that he has been arrested and is being detained at a particular place, unless the attesting witness of the memo of arrest is himself, such a friend or a relative of the arrestee;

237 Joginder Kumar vs. State of Uttar Pradesh, (1994) 4 SCC 260

5. The time, place of arrest and venue of custody of an accused must be notified by the police where the next friend or relative or the accused lives outside the district or town through the Legal Aid Organisation in the district and the police station of the area concerned telegraphically within a period of 8 to 12 hours after the arrest;

6. The person arrested must be made aware of this right to have someone informed of his arrest or detention as soon as he is put under arrest or is detained;

7. An entry must be made in the diary at the place of detention regarding the arrest of the person which shall also disclose the name of the next friend of the person who has been informed of the arrest and the names and particulars of the police officials in whose custody the arrestee is;

8. It shall be the duty of the Magistrate before whom the arrestee is produced to satisfy himself that these requirements have been complied with;

9. The arrestee should, where he so requests, be also examined at the time of his arrest and major and minor injuries, if any present on his body, must be recorded at that time. The "Inspection Memo" must be signed by both the arrestee and the police officer effecting the arrest and its copy provided to the arrestee;

10. The arrestee should be subjected to medical examination by a trained doctor every 48 hours during his detention in custody by a doctor on the panel of approved doctors appointed by Director, Health Services of the concerned State or Union Territory. Director, Health Services should prepare such a panel for all Tehsils and Districts as well;

11. Copies of all the documents including the memo of arrest, referred to above, should be sent to the *illaqa* (area) Magistrate for his record;

12. The arrestee may be permitted to meet his lawyer during interrogation, though not throughout the interrogation;

13. A police control room should be provided at all Districts and State headquarters, where information regarding the arrest and the place of custody of the arrestee shall be communicated by the officer causing the arrest, within 12 hours of effecting the arrest and at the police control room it should be displayed on a conspicuous notice board.

14. Failure to comply with the said requirements shall apart from rendering the concerned official liable for departmental action, also render him liable to be punished for contempt of Court and the proceedings for contempt of court may be instituted in any High Court of the country having jurisdiction over the matter;

15. These requirements would apply with equal force to the other governmental agencies also, like Directorate of Revenue Intelligence, Directorate of Enforcement, Coastal Guard, Central Reserve Police Force, Border Security Force, the Central Industrial Force, the State Armed Police, Intelligence agencies like the Intelligence Bureau, R.A.W., Central Bureau of Investigation, CID, Traffic Police, Mounted Police and ITBP.[238]

Rights of Women Prisoners

16. Female suspects should not be kept in the police lock up in which male suspects are detained. Some police lock ups should be selected in reasonably good localities of the city where only female suspects should be kept and they should be guarded by female constables;
17. The interrogatories of females should be carried out only in the presence of female police officers/constables;
18. A person arrested without a warrant must be immediately informed the grounds of her arrest and in case of every arrest it must be immediately be made known to the arrested person that she is entitled to apply for bail. A pamphlet setting out the legal rights of the arrested person should be forthwith got prepared by the Maharashtra State Board of Legal Aid and Advice and the same is to be printed by the State Government in English, Hindi and in the local language Marathi. The printed copies of such a pamphlet are to be affixed in each cell in every police lock up. Such a pamphlet is to be read out to the arrested personas as soon as she is brought to the police station;
19. On the arrested person being taken to the police lock up, the police are immediately to give intimation of the fact of such arrest to the nearest Legal Aid Committee and such Committee is to take immediate steps to offer legal assistance at State cost to the arrested person;
20. Arrangements are to be made for a Sessions Judge to make surprise visits to police lock ups periodically for providing the arrested persons an opportunity to air their grievances, for ascertaining the conditions in the lock ups, and for finding out whether the provisions of law are being observed and the above directions of the Supreme Court are being carried out. The lapse found in such visits are to be suitably brought to the notice of higher Police officials, to the Home department of the State and if necessary to the Chief Justice of the High Court;
21. Soon after arrest, the Police must obtain from the arrested person the name of any relative or friend whom she would like to be informed about her arrest and the Police should accordingly inform such relative or friend;

238 D.K.Basu vs. State of West Bengal, 1997 Cri.L.J. 743

22. The Magistrate before whom an arrested person is produced shall inquire whether she has any complaint of torture or maltreatment in police custody and inform her that she has a right under Section 54 of the CrPC to be medically examined.[239]

Rights of Children of Women Prisoners

23. 1. A child shall not be treated as an undertrial/convict while in jail with his/her mother. Such a child is entitled to food, shelter, medical care, clothing, education and recreational facilities as a matter of right.

2. **Pregnancy:**

a. Before sending a woman who is pregnant to a jail, the concerned authorities must ensure that jail in question has the basic minimum facilities for child delivery as well as for providing pre-natal and post-natal care for both, the mother and the child.

b. When a woman prisoner is found or suspected to be pregnant at the time of her admission or at any time thereafter, the lady Medical Officer shall report the fact to the superintendent. As soon as possible, arrangement shall be made to get such prisoner medically examined at the female wing of the District Government Hospital for ascertaining the state of her health, pregnancy, duration of pregnancy, probable date of delivery and so on. After ascertaining the necessary particulars, a report shall be sent to the Inspector General of Prisons, stating the date of admission, term of sentence, date of release, duration of pregnancy, possible date of delivery and so on.

c. Gynaecological examination of female prisoners shall be performed in the District Government Hospital. Proper pre-natal and post-natal care shall be provided to the prisoner as per medical advice.

3. **Child Birth in Prison**:

a. As far as possible and provided she has a suitable option, arrangements for temporary release/parole (or suspended sentence in case of minor and casual offender) should be made to enable an expectant prisoner to have her delivery outside the prison. Only exceptional cases constituting high security risk or cases of equivalent grave descriptions can lead to the denial of this facility.

239 Sheela Barse vs. State of Maharashtra, 1993 Cri.L.J. 642

b. Births in prison, when they occur, shall be registered in the local birth registration office. But the fact that the child has been born in the prison shall not be recorded in the certificate of birth that is issued. Only the address of the locality shall be mentioned.

c. As far as circumstances permit, all facilities for the naming rites of children born in prison shall be extended.

4. **Female Prisoners and Their Children**:

a. Female prisoners shall be allowed to keep their children with them in jail till they attain the age of six years.

b. No female prisoner shall be allowed to keep a child who has completed the age of six years.

Upon reaching the age of six years, the child shall be handed over to a suitable surrogate as per the wishes of the female prisoner or shall be sent to a suitable institution run by the Social Welfare Department. As far as possible, the child shall not be transferred to an institution outside the town or city where the prison is located in order to minimise undue hardships on both mother and child due to physical distance.

c. Such children shall be kept in protective custody until their mother is released or the child attains such age as to earn his/her own livelihood.

d. Children kept under the protective custody in a home of the Department of Social Welfare shall be allowed to meet the mother at least once a week. The Director, Social Welfare Department, shall ensure that such children are brought to the prison for this purpose on the date fixed by the Superintendent of Prisons.

e. When a female prisoner dies and leaves behind a child, the Superintendent shall inform the District Magistrate concerned and he shall arrange for the proper care of the child. Should the concerned relative(s) be unwilling to support the child, the District Magistrate shall either place the child in an approved institution/home run by the State Social Welfare Department or hand the child over to a responsible person for care and maintenance.

5. **Food, clothing, medical care and shelter**:

a. Children in jail shall be provided with adequate clothing suiting the local climatic requirement for which the State/U.T. Government shall lay down the scales.

b. State/U.T. Governments shall lay down dietary scales for children keeping in view the calorific requirements of growing children as per medical norms.

c. A permanent arrangement needs to be evolved in all jails, to provide separate food with ingredients to take care of the nutritional needs of children who reside in them on a regular basis.

d. Separate utensils of suitable size and material should also be provided to each mother prisoner for using to feed her child.

e. Clean drinking water must be provided to the children. This water must be periodically checked.

f. Children shall be regularly examined by the Lady Medical Officer to monitor their physical growth and shall also receive timely vaccination. Vaccination charts regarding each child shall be kept in the records. Extra clothing, diet and so on may also be provided on the recommendation of the Medical Officer.

g. In the event of a woman prisoner falling ill, alternative arrangements for looking after any children falling under her care must be made by the jail staff.

h. Sleeping facilities that are provided to the mother and the child should be adequate, clean and hygienic.

i. Children of prisoners shall have the right of visitation.

j. The Prison Superintendent shall be empowered in special cases and where circumstances warrant admitting children of women prisoners to prison without court orders provided such children are below 6 years of age.

6. **Education and Recreation for Children of Female Prisoners**:

a. The child of female prisoners living in the jails shall be given proper education and recreational opportunities and while their mothers are at work in jail, the children shall be kept in crèches under the charge of a matron/female warder. This facility will also be extended to children of warders and other female prison staff.

b. There shall be a crèche and a nursery attached to the prison for women where the children of women prisoners will be looked after. Children below three years of age shall be allowed in the creche and those between three and six years shall be looked after in the nursery. The prison authorities shall preferably run the said creche and nursery outside the prison premises.

7. In many states, small children are living in sub-jails that are not at all equipped to keep small children. Women prisoners with children

should not be kept in such sub-jails, unless proper facilities can be ensured which would make for a conducive environment there, for proper biological, psychological and social growth.

8. The stay of children in crowded barracks amidst women convicts, undertrials, offenders relating to all types of crimes including violent crimes is certainly harmful for the development of their personality. Therefore, children deserve to be separated from such environments on a priority basis.

9. Dietary scale for institutionalised infants/children recommends exclusive breastfeeding on the demand of the baby day and night. If for some reason, the mother cannot feed the baby, undiluted fresh milk can be given to the baby. It is emphasised that "dilution is not recommended" for a balanced diet for infants and children ranging from 6 months to 6 years of age it recommends right proportion for children from the ages of 6-12 months, 1-3 years and 4-6 years: Cereals and Millets; Pulses; Milk; Roots and Tubers; Green Leafy Vegetables; Other Vegetables; Fruits; Sugar; and Fats/Oils (Visible). One portion of pulse may be exchanged with one portion (50 grams) of egg/meat/chicken/fish. It is essential that the above food groups to be provided in the portions mentioned in order to ensure that both macronutrients and micronutrients are available to the child in adequate quantities.

10. Jail Manual and/or other relevant Rules, Regulations, instructions etc. shall be suitably amended within three months so as to comply with the above directions. If in some jails, better facilities are being provided, same shall continue.

11. Schemes and laws relating to welfare and development of such children shall be implemented in letter and spirit. State Legislatures may consider passing of necessary legislations, wherever necessary, having regard to what is noticed in this judgment.

12. The State Legal Services Authorities shall take necessary measures to periodically inspect jails to monitor that the directions regarding children and mother are complied with in letter and spirit.

13. The Courts dealing with cases of women prisoners whose children are in prison with their mothers are directed to give priority to such cases and decide their cases expeditiously.

14. Copy of the judgment shall be sent to Union of India, all State Governments/Union Territories, High Courts.

15. Compliance report stating steps taken by Union of India, State Governments, Union territories and State Legal Services Authorities shall be filed in four months whereafter matter shall be listed for directions.[240]

240 RD Upadhyay Vs. State of A.P, AIR2006SC1946

Rights against Torture

24. Using any form of torture for extracting any kind of information would neither be right nor just nor fair and therefore, would be impermissible being offensive under Article 21;

25. Some punitive provisions are contained in the Indian Penal Code, which seek to punish violation of right to life. Section 220 provides for punishment to an officer or authority who detains or keeps a person in confinement with a corrupt or malicious motive. Sections 330 and 331 provide for punishment of those who inflict injury or grievous hurt on a person to extort confession or information in regard to commission of an offence. Illustration (a) and (b) to Section 330 make a police officer guilty of torturing a person in order to induce him to confess the commission of a crime or to induce him to point out places where stolen property is deposited. Section 330, therefore, directly makes torture during interrogation and investigation punishable under the Indian Penal Code. Prosecution of the offender is an obligation of the State in case of every crime;

26. These statutory provisions are inadequate to repair the wrong done to the citizen. The court, where the infringement of the fundamental right is established, therefore, cannot stop by giving a mere declaration. It must proceed further and give compensatory relief, not by way of damages as in a civil action but by way of compensation under the public law jurisdiction for the wrong done due to the breach of public duty by the State of not protecting the fundamental right to life of the citizen. To repair the wrong done and give judicial redress for legal injury is a compulsion of judicial conscience;

27. The claim in public law for compensation for unconstitutional deprivation of fundamental right to life and liberty, the protection of which is guaranteed under the Constitution, is a claim based on strict liability and is in addition to the claim available in private law for damages for tortuous acts of public servants. Public law proceedings serve a different purpose than the private law proceedings. Award of compensation for established infringement of the indefeasible rights guaranteed under Article 21 of the Constitution is a remedy available in public law since the purpose of public law is not only to civilise public power but also to assure the citizens that they live under a legal system wherein their rights and interests shall be protected and preserved. Grant of compensation in proceedings under Articles 32 or 226 of the Constitution of India for the established violation of the fundamental rights guaranteed under Article 21, is an exercise of the Courts under the

public law jurisdiction for penalising the wrong doer and fixing the liability for the public wrong on the State which failed in the discharge of its public duty to protect the fundamental rights of the citizen;[241]

28. International Conventions and Covenants ratified by India which elucidate and effectuate the fundamental rights guaranteed by the Constitution of India, can be relied upon by courts in India as facets of those fundamental rights and hence enforceable as such. The conventions ratified by India include the International Covenant on Civil and Political Rights, the International Covenant on Social, Economic and Cultural Rights, the International Covenant on Rights of a Child (CRC) and the Convention on the Elimination of Discrimination against Women (CEDAW);[242]

29. The exaggerated adherence to and insistence upon the establishment of proof beyond every reasonable doubt, by the prosecution, ignoring the ground realities, the factual situations and the peculiar circumstances in cases of custodial death and torture, often result in miscarriage of justice and makes the justice delivery system a suspect. Tortures in police custody, which of late are on the increase, receive encouragement by this type of an unrealistic approach of the courts because it reinforces the belief in the mind of the police that no harm would come to them if an odd prisoner died in the lock up, because there would hardly be any evidence available to the prosecution to directly implicate them within the torture. The courts are required to have a change in their outlook and attitude, particularly, in cases involving custodial crimes and they should exhibit more sensitivity and adopt a realistic rather than a narrow technical approach, while dealing with the cases of custodial crimes so that as far as possible within their powers, the guilty should not escape.[243]

Right to Speedy Trial

30. Fair, just and reasonable procedure implicit in Article 21 of the Constitution creates a right in the accused to be tried speedily. Right to speedy trial is the right of the accused. The fact that a speedy trial is also in public interest or that it serves the social interest also, does not make it any the less the right of the accused. It is in the interest of all concerned that the

241 Rudal Sah vs. State of Bihar, AIR 1983 SC 1086; Sebastian M.Hongrey vs. Union of India, AIR 1984 SC 956; Smt. Nilabati Behera vs. State of Orissa, (1993)2 SCC 746 and D.K.Basu vs. State of West Bengal, 1997 Cri.L.J. 743

242 People's Union for Civil Liberties vs. Union of India, (1997) 3 SCC 433

243 State of Madhya Pradesh vs. Shyamsunder Trivedi, (1995) 4 SCC 262

guilt or innocence of the accused is determined as quickly as possible in the circumstances;

31. Right to speedy trial flowing from Article 21 encompasses all the stages, namely the stage of investigation, inquiry, trial, appeal, revision and retrial. That is how the Supreme Court has understood this right and there is no reason to take a restricted view;

32. The concerns underlying the right to speedy trial from the point of view of the accused are:

    a) The period of remand and pre-conviction detention should be as short as possible. In other words, the accused should not be subjected to unnecessary and unduly long incarceration prior to his conviction;

    b) The worry, anxiety, expense and disturbance to his vocation and peace, resulting from an unduly prolonged investigation, inquiry or trial should be minimal; and

    c) Undue delay may well result in impairment of the ability of the accused to defend himself, whether on account of death, disappearance or non-availability of witnesses or otherwise;

33. At the same time, one cannot ignore the fact that it is usually the accused that is interested in delaying the proceedings. As is often pointed out, 'delay is a known defence tactic'. Since the burden of proving the guilt of the accused lies upon the prosecution, delay ordinarily prejudices the prosecution. Non-availability of witnesses, disappearance of evidence by lapse of time really works against the interest of the prosecution. Of course, there may be cases where the prosecution, for whatever reason, also delays the proceedings. Therefore, in every case, where the right to speedy trial is alleged to have been infringed the first question to be put and answered is -- who is responsible for the delay? Proceedings taken by either party in good faith, to vindicate their rights and interest, as perceived by them, cannot be treated as delaying tactics nor can the time taken in pursuing such proceedings be counted towards delay. It goes without saying that frivolous proceeding or proceedings taken merely for delaying the day of reckoning cannot be treated as proceedings taken in good faith. The mere fact that an application/ petition is admitted and an order of stay granted by a superior court is by itself no proof that the proceeding is not frivolous. Very often these stays are obtained on ex parte representation;

34. While determining whether undue delay has occurred (resulting in violation of right to speedy trial) one must have regard to all the attendant circumstances including nature of offence, number of accused and

witnesses, the workload of the court concerned, prevailing local conditions and so on, including the systemic delays. It is true that it is the obligation of the State to ensure a speedy trial and State includes judiciary as well, but a realistic and practical approach should be adopted in such matters instead of a pedantic one;

35. Each and every delay does not necessarily prejudice the accused. However, inordinately long delay may be taken as presumptive proof of prejudice. In this context, the fact of the incarceration of the accused will also be a relevant fact. The prosecution should not be allowed to become a persecution. But when does the prosecution become persecution, again depends upon the facts of a given case;

36. We cannot recognise or give effect to, what is called the 'demand rule'. An accused cannot try himself; the court at the behest of the prosecution tries him. Hence, an accused's plea of denial of speedy trial cannot be defeated by saying that the accused did at no time demand a speedy trial. If in a given case, he did make such a demand and yet he was not tried speedily, it would be a plus point in his favour, but the mere non-asking for a speedy trial cannot be put against the accused;

37. Ultimately, the court has to balance and weigh the several relevant factors- 'balancing test' or 'balancing process' -- and determine in each case whether the right to speedy trial has been denied in a given case;

38. Ordinarily speaking, where the court comes to the conclusion that right to speedy trial of an accused has been infringed the charges or conviction, as the case may be, shall be quashed. However, the nature of the offence and other circumstances in a given case may be such that quashing of proceedings may not be in the interest of justice. in such a case, it is open to the court to make such other appropriate order -- including an order to conclude the trial within a fixed time where the trial is not concluded or reducing the sentence whether the trial has concluded -- as may be deemed just and equitable in the circumstances of the case;

39. It is neither advisable nor practicable to fix any time limit for trial of offences. Any such rule is bound to be a qualified one. Such rule cannot also be evolved merely to shift the burden of proving justification on to the shoulders of the prosecution. In every case of complaint of denial of right to speedy trial, it is primarily for the prosecution to justify and explain the delay. At the same time, it is the duty of the court to weigh all the circumstances of a given case before pronouncing upon the complaint;

40. An objection based on the denial of right to speedy trial and for relief on that account, should be first addressed to the High Court. Even if the High

Court entertains such a plea, ordinarily it should not stay the proceedings, except in a case of grave and exceptional nature. Such proceedings in High Court must, however, be disposed of on a priority basis.[244]

41. No length of time is per se too long to pass scrutiny under this principle nor the accused is called upon to show the actual prejudice by delay of disposal of cases. On the other hand, the court has to adopt a balancing approach by taking note of the possible prejudices and disadvantages to be suffered by the accused by avoidable delay and to determine whether the accused in a criminal proceeding has been deprived of his right of having speedy trial with unreasonable delay which could be identified by the factors -- (1) length of delay, (2) the justification for the delay, (3) the accused's assertion of his right to speedy trial, and (4) prejudice caused to the accused by such delay. However, the fact of delay is dependent on the circumstances of each case because reasons for delay will vary, such as delay in investigation on account of the widespread ramification of crimes and its designed network either nationally or internationally, the deliberate absence of witness or witnesses, crowded dockets on the file of the court, etc.[245]

42. The Supreme Court in the Common Cause judgments[246] issued the following directions to ensure that criminal prosecutions do not operate as engines of oppression:

a) Where the offences under IPC or any other law for the time being in force for which the accused are charged before any criminal court are punishable with imprisonment not exceeding three years with or without fine and if trials for such offences are pending of one year or more and the accused concerned have not been released on bail but are in jail for a period of six months or more, the criminal court concerned shall release the accused on bail or on personal bond to be executed by the accused and subject to such conditions, if any, as may be found necessary, in the light of Section 437 of the CrPC;

b) Where the offences under IPC or any other law for the time being in force for which the accused are charged before any criminal court are punishable with imprisonment not exceeding five years with or without fine and if trials for such offences are pending of two years or more and the accused concerned have not been released on bail but are in jail for a period of six months or more, the criminal court concerned shall release the accused on bail or on personal bond to be executed by the accused

244 A.R.Antulay vs. R.S.Nayak, (1992)1 SCC 225

245 Kartar Singh vs. State of Punjab, (1994) 3 SCC 569

246 Common Cause vs. Union of India, 1996 SCC (Cri) 589 and (1996) 8 Supreme 3Q2

and subject to such conditions, if any, as may be found necessary, in the light of Section 437 of the CrPC;

c) Where the offences under IPC or any other law for the time being in force for which the accused are charged before any criminal court are punishable with seven years or less, with or without fine, and if trials for such offences are pending of two years or more and the accused concerned have not been released on bail but are in jail for a period of one year or more, the criminal court concerned shall release the accused on bail or on personal bond to be executed by the accused and subject to such conditions, if any, as may be found necessary, in the light of Section 437 of the CrPC;

d) The period of pendency of criminal cases shall be calculated from the date the accused are summoned to appear in the court;

e) The trial shall be deemed to have commenced when charges are framed or plea recorded of the accused by the trial court;

f) The above directions set out shall not apply to offences involving corruption, misappropriation of public funds, cheating whether under the IPC, Prevention of Corruption Act or any other statute, smuggling, foreign exchange violation and offences under the Narcotic Drugs and Psychotropic Substances Act, Essential Commodities Act, Food Adulteration Act, Acts dealing with environment or any other economic offences, offences under the Arms Act, Explosive Substances Act, Terrorists and Disruptive Activities Act, offences relating to the Army, Navy and Air Force, offences against public tranquility, offences relating to public servants, offences relating to coins and government stamp, offences relating to elections, offences relating to giving false evidence and offences against public justice and any other type of offences against the State, offences under the taxing enactment, offences of defamation, matrimonial offences, offences under the Negotiable Instruments Act, offences relating to criminal misappropriation of property of the complainant as well as offences relating to criminal breach of trust, offences pertaining to rash and negligent acts, offences affecting the public health, safety, convenience, decency and morals as listed in the IPC or such similar offences which are made punishable under any law for the time being in force.

43. In addition to the aforementioned propositions, the following proposition was laid down in Raj Deo Sharma's cases[247]:

247 Raj Deo Sharma vs. State of Bihar, (1998) 7 SCC 507 and (1999) 7 SCC 602

a) In cases where the trial is for an offence punishable with imprisonment for a period not exceeding seven years, if the accused has been in jail for a period of not less than one-half of the maximum period of punishment prescribed for the offence, the trial court shall release the accused on bail forthwith on such conditions as it deems fit;

44. The Common Cause and Rajdeo Sharma decisions have been overturned by a Constitution Bench of the Apex Court recently in P. Ramchandra Rao vs State of Karnataka[248] only with regards to the directions regarding trial and discharge/acquittal and not with regards to enlargement of bail. In this judgment the Court held that Antulay's case is still good law and the question of delay has to be decided by the court having regard to the totality of circumstances of an individual case. The test is whether delay is such that it can be called oppressive or unwarranted.

45. Person who has been in custody as an undertrial prisoner for the period exceeding the maximum sentence imposable by law should be released and the case against him quashed.[249]

46. In Moti Lal Saraf vs State of Jammu & Kashmir,[250] not a single witness could be examined by the prosecution in 26 years without there being any lapse on behalf of the appellant. Permitting the State to continue with the prosecution and trial, the court held any further delay would be total abuse of the process of law. Consequently, the criminal proceedings were quashed.

47. The Supreme Court while dealing with case of delay in delivery of judgments in criminal appeals, in Anil Rai's case gave guidelines as a mandate to all High Courts regarding pronouncement of judgments:

i) The Chief Justices of the High Courts may issue appropriate directions to the Registry that in a case where the judgment is reserved and is pronounced later, a column be added in the judgment where, on the first page, after the cause-title date of reserving the judgment and date of pronouncing it be separately mentioned by the court officer concerned.

ii) That Chief Justices of the High Courts, on their administrative side, should direct the Court Officers/Readers of the various benches in the High Courts to furnish every month the list of cases in the matters where the judgments reserved are not pronounced within the period of that month.

---

248 (2000) 4 SCC 578

249 Hussainara Khatoon vs. State of Bihar, (1980) 1 SCC 91;Veena vs. State of Bihar, AIR 1983 SC 339; Ravidas vs. State of Bihar, AIR 1987 SC 1333

250 (2006) 10 SCC 560

iii) On noticing that after conclusion of the arguments the judgment is not pronounced within a period of two months the concerned Chief Justice shall draw the attention of the Bench concerned to the pending matter. The Chief Justice may also see the desirability of circulating the statement of such cases in which the judgments have not been pronounced within a period of six weeks from the date of conclusion of the arguments amongst the judges of the High Court for their information. Such communication be conveyed as confidential and in a sealed cover.

iv) Where a judgment is not pronounced within three months from the date of reserving judgment any of the parties in the case is permitted to file an application in the High Court with prayer for early judgment. Such application, as and when filed, shall be listed before the bench concerned within two days excluding the intervening holidays.

v) If the judgment, for any reason, is not pronounced within a period of six months any of the parties of the said list shall be entitled to move an application before the Chief justice of the High Court with a prayer to withdraw the said case and to make it over to any other bench for fresh arguments. It is open to the Chief Justice to grant the said prayer or to pass any other order as he deems fit in the circumstances.[251]

Legal Aid

48. Free legal service is an unalienable element of 'reasonable, fair and just' procedure for without it a person suffering from economic or other disabilities would be deprived of the opportunity for securing justice. The right to free legal service is, therefore, clearly an essential ingredient of ' reasonable, fair and just' procedure for a person accused of an offence and it must be held implicit in the guarantee of Article 21 from the stage of remand itself.[252]

49. When the undertrial prisoner is produced before a Magistrate and he has been in detention for 90 days or 60 days, as the case may be, from the date of arrest, the Magistrate must, before making an order of further remand to judicial custody, point out to the undertrial prisoner that he is entitled to be released on bail. The State Government must also provide at its own cost a lawyer to the undertrial with a view to enabling him to apply for bail in exercise of his right and the Magistrate must take care to see that legal aid is provided.[253]

---

251 Anil Rai vs Stata of Bihar (2001) 7 SCC 318
252 Hussainara Khatoon vs. State of Bihar, (1980) 1 SCC 98
253 Hussainara Khatoon vs. State of Bihar, (1980) 1 SCC 108

Handcuffing

50. As a rule, handcuffs or other fetters shall not be forced on a prisoner-convicted or undertrial -- while lodged in a jail anywhere in the country or while transporting or in transit from one jail to another or from jail to court and back. The police and the jail authorities, on their own, shall have no authority to direct the handcuffing of any inmate of a jail in the country or during transport from one jail to another or from jail to court and back;

51. Where the police or the jail authorities have well-grounded basis for drawing a strong inference that a particular prisoner is likely to jump jail or break out of the custody then the said prisoner be produced before the Magistrate concerned and a prayer for permission to handcuff the prisoner be made before the said Magistrate. Save in rare cases of concrete proof regarding proneness of the prisoner to violence, his tendency to escape, he being so dangerous/desperate and the finding that no other practical way of forbidding escape is available, the Magistrate may grant permission to handcuff the prisoner.

52. In all the cases where a person arrested by police is produced before the Magistrate and remand- judicial or non-judicial- is given by the Magistrate, the person concerned shall not be handcuffed unless special orders in that respect are obtained from the Magistrate at the time of the grant of the remand.

53. When the police arrests a person in execution of a warrant of arrest obtained from a Magistrate, the person so arrested shall not be handcuffed unless the police have also obtained orders from the Magistrate for the handcuffing of the person to be so arrested.

54. Where a person is arrested by the police without warrant the police officer concerned may if he is satisfied, on the basis of the guidelines given in the above paragraphs, that it is necessary to handcuff such a person, he may do so till the time he is taken to the police station and thereafter his production before the Magistrate. Further use of fetters thereafter can only be under the orders of the Magistrate as already indicated.

55. All ranks of police and the prison authorities are directed to meticulously obey the above directions. Any violation of any of the directions issued by any rank of police in the country or member of the jail establishment shall be summarily punishable under the Contempt of Courts Act apart from other penal consequences under law.[254]

254 Citizens for Democracy vs. State of Assam, (1995) 3 SCC 743

Prisoners' Rights and Prison Reform

56. Solitary confinement is not sanctioned though prisoners under sentence of death can be kept separate from the rest of the prison community during hours when prisoners are generally locked in. Such prisoners can be kept under special watch, however, conceding to minimum human privacy. However these prisoners shall mean not those sentenced to death by any court but whose mercy petitions the President or the Governor has rejected as the case may be. These prisoners shall not be denied any of the community amenities, including games, newspapers, books, moving around and meeting prisoners and visitors, subject to reasonable regulation of prison management. More importantly, if the prisoner desires loneliness for reflection and remorse, for prayers and making peace with his maker, or opportunities for meeting family or friends, such facilities shall be liberally granted.

57. Absent provision for independent review of preventive and punitive action, for discipline or security, such action shall be invalid as arbitrary, unfair and unreasonable. The prison officials will then be liable civilly and criminally for harm to the person of the prisoner. The State will urgently set up or strengthen the necessary infrastructure and process in this behalf.

58. Legal aid shall be given to prisoners to seek justice from prison authorities, and if need be, to challenge the decision in court in cases where they are too poor to secure it on their own. If lawyer's services are not given, the decisional process becomes unfair and unreasonable, especially because the rule of law perishes for a disabled prisoner if counsel is unapproachable and beyond purchase. By and large, prisoners are poor, lacking legal literacy, under the trembling control of the jailer, at his mercy as it were, and unable to meet relations or friends to take legal action. Where a remedy is all but dead the right lives only in print. Article 39A is relevant in the context. Article 19 will be violated in such cases, as the process will be unreasonable. Article 21 will be infringed since the procedure is unfair and is arbitrary.[255]

59. The Districts Magistrates should inspect the jails every week and perform the following functions:

    a) Inspect the barracks, cells, wards, workshed and other buildings of the jail generally and the cooked food;

    b) Ascertain whether considerations such as health, cleanliness and security are attended to, whether proper management and discipline are maintained in every respect, and whether any prisoner is illegally detained or is detained for an undue length of time while awaiting trial;

255 Sunil Batra vs. Delhi Administration, (1978) 4 SCC 494

c) Examine jail registers and records;

d) Hear, attend to all representations and petitions made, by or on behalf of prisoners;

e) Direct, if deemed advisable, that any such representation or petitions be forwarded to the government; and

60. No prisoner shall be punished for any statement made by him to a visitor unless an inquiry made by magistrate results in a finding that it is false.

61. If the District Magistrate is unable to visit, he should depute a magistrate subordinate to him. The District Magistrate should exercise this function in his capacity as a judicial officer and not an executive head and should meet the prisoners separately if they have any grievance and not in the presence of warders or officials. He must ensure that his inquiry is confidential although subject to natural justice and does not lead to reprisals by jail officials. All orders by him shall be immediately complied with. In the event of non-compliance, he should immediately inform the government about such disobedience and advise the prisoner to forward his complaint to the High Court under Article 226 together with a copy of his own report to help the High Court exercise its habeas corpus power. The Magistrate should keep a grievance box in each ward to which free access shall be afforded to every inmate. It should be kept locked and sealed by him and on his periodical visit, he alone or his surrogate should open the box, find out the grievances, investigate their merits and take remedial action if justified.

62. The Sessions Judge, District Magistrate or their nominees shall hear complaints, examine all documents, take evidence, interview prisoners and check to see if there is deviance, disobedience, delinquency or the like which infringes upon the right of prisoners. They have a duty to hear and bring to notice any complaint or representation made to him by any prisoner. The Sessions Court Judges concerned, under their lock and seal, should keep a requisite number of grievance boxes in the prison and give necessary directions to the Superintendent to see that free access is afforded to put in complaints of encroachments, injuries or torture by any prisoner, where he needs remedial action. Such boxes shall not be tampered with by anyone and shall be opened only under the authority of the Sessions Judge. The Sessions Judge must sensitively exercise the utmost vigilance and authority in this situation since prisoner's personal liberty depends in this undetectable campus upon his awareness, activism, adjudication and enforcement. Constitutional rights shall not be emasculated by the insouciance of judicial officers.

63. The prison authorities shall not in any manner obstruct or non-co-operate with reception or inquiry into the complaints. Otherwise, prompt punitive action must follow. The High Court or the Supreme Court shall be apprised of the grievance so that habeas corpus may issue after due hearing.

64. All visitors shall be afforded every facility for observing the state of the jail and the management thereof, and shall be allowed access under proper regulations, to all parts of the jail and to every prisoner confined therein.

65. All visitors should have the power to call for and inspect any book or other record in the jail unless the Superintendent, for reasons to be recorded in writing, declines on the ground that its production is undesirable. Similarly, every visitor should have the right to see any prisoner and to put any questions to him out of the hearing of any jail officer. There should be one Visitor's Book for both classes of Visitors, their remarks should in both cases be forwarded to the Inspector General who should pass such order as he thinks necessary, and a copy of the Inspector General's order should be sent to the visitor concerned.

66. The treatment of prisoners should emphasize not their exclusion from the community but their continuing part in it. Community agencies should, therefore, be enlisted where possible to assist the staff of the institution in the task of social rehabilitation of the prisoners. There should be in connection with every institution social workers charged with the duty of maintaining and improving all desirable relations of a prisoner with his family and with valuable social agencies. Steps should be taken to safeguard, to the minimum extent compatible with the law and the sentence, the rights relating to civil interests, social security rights and other social benefits of prisoners.

67. Lawyers nominated by the District Magistrate, Sessions Judge High Court and the Supreme Court will be given all facilities for interviews, visits and confidential communication with prisoners subject to discipline and security considerations. This has roots in the visitorial and supervisory judicial role. The lawyers so designated shall be bound to make periodical visit and record and report to the concerned court results, which have relevance to legal grievances.

68. No solitary or punitive cell, no hard labour or dietary change as painful additive, no other punishment or denial of privileges and amenities, no transfer to other prisons with penal consequences, shall be imposed without judicial appraisal of the Sessions Judge and where such intimation, on account of emergency, is difficult, such information shall be given within two days of the action.

69. There should be accommodation for proper classification for undertrials, females, habituals, casuals, juveniles, political prisoners, etc.

70. The State shall prepare in Hindi, a Prisoner's Handbook and circulate copies to bring legal awareness home to the inmates. Periodical jail bulletin stating how improvements and rehabilitative programmes are brought into the prison that may create a feeling of fellowship among prisoners to ease tensions. A prisoner's wallpaper that will freely ventilate grievances will also reduce stress.

71. The State shall take steps to keep up to the Standard Minimum Rules for Treatment of Prisoners recommended by the United Nations, especially those relating to work and wages, treatment with dignity, community contact and correctional strategies.

72. The Prisons Act needs rehabilitation and the Prison Manual total overhaul, even the Model Manual being out of focus with healing goals. A correctional-cum-orientation course is necessitous for the prison staff inculcating the constitutional values, therapeutic approaches and tension-free management.

73. The Court shall protect the prisoners' rights by its writ jurisdiction plus contempt power. To make this jurisdiction viable, free legal services to the prisoner programmes shall be promoted by professional organisations recognised by the court. The District Bar shall, keep a cell for prisoner relief.[256]

74. In State of Gujarat vs. Hon'ble High Court of Gujarat,[257] the Supreme Court concluded that:

    a) It is lawful to employ the prisoners sentenced to rigorous imprisonment to do hard labour whether he consents to do it or not;

    b) It is open to the jail officials to permit other prisoners also to do any work which they choose to do provided such prisoners make a request for that purpose;

    c) It is imperative that the prisoners should be paid equitable wages for the work done by them. In order to determine the quantum of equitable wages payable to prisoners, the State concerned shall constitute a wage-fixation body for making recommendations as early as possible;

    d) Until the State Government takes any decision on such recommendations, every prisoner must be paid for work done by him at such rates or revised rates as the Government concerned fixes in the light of the above recommendations;

256 Sunil Batra vs. Delhi Administration (II), (1980) 3 SCC 488
257 1998 (7) SCC 392

e) The State concerned may make law for setting apart a portion of the wages earned by the prisoners to be paid as compensation to deserving victims of the offence, the commission of which entailed the sentence of imprisonment to the prisoner, either directly or through a common fund to be created for this purpose or in any other feasible mode;

f) The request of the Government to permit them to deduct the expenses incurred for food and clothes of the prisoners from the minimum wages rates is a reasonable request. There is nothing uncivilised or unsociable in it. But the Government cannot deduct any substantial portion from the wages on that account. The Government can arrive at the reasonable percentage to be deducted from the minimum wages taking into account the average amount, which the Government is spending per prisoner for providing food, clothes and other amenities to him.

75. Where there is an undue delay in executing a sentence of death after its confirmation or in disposing of a mercy petition by the President or Governor, it involves a cruel punishment because the mental worry and agony that is caused by the intervening period of suspense is an additional penalty over and above the death penalty which was awarded by the court on trial. In these circumstances, the court would convert the sentence of death into one of life imprisonment, though no period could be set out as a benchmark for the commutation.[258]

76. In Rama Murthy vs State of Karnataka[259], the Court held that the literature on prison justice and prison reform shows that there are nine major problems which afflict the system and which need immediate attention. These are : (1) overcrowding: (2) delay in trial; (3) torture and ill-treatment; (4) neglect of health and hygiene; (5) insubstantial food and inadequate clothing; (6) prison vices; (7) deficiency in communication; (8) streamlining of jail visits; and (9) management of open air prisons. The Court took each of the problems separately and expressed its view as to what could reasonably be done and should be done to take care of the same.

77. **Overcrowding**

- Even if overcrowding be not constitutionally impermissible, there is no doubt that the same does affect the health of prisoners for the reasons noted above. The same also very adversely affects hygienic conditions. It is, therefore, to be taken care of.

---

258 Triveniben vs. State of Gujarat,(1989)1 SCC 678; Daya vs. Union of India, 1991 Cr.L.J. 1903; Madhu vs. Union of India, (1989)4 SCC 62; Juman vs. State of UP, (1991) 1 SCJ 444; Javed vs. State of Maharashtra, AIR 1985 SC 231

259 (1997)2SCC642

- The recent decision of this Court requiring release on bail of certain categories of undertrial prisoners, who constitute the bulk of prison population, has to result in lessening the over capacity. It would he useful to refer here to the Seventy-Eighth Report of the Law Commission of India on 'Congestion of Undertrial Prisoners in Jails'. The Commission has in chapter 9 of the Report made some recommendations acceptance of which would relieve congestion in jails. These suggestions include liberalisation of conditions of release on bail. It may be pointed out that it has already been held by this Court in Babu Singh v. State of U.P. MANU/SC/0059/1978; and Gurbaksh Singh Sibbia v. State of Punjab MANU/SC/0215/1980 that imposing of unjust or harsh conditions, while granting bail, are violative of Article 21.
- We require the concerned authorities to take appropriate decision on the recommendations of the Law Commission within six months from today.
- Overcrowding may also be taken care of by taking recourse to alternatives to incarceration. These being: (1) Fine: (2) civil commitment; and (3) probation. There is an enlightened discussion on these judicial choices in Chapter IV of "Justice, Punishment, Treatment" by Leonard Orland. In that chapter (of 1983 edition) the learned author has referred to may case on this subject and has pointed out the difference between "civil" and "penal" institutions from the perspective of the inmate. As to release on probation, it may be stated that it really results in suspension of sentence, as the person released on probation is required to execute bond under the provisions of the Probation of Offenders Act, 1958, requiring maintenance of good conduct during the probationary period, the failure to do which finds the concerned person in prison again. That Act has provision of varying conditions of probation and has also set down the procedure to be followed in case of the offenders failing to observe conditions.
- Overcrowding is reduced by release on parole as well, which is a conditional release of an individual from prison after he has served part of the sentence imposed upon him. Various aspects of parole have been dealt in Chapter 11 of Professor Orland's aforesaid book. In Suresh Chandra and Krishan Lal (supra) liberal use of parole was recommended by this Court.
- Reference may also be made in this connection to Chapter 20 of the Report of All India Committee on Jail Reforms (headed by Justice A.N. Mulla) (1980-83) Vol. 1. That chapter deals with the system of remission, leave and premature release. The Committee has mentioned about various types of remission and has made some recommendations to streamline the remission system. As to premature release, which is

the effect of parole, the Committee has stated that this is an accepted mode of incentive to a prisoner, as it saves him from the extra period of incarceration; it also helps in reformation and rehabilitation. The Committee has made certain suggestions in this regard too. We direct the concerned authorities to take appropriate decision on the suggestions within a period of six months from today. It may be pointed out that there is really a grievance about allowing the recommendations to remain in cold storage. (See article of T. Ananthachari "Human Rights Behind Prison Walls" published at pp. 35-47 of the 1995 report by Commonwealth Human Rights Initiative (ANGO) titled 'Behind Prison Walls - Police, Prisons and Human Rights'). While taking appropriate decision, the authorities may apprise themselves of what has been in Chapter 6 (headed 'Parole') of the British White Paper on "Crime, Justice and Protecting the Public' (1990).

- There is yet another baneful effect of overcrowding. The same is that it does not permit segregation among convicts - Those punished for serious offences and for minor. The result may be that hardened criminals spread their influence over others. Then, juvenile offenders kept in jails (because of inadequacy of alternative places where they are required to be confined) get mixed up with others and they are likely to get spoiled further. So, problem of overcrowding is required to be tackled in right earnest for a better future.

78. Delay in Trial

- It is apparent that delay in trial finds an undertrial prisoner (UTP) in jail for a longer period while awaiting the decision of the case. In the present proceeding, we are really not concerned regarding the causes of delay and how to remedy this problem. Much has been said in this regard elsewhere and we do not propose to burden this judgment with this aspect. We would rather confine ourselves as to how to take care of the hardship which is caused to a UTP because of the delay in disposal of this case. The recent judgments of this Court (noted above) requiring release of UTP on bail where the trial gets protracted would hopefully take care to a great extent the hardship caused in this regard. We desire to see full implementation of the directions given in the aforesaid cases.
- Another aspect to which we propose to advert is the grievance very often made about non-production of (UTP) in courts on remand dates. The District Judge in his report has also found this as a fact. The reason generally advanced for such non-production is want of police escorts. It has to be remembered that production before the court on remand dates is a statutory obligation and the same has a meaning also inasmuch as that the production gives an opportunity to the prisoner to bring to the

notice of the Court, who had ordered for his custody, if he has faced any ill-treatment or difficulty during the period of remand. It is for this reason that actual production of the prisoner is required to be insured by the trial court before ordering for further remand, as pointed out in a number of decisions by this Court.

- We are also conscious of the fact that police force in the country is rather overworked. It has manifold duties to perform. In such a situation it is a matter for consideration whether the duty of producing UTP on remand dates should not be entrusted to the prison staff. To enable the prison staff to do so, it would, however, need escorts vehicles.
- We could require the concerned authorities to take appropriate decision in this regard within a period of six months from today.

79. **Torture and Ill-treatment**

- There are horror stories in this regard. The cellular jail in Port Blair resounds with the cries of the prisoners who were subjected to various forms of torture. This is now being brought home in the Light and Sound programme being organised in that jail, which after Independence has been declared as a national monument. Other jails would also tell similar stories.
- Apart from torture, various other physical ill-treatment like putting of fetters, iron bars are generally taken recourse to in jails. Some of these are under the cover of provisions in Jail Manuals. The permissible limits of these methods has been spelt out well in many earlier decisions of this Court to which reference has been already made. We do not propose to repeat.
- What we would rather state is that if what is being done to prisoners in the above regard is to enforce prison discipline mentioned in various Jail Manuals, there exists a strong need for a new All India Jail Manual to serve as a model for the country, which Manual would take note of what has been said about various punishments by this Court in its aforesaid decisions. Not only this, the century old Indian Prison Act, 1894, needs a thorough look and is required to be replaced by a new enactment which would take care of the thinking of the Independent India and of our constitutional moores and mandate. The National Human Rights Commission has also felt that need for such exercise, mention about which has been made in para 4.18 and 4.21 of the aforesaid Report.
- A reading of the Chapter IX on 'Prison Discipline' in RN Datir's book on 'Prison as a Social System', shows that in some Jail Manuals even flogging/whipping has been retained as a punishment, which would not be permissible in view of the right enshrined in Article 21 of the

Constitution. We have mentioned about this only to highlight the need for a new model All India Jail Manual.

- It would be apposite in this context to refer to the recent decision of the United States Supreme Court in Hudson v. Mc Million, 403 US 1, in which that Court was required to decide whether the use of excessive physical force against a prisoner may constitute cruel and unusual punishment even when the inmate does not suffer serious injury. This question was answered in affirmative by majority of 7 : 2. As already mentioned, Article 21 of our Constitution also does not permit cruel punishment.
- May we say that the ideal prison and the advance prison system which the enlightened segment of the society visualise would not permit torture and ill-treatment of prisoners. Of course, if for violating prison discipline some punishment is required to be given, that would be a different matter.

80. Neglect of Health and Hygiene

- The Mulla Committee has dealt with this aspect in Chapter 6 and 7 of its Report, a perusal of which shows the pathetic position in which most of the jails are placed insofar as hygienic conditions are concerned. most of them also lack proper facilities for treatment of prisoners. The recommendations of the Committee in this regard are to be found in Chapter 29. We have nothing useful to add except pointing out that society has an obligation towards prisoners' health for two reasons. First, the prisoners do not enjoy the access to medical expertise that free citizens have. Their incarceration places limitations on such access; no physician of choice, no second opinions, and few if any specialists. Secondly, because of the conditions of their incarceration, inmates are exposed to more health hazards than free citizens. Prisoners therefore, suffer from a double handicap.
- In 'American Prison System' (supra) there is a discussion at pages 411-13 as to whether a prisoner can seek any relief from the Court because of neglect of medical treatment on the ground of violation of their constitutional right. Policy makers may bear this also in mind while deciding about the recommendations of the Mulla Committee Report, which they would so do within six months from today.

81. Insubstantial Food and Inadequate Clothing

- There is not much to doubt that the rules contained in concerned Jail Manual dealing with food and clothing etc. to be given to prisoners are not fully complied with always. All that can usefully be said on this aspect is the persons who are entitled to inspect jails should do so after giving shortest notice so that the reality becomes known on inspection. The system of complaint box introduced in Tihar Jail during some period needs to be adopted in other jails also. The complaint received must be fairly inquired and appropriate actions against the delinquent must be taken. On top of all, prisoners must receive full assurance that whoever would lodge a complaint would not suffer any evil consequence for lodging the same.

82. Prison Vices

- On this aspect nothing more is required to be said than what was pointed out in Sunil Batra (II). It may only be stated that some vices may be taken care of if what is being stated later on the subject of jail visits is given concrete shape. We have said so because many of the vices are related to sexual urge, which remains unsatisfied because of snapping of marital life of the prisoner. If something could be done to keep the thread of family life unbroken some vices may take care of themselves, as sexual frustration may become tolerable.
- The aforesaid seems to us a more rational way to deal with prison vices rather than awarding hard punishment to them. We may not suggest that, however, the jail authorities need not take action against the prisoners indulging in vices; but in the situation in which they are placed, a sympathetic approach is also required.

83. Deficiency in Communication

- While in jail, communication with outside world gets snapped with a result that the inmate does not know what is happening even to his near and dear ones. This causes additional trauma. A liberalised view relating to communication with kith and kin specially is desirable. It is hoped that the model All India Jail Manual, about the need of which we have already adverted, would make necessary provision in this regard. It may be pointed out that though there may be some rationale for restricting visits, to which aspect we shall presently address, but insofar as communication by post is concerned, there does not seem (sic) be any plausible reason to deny easy facility to an inmate.

84. Streamlining of Jail Visits

- Prison visits fall into three categories: (1) relatives and friends; (2) professionals; and (3) lay persons. In the first category comes the spouse. Visit by him/her has special significance because a research undertaken on Indian prisoners sometime back showed that majority of them were in the age group of 18 to 34, which shows that most of them were young and were perhaps having a married life before their imprisonment. For such persons, denial of conjugal life during the entire period of incarceration creates emotional problems also. Visits by a spouse is, therefore, of great importance.

- It is, of course, correct that at times visit may become a difficult task for the visitors. This would be so where prisoners are geographically isolated. This apart, in many jails facilities available to the visitors are degrading. At many places even privacy is not maintained. If the offenders and visitors are screened, the same emphasises their separation rather than retaining common bonds and interests. There is then urgent need to streamline these visits.
- Dr. Mir Mehrajuddin in his book *Crime and Criminal Justice System in India* has dealt with different aspects of prison visits in Chapter VI headed 'Resocialisation : Search for Goals'. The learned author has said that frequent jail visits by family members go a long way in acceptance of the prisoner by his family and small friendly group after his release from jail finally, as the visits continue the personal relationship during the term of imprisonment, which brings about a psychological communion between him and other members of the family.
- As to visits by professionals, i.e. the lawyer, the same has to be guaranteed to the required extent, if the prisoner be a pre-trial detainee, in view of the right conferred by Article 22(1) of the Constitution.

85. Management of Open Air Prisons

- Open air prisons play an important role in the scheme of reformation of a prisoner which has to be one of the desideratum of prison management. They represent one of the most successful applications of the principle of individualisation of penalties with a view to social readjustment as stated by B. Chandra in the Preface to his book titled *Open Air Prisons*. It has been said so because release of offenders on probation, home leave to prisoners, introduction of wage system, release on parole, educational, moral and vocational training of prisoners are some of the features of the open air prison (camp) system. Chandra has stated in the concluding portion of Chapter 3 at page 150 (of 1984 edition) that in terms of finances, open institution is far less costly than a closed establishment and the scheme has further advantage that the Government is able to employ in work, for the benefit of the public at large, the jail population which would have otherwise remained unproductive. According to the author, the monetary returns are positive, and once put into operation, the camps pay for itself.
- Reference may also be made to what has been stated in Chapter 5 about the change in the humans and social outlook, which activities

and programmes of these camps bring about. The whole thrust is to see that after release the prisoners may not relapse into crimes, for which purpose they are given incentives to live normal, life, as they are trained in the fields of agriculture, horticulture etc. Games, sports and other recreational facilities, which form part of the routine life at the open air camps, inculcate in the prisoners a sense of discipline and social responsibility. The prayers made regularly provide spiritual strength.

- While on the subject of prayer, mention may be made about the experiment carried out even in the closed Tihar Jail sometime in 1993-94, when *Vipassana* meditation was introduced in a big way, which according to Tarsem Kumar, one of the Superintendents of the Jail, brought about a radical change in the living and thinking of the prisoners, as narrated in his book titled "Freedom Behind Bars".
- Open air prisons, however, create their own problem which are basically of management. We are, however, sure that these problems are not such which cannot be sorted out. For the greater goods of the society, which consists in seeing that the inmates of a jail come out, not as a hardened criminal but as a reformed person, no managerial problem is insurmountable. So, let more and more open air prisons be opened. To start with, this may be done at all the District Headquarters of the country.

86. Conclusion

- We have travelled a long path. Before we end our journey, it would be useful to recapitulate the directions we have given on the way to various authorities. These are:

(1) To take appropriate decision on the recommendations of the Law Commission of India made in its 78th Report on the subject of 'Congestion of undertrial prisoners in jail' as contained in Chapter 9, (Para 20A).

(2) To apply mind to the suggestions of the Mulla Committee as contained in Chapter 20 of Volume I of its Report relating to streamlining the remission system and premature release (parole), and then to do the needful). (Para 23).

(3) To consider the question of entrusting the duty of producing UTPs on remand dates to the prison staff. (Para P7).

(4) To deliberate about enacting of new Prison Act to replace century old Indian Prison Act, 1894'. (Para 31). We understand that the National

CHAPTER 8

SOME PENAL OFFENCES

The earliest codification of the present penal system was the Indian Penal Code in 1860 and the same continues to be the major penal statute to date. There are several other penal statutes, some of which are state legislations and many penal provisions are contained in acts that are not primarily penal statutes such as the Negotiable Instruments Act and the labour laws. The Indian Penal Code is also important as all penal statutes borrow their basic concepts form it, whether it be in the manner the offences are defined (individualisation of the crime), or the basic explanations and concepts applied to offences. The Indian Penal Code or the IPC in short comprises of 23 chapters and 511 sections. The description of the offences begins only from Chapter VI and the Chapters II to V are of importance and apply to all criminal proceedings, as they lay down the basic criminal structure of the system. Chapter II contains General Explanations, Chapter III is on Punishments, Chapter IV the General Exceptions, Chapters V and VA define Abetment and Criminal Conspiracy.

General Exceptions

Under Section 105 of the Indian Evidence Act, the burden of proving that the case of the accused comes under the general exceptions is on the defence. However it does not absolve the prosecution from bringing any material that proves that the act was done under these exceptional circumstances that it is aware of before the court.[263] It is also the primary responsibility of the prosecution to prove that the act was done with the requisite mens rea, and only then does the burden shift to the accused.[264]

1. **Mistake of Fact**

   Nothing is an offence if done by a person who due to a mistake of fact in good faith believes himself to be bound or justified by law, in doing it. However mistake of law is not a defence. (Sections 76 and 79).

2. **Act of Judge**

   Nothing is an offence if done by a Judge when acting judicially in the exercise of any power which is given to him or which he, in good faith, believes is given to him or anything which is done in good faith, in pursuance of, or is warranted by the judgment or order of the Court, while it is in force, though the court may not have the jurisdiction to pass such judgment or order. (Sections 77 and 78)

263 Saraswati vs. State of Maharashtra, 1993 Mah.L.J. 1529

264 AIR 1964 SC 1563

3. Accident

Nothing is an offence, which is done by accident or misfortune, and without any criminal intention or knowledge in the doing of a lawful act in a lawful manner by lawful means and with proper care and caution (Section 80).

4. Act Done in Good Faith

Nothing is an offence if it is done, with the knowledge that it will cause harm, but without any criminal intention to cause harm and in good faith for the purpose of preventing or avoiding other harm to person or property, provided that the harm to be prevented or avoided was of such a nature and so imminent as to justify or excuse the risk of doing the act. (Section 81) No communication made in good faith is an offence by reason of any harm to the person to whom it is made, if it is made for the benefit of that person. (Section 93). An example of this is when a person hearing of his impending death from a doctor, dies of shock.

Nothing is an offence by reason of any harm which it may cause to a person for whose benefit it is done in good faith, even without that person's consent if the circumstances are such that it is impossible for that person to signify consent or if that person is incapable of giving consent, and has no guardian or other person in lawful charge of him from whom it is possible to obtain consent in time for the thing to be done with benefit. Provided that this shall not extend to the intentional causing of death or attempt to cause death, or doing anything which the person doing it knows to be likely to cause death, for any purpose other than the preventing death or grievous hurt or the curing of any grievous disease or infirmity. It shall not extend to the voluntary causing of hurt or attempt to cause hurt, except to prevent death or hurt and shall not extend to the abetment of any offence, to the committing of which offence it would not extend. The benefit here would not include mere pecuniary benefit (Section 92).

Hurt has been defined by Section 319 of the IPC as bodily pain, disease or infirmity. Grievous hurt is emasculation, permanent privation of the sight of either eye, permanent privation of the hearing of either ear, privation of any member joint or the destruction or permanent impairing of the powers of any member or joint, permanent disfiguration of the head or face, fracture or dislocation of a bone or tooth, or any hurt which endangers life or which causes the sufferer to be in severe bodily pain or unable to follow his ordinary pursuits for twenty days (Section 321).

5. Act of a Child

Nothing is an offencc if done by a child below 7 years of age and if done by a child above 7 but below 12, who has not attained sufficient maturity of understanding to judge the nature and consequences of his conduct on that occasion. (Sections 82 and 83)

6. Act of Person of Unsound Mind

Nothing is an offence, which is done by a person who at the time of doing it was incapable of knowing the nature of the act or that that he was doing what is either wrong or contrary to law, due to unsoundness of mind. (Section 84). Legal insanity is the state of mind at the time of the commission of the offence and is determined by factors including the conduct of the person immediately preceding and succeeding the act.[265]

7. Act of Intoxicated Person

Nothing is an offence when done by a person, who at the time of doing it is, by reason of intoxication, incapable of knowing the nature of the act or that he is doing what is either wrong or contrary to law, provided that the thing which intoxicated him was administered to him without his knowledge or against his will. Where the person was voluntarily drunk, he cannot take advantage of this provision even where an act done is not an offence unless done with the particular knowledge or intent. He shall be presumed to have had the requisite knowledge or intent (Sections 85 and 86).

8. Consent

Any act which is done without intention to cause death or grievous hurt, and which is not known by the doer to be likely to cause death or grievous hurt, which causes harm or is intended to cause harm, if done with the express or implied consent of a person above 18 years of age, to suffer the risk of the harm, will not be an offence (Section 87). Examples of these are hurt caused in sporting encounters. Likewise nothing which is not intended to cause death, is an offence by reason of any harm which it may cause or be intended by the doer to cause or be known by the doer to be likely to cause, to any person for whose benefit it is done in good faith, and who has given a consent, whether express or implied, to suffer that harm or to take the risk or that harm (Section 88).

Similarly any harm caused or intended to cause or known likely to be caused by an act done in good faith for the benefit of a person below 12 years or of unsound mind, by or by the consent of the guardian, will not amount to an offence. Provided that this harm shall not extend to the intentional causing of death or attempt to cause death, or doing anything which the doer knows is likely to cause death, or the voluntary causing of grievous hurt or attempt to cause hurt for any purpose other than the preventing of death or grievous hurt or the curing of any grievous disease or infirmity, or the abetment of any of the above offences (Section 89).

Consent given due to any fear of injury or under a misconception of fact, which is known, to the doer would not amount to consent. Similarly a

265 State vs. Mohinder Singh, (1983) 2 SCC 274

consent given by a child below 12 years, or a person who, from unsoundness of mind, or intoxication is unable to understand the nature and consequence of that to which he gives his consent, will also not amount to a consent within the meaning of these sections (Section 90). These exceptions also do not extend to acts that are offences independent of any harm caused with the consent, such as causing miscarriage with the consent of the woman or her guardian (Section 91).

9. Act by Compulsion

Except murder and offences against the State punishable with death, nothing is an offence which is done by a person who is compelled to do it by threats, which at the time of doing it, reasonably cause the apprehension that instant death to that person will otherwise be the consequence, provided that the person did not of his own accord or from a reasonable apprehension of harm to himself short of instant death, place himself in the situation where he became the subject to such constraint (Section 94).

10. Act Causing Slight Harm

Nothing is an offence by reason that it causes, or that it is intended to cause, or that it is known to be likely to cause, any harm if that harm is so slight that no person or ordinary sense and temper would complain of such harm (Section 95). The Supreme Court has held that while the section is intended to prevent penalisation of negligible wrongs or of offences of trivial character, whether an act would be so would depend upon the nature of injury, the position of the parties, the knowledge or intention with which the offending act was done and other related circumstances, and not solely by the measure of physical or other injury caused.[266]

11. Private Defence

Sections 96 to 106 deal with the right to private defence. Every person has a right to defend his own body and the body of any other person against any offence affecting the human body, and his own or any other person's property, whether movable or immovable, against any act which amounts to an offence of theft, robbery, mischief or criminal trespass or an attempt to commit any of these.

Mischief has been defined by Section 425 as the destruction of any property or any such change in any property or in the situation thereof as destroys or diminishes its value or utility or affects it injuriously, if caused intentionally or knowing it to be likely to cause wrongful loss or damage to the public or to any person. It is not necessary that the loss or damage

266 Veeda Menezes vs. Yusuf Khan, AIR 1966 SC 1773; Rupan Deol Bajaj vs. K.P.S. Gill, AIR 1996 SC 309

should be intended to be caused to the owner, and what is relevant is that the injury to the property should cause or intend to cause wrongful loss or damage to any person whether the property belongs to that person or not. Mischief can also be committed by an act affecting property belonging to the person who commits the act or to that person and others jointly. An example of this is given in Illustration (e) of the section. A having insured a ship voluntarily causes the same to be cast away, with the intention of causing damage to the underwriters. A has committed mischief.

The right to private defence of the body commences as soon as a reasonable apprehension of danger to the body arises from an attempt or threat to commit the offence though the offence may not have been committed and it continues as long as such apprehension of danger to the body continues.

The right to private defence of the property commences when a reasonable apprehension of danger to the property commences. The right against theft continues till the offender has effected his retreat with the property or either the assistance of the public authorities is obtained or the property has been recovered. The right against robbery continues as long as the offender cause or attempts to cause to any person death or hurt or wrongful restraint or as long as the fear of instant death or of instant hurt or of instant personal restraint continues. The right against criminal trespass or mischief continues as long as the offender continues in the commission of criminal trespass or mischief. The right against housebreaking continues as long as the house-trespass that has been begun by such housebreaking continues.

The right to private defence is available against a person who is entitled to the benefit of immunity on ground of being a child, of unsound mind or intoxicated or by reason of any misconception of his part.

There is no right to private defence against an act which does not reasonably cause the apprehension of death or of grievous hurt, if done or attempted to be done by or under direction of a public servant, acting in good faith under colour of office though that act may not be strictly justified by law. A person is not deprived of the right of private defence against an act done, or attempted to be done, by a public servant, as such unless he knows or has reason to believe that the person doing that act is such public servant. A person is not deprived of the right of private defence against an act done or attempted to be done, by the direction of a public servant unless he knows, or has reason to believe, that the person doing the act is acting by such direction or unless such person states the authority under which he acts, or if he has authority in writing unless he produces such authority, if demanded.

There is also no right to private defence in cases in, which there is time to have recourse to the protection of the public authorities. The right to private defence in no case extends to inflicting more harm than it is necessary to inflict for the purpose of defence.

The right of private defence of the body extends to the voluntary causing of death or of any other harm to the assailant, if the offence which occasions the exercise of the right were of any of the following descriptions:

a) Such an assault as may reasonably cause the apprehension that death will otherwise be the consequence of such assault;

b) Such as assault as may reasonably cause the apprehension that grievous hurt will otherwise be the consequence of such assault;

c) An assault with the intention of committing rape;

d) An assault with the intention of gratifying unnatural lust;

e) An assault with the intention of kidnapping or abducting;

f) An assault with the intention of wrongfully confining a person under circumstances which may reasonably cause him to apprehend that he will be unable to have recourse to the public authorities for his release.

g) If the offence is not any of the above, then the right does not extend to the voluntary causing of death of the assailant.

The right of private defence of property extends to the voluntary causing of death or of any other harm to the assailant, if the offence which occasions the exercise of the right were of any of the following descriptions:

a) Robbery;

b) House-breaking by night;

c) Mischief by fire committed on any building, tent or vessel which building, tent or vessel is used as a human dwelling, or as a place of custody of property;

d) Theft, mischief or house-trespass, under such circumstances as may reasonably cause apprehension that death or grievous hurt will be the consequence if such right of private defence is not exercised.

If the offence is not any of the above, then the right does not extend to the voluntary causing of death of the wrongdoer.

If in the exercise of the right of private defence against an assault, which reasonably causes the apprehension of death, the defender were so situated that he cannot effectually exercise that right without risk of harm to an innocent person, his right of private defence extends to the running of that risk.

The right to self-defence has been held to be a very valuable right and ought not be constructed narrowly. The plea of private defence need not always be taken by the accused and the court can consider it if circumstances show that right of private defence was legitimately exercised. The number of injuries on the person is not the criterion for determining whether the person was exercising his right of private defence. In order to find whether right of private defence is available or not, the injuries received by the accused, the imminence of threat to his safety, the injuries caused by the accused and the circumstances whether the accused had time to have recourse to public authorities are all relevant factors to be considered. But a right to self-defence does not include the right to launch an offensive, particularly when the need to defend no longer survives.[267] The right to defence over property would lie with the person in settled possession. Stray or intermittent acts of trespass do not give this right against the true owner. The Supreme Court has in Puran Singh vs State of Punjab[268], held that the nature of possession which may entitle a trespasser to exercise the right of private defence of property and person should contain the following attributes:

- The trespasser must be in actual physical possession of the property over a sufficiently long period
- The possession must be to the knowledge either express or implied of the owner or without any attempt at concealment and which contains an element of animus possidendi. The nature of possession of the trespasser would be a matter to be decided on facts and circumstances of each case
- The process of dispossession of the true owner by the trespasser must be complete and final and must be acquiesced in by the true owner
- One of the usual tests to determine the quality of settled possession, in the case of cultivable land, would be whether or not the trespasser, after having taken possession, had grown any crop. If the crop had been grown by the trespasser then even the true owner has no right to destroy the crop grown by the trespasser and take forcible possession, in which case the true owner will have no right of private defence.

The court further held that the right of private defence of person or property is to be exercised under the following limitations:

- That if there is sufficient time for recourse to the public authorities, the right is not available

267 V.Subramani vs State of Tamil Nadu, AIR 2005 SC 1983; Lakshmi Singh vs State of Bihar, AIR 1976 SC 2263; Biran Singh vs State of Bihar, AIR 1975 SC 87; Wassan Singh vs State of Punjab, (1996)1 SCC 458; Sekar vs State represented by Inspector of Police, TN (2002)8 SCC 354; Vidhya Singh vs State of MP, AIR 1971 SC 1857

268 AIR 1975 SC 1674. Also see Munshi Ram vs Delhi Admnistration, AIR 1968 SC 702

- That more harm than necessary should not be caused
- That there must be a reasonable apprehension of death or of grievous hurt to the person or damage to the property concerned.

Custodial Violence

While custodial violence including use of torture and deaths in custody due to violence have been assailed as being violative of Article 21 and public law remedy for the same has been held to be compensation apart from criminal law action, there is rarely evidence of the illegality of custodial violence having an impact at the ground level. There are very few convictions in cases of custodiai deaths and lack of evidence is generally responsible for the same as these crimes are committed in circumstances under the control of the accused police officials and the witnesses to these crimes are other accused who are themselves in the custody of these custodians of law and therefore vulnerable to similar ends. In its 113th Report, the Law Commission recommended that the Indian Evidence Act be amended to provide that in prosecutions of police officers for an alleged offence of having caused bodily injuries to a person while in police custody. If there is evidence that the injury was caused during the period when the person was in the police custody, the court may presume that the injury was caused by the police officer having custody of the person unless the police officer proves to the contrary. But neither the 2005 nor the 2006 amendments of the CrPC have incorporated these changes.

In State of MP vs Shyamsundar Trivedi's case[269], the Supreme Court while deciding a case of custodial death found that the presence of the accused police officials was established and the victim had died as a result of excessive beating by the police, but the court held that it could not be said that they intended to cause death of the victim and therefore set aside the conviction under Section 302 and instead convicted them for offence under Section 304 Part II/34 IPC, and awarded the accused one to two years of imprisonment and ordered the payment of fine to be given to the victim's family as compensation. The Court however observed that, "The exaggerated adherence to and insistence upon the establishment of proof beyond every reasonable doubt by the prosecution, at times even when the prosecuting agencies are themselves fixed in the dock, ignoring the ground realities, the fact-situation and the peculiar circumstances of a given case, as in the present case, often results in miscarriage of justice and makes the justice delivery system suspect and vulnerable. In the ultimate analysis the society suffers and a criminal gets encouraged. Tortures in police custody, which of late are on the increase, receive encouragement by this type of an unrealistic approach at times of the courts as well because it reinforces the belief in the mind of the police that no harm would come to them if one prisoner dies in the lock-up because there would hardly be any evidence available to the

269 (1995) 4 SCC 262

prosecution to directly implicate them with the torture. The courts must not lose sight of the fact that death in police custody is perhaps one of the worst kind of crimes in a civilized society, governed by the rule of law and poses a serious threat to an orderly civilized society. Torture in custody flouts the basic rights of the citizens recognised by the Indian Constitution and is an affront to human dignity. Police excesses and the mal-treatment of detainees/ under-trial prisoners or suspects tarnishes the image of any civilized nation and encourages the men in 'Khaki' to consider themselves to be above the law and sometimes even to become law unto themselves. Unless stern measures are taken to check the malady of the very fence eating the crops, the foundations of the criminal justice delivery system would be shaken and the civilization itself would risk the consequence of heading; towards total decay resulting in anarchy and authoritarianism reminiscent of barbarism. The courts must, therefore, deal with such cases in a realistic manner and with the sensitivity which they deserve, otherwise the common man may tend to gradually lose faith in the efficacy of the system of judiciary itself, which if it happens will be a sad day, for any one to reckon with" and recommended that the Law Commission's recommendations be incorporated in law.

The Supreme Court in Sahadevan alias Sagadevan vs State represented by Inspector of Police, Chennai[270] reversed the acquittal of the policemen responsible for the murder by the High Court and confirmed conviction recorded by the judgment and order of the Trial Court for murder. In that case too, the dead body's identity was disputed and the eyewitnesses to the torture were "hardened criminals". The defence was also lack of motive and the person having escaped from custody. The Supreme Court had held that on the basis of the direct and circumstantial evidence the offence was said to be proved. It is also well settled legal position in murder cases where the *corpus delicti* is not found that the same is not necessary in cases where there is direct or circumstantial evidence leading to the inescapable conclusion that the person has died and that the accused are the persons who have committed the murder. The Court further held that it could not be oblivious to the fact that the case involved policemen and the investigation had been ordered by the High Court and hence the benefit of the acts and omissions of the investigation could not go to the accused in the interest of justice.

In Shakila Abdul Gafar Khan vs Vasant Raghunath Dhoble[271] the Supreme Court held that the case was not proved due to the delay in one year in filing of the private complaint in the case of custodial death after the State failed to register the offence and due to the non-complaint of torture. The Court had expressed its disturbance over the partisan nature of state action in failing to register the FIR. The court also disbelieved the evidence of the witnesses whom it found

270 (2003) 1 SCC 534
271 (2003) 7 SCC 749

unreliable as it doubted their very presence at the spot. Having upheld the acquittal of the accused the Court opined that "there are several loose ends, which as admitted by the prosecution, were not taken note of. Even according to the version of the accused, the deceased was taken to the hospital and was examined by DW-3. What was the occasion for this being done still remains shrouded in mystery. The post-mortem report reveals 16 injuries, though of simple nature. If none of these injuries was sustained by the deceased in police custody, there was no necessity of bringing the deceased to the hospital on 15-10-1983 at 11.00 a.m. DW-2 has admitted that he had taken the deceased for examination by DW-3. The Court could have asked him as to what was the necessity for doing so. That admittedly has not been done." Thereafter the court proceeded to grant Rs 1 lakh as compensation to the victim's family. In Munshi Singh Gautam vs State of M.P[272] the Supreme Court again disbelieved the evidence of the eyewitnesses one of whom stated that he was also tortured along with the deceased but did not make a grievance of the same before the Magistrate when he was produced after arrest. The court acquitted all the accused except one which it convicted on the basis of the statement under Section 313 of the Cr.PC. More worrying is an observation by the Supreme Court in both the cases about the "disturbing trend of increase in cases where false accusations of custodial torture are made, taking advantage of the serious concern shown and the stern attitude reflected by the courts while dealing with custodial violence"[273].

In Sadashio Mundaji Bhalerao vs State of Maharashtra[274], the Supreme Court reversed the conviction for the murder of an accused by the police officers and upheld the acquittal by the trial court. In the said case, the deceased had been last seen alive in the police lock up and four inmates of the lock up had testified that they saw him being badly beaten up by the accused. The body was later removed and disposed of in a canal. The body was recovered by another police team but it was highly decomposed and post mortem was inconclusive. The body was identified by the fingerprint. The trial court discared the identification evidence and disbelieved the testimony of eyewitnesses. The lower court disbelieved all evidence of direct nature as being not reliable. The court held that the policemen had no motive for committing the offence. The *corpus delicti* of the crime was held to be not found and since there was no evidence that the victim had died, the murder was not proved. The lower court believed the defence of the accused that the victim ran away from the police station and disbelieved the prosecution case and therefore acquitted the accused. The Supreme Court held that it could not be proved that the body recovered was indeed that of the accused and hence reversed the conviction by the High Court.

---

272 (2005)9SCC631

273 Shakila Abdul Gafar Khan vs Vasant Raghunath Dhoble, (2003) 7 SCC 749 and Munshi Singh Gautam vs State of M.P, (2005)9SCC631

274 2006(12)SCALE470; MANU/SC/8601/2006

In Sube Singh vs State of Haryana[275], the Supreme Court stated that in cases where custodial death or custodial torture or other violation of the rights guaranteed under Article 21 is established, courts may award compensation in a proceeding under Article 32 or 226. However, before awarding compensation, the Court will have to pose to itself the following questions:

(a) Whether the violation of Article 21 is patent and incontrovertible,

(b) Whether the violation is gross and of a magnitude to shock the conscience of the court,

(c) Whether the custodial torture alleged has resulted in death or whether custodial torture is supported by medical report or visible marks or scars or disability.

Where there is no evidence of custodial torture of a person except his own statement, and where such allegation is not supported by any medical report or other corroboration evidence, or where there are clear indications that the allegations are false or exaggerated fully or in part, courts may not award compensation as a public law remedy under Article 32 or 226, but relegate the aggrieved party to the traditional remedies by way of appropriate civil/criminal action. But the court stated that it should not be understood as holding that harassment and custodial violence is not serious or worthy of consideration, where there is no medical report or visible marks or independent evidence. Harassment or custodial violence cannot always be supported by a medical report or independent evidence or proved by marks or scars. Every illegal detention irrespective of its duration, and every custodial violence, irrespective of its degree or magnitude, is outright condemnable and per se actionable. Remedy for such violation is available in civil law and criminal law. The public law remedy is additionally available where the conditions mentioned above are satisfied.

The Court further stated that to combat the Custodial violence requires to be tackled from two ends, that is, by taking measures that are remedial and preventive. Award of compensation is one of (Page 847) the remedial measures after the event. Effort should be made to remove the very causes, which lead to custodial violence, so as to prevent such occurrences. Following steps, if taken, may prove to be effective preventive measures:

a) Police training should be re-oriented, to bring in a change in the mindset and attitude of the Police personnel in regard to investigations, so that they will recognise and respect human rights, and adopt thorough and scientific investigation methods.

b) The functioning of lower level Police Officers should be continuously monitored and supervised by their superiors to prevent custodial violence and adherence to lawful standard methods of investigation.

275 (2006)3SCC178

c) Compliance with the eleven requirements enumerated in DK Basu (supra) should be ensured in all cases of arrest and detention.

d) Simple and fool-proof procedures should be introduced for prompt registration of first information reports relating to all crimes.

e) Computerization, video-recording, and modern methods of records maintenance should be introduced to avoid manipulations, insertions, substitutions and ante-dating in regard to FIRs, Mahazars, inquest proceedings, Port-mortem Reports and Statements of witnesses etc. and to bring in transparency in action.

f) An independent investigating agency (preferably the respective Human Rights Commissions or CBI) may be entrusted with adequate power, to investigate complaints of custodial violence against Police personnel and take stern and speedy action followed by prosecution, wherever necessary.

The endeavour should be to achieve a balanced level of functioning, where police respect human rights, adhere to law, and take confidence building measures (CBMs), and at the same time, firmly deal with organised crime, terrorism, white-collared crime, deteriorating law and order situation, etc.

Offences Relating to Women

Some of the specific offences that relate to women in the IPC are dealt with in this section. Though there is no separate chapter on offences against women, there are several provisions in the IPC, which specifically relate to women. Most of these provisions are contained in the chapters relating to the general offences of similar nature. So rape and dowry death are dealt with in Chapter XVI which relates to Offences against Human Body. The chapter on Offences Relating to Marriage (XX) and Cruelty by Husband or Relatives of Husband (XXA) are relevant chapters too, but as the name denotes and as the Supreme Court has pointed out, Chapter XX is meant to protect marriage and not women. Section 198 of the CrPC also specifies that no court shall take cognizance of an offence punishable under Chapter XX of the IPC except upon a complaint made by the person aggrieved by the offence, and where the person is unable to approach the court, by another person who is either the legal guardian or a relative by blood, marriage or adoption, with the leave of the court. The other general provisions in the IPC and other criminal law also apply equally to women and Section 405 which defines Criminal breach of trust has been interpreted to deal with cases of refusal to return the streedhana of a woman by the Supreme Court.[276]

Given below is a table, which summarises most of the important provisions relating to women in the IPC.

276 Pratibha Rani v. Suraj Kumar, (1985) 2 SCC 370.

SECTION	OFFENCE	PUNISHMENT	TYPE OF OFFENCE
498A	**Husband or his relative subjecting a woman to cruelty**. Cruelty means: (a) Any willful conduct which is of such a nature as is likely to drive a woman to commit suicide or to cause grave injury or danger to life, limb or health, both physical or mental, of woman; (b) Harassment of the woman to coerce her or her relative to meet any dowry demand or because of her failure to meet such demand.	Upto three years and also fine	Cognizable if the complaint is made by the person aggrieved or by her father, mother, brother, sister, uncle or aunt or other person related by blood with the leave of the court. Non-bailable Triable by Magistrate of the First Class
304B	Dowry Death: Death of a woman caused by any burns or bodily injury or occurs under unnatural circumstances within seven years of marriage where the husband or his relative subjected her to cruelty or harassment for or in connection with a dowry death. Husband or relative shall be deemed to have caused her death.	Minimum seven years and maximum penalty upto life imprisonment	Cognizable Non-bailable Triable by the Sessions Court
494	Bigamy: Whoever having a husband or wife living, marries again without obtaining a divorce and where the personal law does not permit a second marriage without divorce or annulment. Provided that where the spouse has been continually absent for a period of seven years and has not been heard of as being alive, and has informed the second spouse of the same.	Upto Seven years and fine	Non-cognizable Non-bailable Triable by Magistrate of the first class
497	Adultery: A person having sexual intercourse, not amounting to rape, with a woman he knows or has reason to believe is married, without her husband's consent or connivance. Wife is not punishable as abettor	Upto five years or fine or both	Non-cognizable Non-bailable Triable by Magistrate of the first class

SECTION	OFFENCE	PUNISHMENT	TYPE OF OFFENCE
405/406	Criminal Breach of Trust: Whoever, being in any manner entrusted with property or with dominion over property, dishonestly misappropriates or converts to his own use that property or disposes of that property in violation of any law or legal contract, express or implied which he has made touching the discharge of the trust, or willfully suffers another person to do so.	Imprisonment upto three years or fine or both	Cognizable Non-bailable Triable by Magistrate of the First Class
306	Abetment of Suicide: If any person commits suicide, whoever abets the commission of such suicide.	Imprisonment upto ten years and fine	Cognizable Non-bailable Triable by the Sessions Court
363	Kidnapping and Abduction: Kidnapping is taking a person out of India without her consent or taking a girl below 18 years or of mentally unsound mind out of the keeping of her guardian without the consent of such guardian; Abduction is compelling by force or inducing by any deceitful means, a person to go from a place.	Imprisonment upto seven years and fine	Cognizable Bailable Triable by Magistrate of the First Class
366	Kidnapping per se is an offence Kidnapping, abducting or inducing a woman to compel her to marry against her will or to force or seduce her to illicit intercourse; Illicit intercourse is intercourse outside marriage.	Imprisonment upto 10 years and fine	Cognizable Non-bailable Triable by the Sessions Court
366A&B	Procuration of minor girl Importation of girl from foreign country.	Ditto	Ditto
367	Kidnapping or abducting in order to subject person to grievous hurt, slavery or unnatural lust.	Ditto	Ditto
368	Wrongfully concealing or confining a kidnapped or abducted person.	Ditto	Ditto

SECTION	OFFENCE	PUNISHMENT	TYPE OF OFFENCE
372	Selling minor for purposes of prostitution or illicit intercourse or for any unlawful and immoral purpose.	Ditto	Ditto
373	Buying minor for purposes of prostitution or illicit intercourse or for any unlawful and immoral purpose.	Ditto	Ditto
374	Any sale or purchase made to or by a brothel keeper or prostitute will be presumed to be for purposes of prostitution.	Ditto	Ditto
375	**Rape** Sexual intercourse between man and woman, which is against the will of the woman concerned or without her consent. Or If consent is obtained by circumstances involving force, coercion, undue influence Or Where consent is vitiated due to recognised legal inability on the woman's part, such as her age being under 16 years of age, or her being mentally ill or intoxicated by the man except where the woman is the wife and above 15 years of age.	Mnimum seven years extending upto life imprisonment and /or fine except where the wife is above 12 years of age, then two years	Cognizable Non-bailable Triable by Sessions Court Non cognizable Bailable Court of Session
376	Custodial rape by police, hospital staff or institutional staff of women under the custody of the accused, gang rape (i.e. rape of a woman by more than one man), rape of a pregnant woman whom he knows to be pregnant and rape of a girl below 12 years of age; Intercourse by man with separated wife.	Minimum ten years extending to life imprisonment and fine	Cognizable Non Bailable Court of Session
376A	Intercourse by public servant with woman in his custody not amounting to rape	Two years and fine	Non Cognizable Bailable Triable by Sessions Court Cognizable bailable Triable by Sessions Court

SECTION	OFFENCE	PUNISHMENT	TYPE OF OFFENCE
376B	Intercourse by Superintendent of Jail, Remand Home or children or women's instititution with female inmate not amounting to rape	Upto five years and fine	Ditto
376B	Intercourse by public servant with woman in his custody not amounting to rape	Two years and fine	Non Cognizable Bailable Triable by Sessions Court Cognizable bailable Triable by Sessions Court
376C	Intercourse by Superintendent of Jail, Remand Home or children or women's instititution with female inmate not amounting to rape	Upto five years and fine	Ditto
376D	Intercourse by management or staff of hospital with woman in hospital not amounting to rape	Ditto	Ditto
377	Unnatural Offences: having voluntary carnal intercourse against the order of nature with any man, woman or animal Penetration is sufficient to constitute carnal intercourse	Imprisonment for life or upto ten years and fine	Cognizable Non-bailable Triable by Magistrate of the First Class
354	Outraging Modesty of a Woman: Whoever assaults or uses criminal force to any woman intending or knowing it to be likely that he would outrage her modesty.	Imprisonment for two years or fine or both	Cognizable Bailable Triable by any Magistrate
509	Whoever, intending to insult the modesty of any woman utters any word, makes any sound or gesture, or exhibits any object intending that it shall be witnessed by the woman or intrudes upon the privacy of the woman	Simple imprisonment for one year or fine or both	Ditto

Streedhana

Streedhan refers to any property that is gifted to the woman during and around the time of her marriage, or has been left to her in a will. This includes property that has been gifted to her by her parents, siblings and in-laws. She is the "absolute owner" of this property and can deal with it in any way that she likes. Since the husband has no ownership rights over this property,[277] she may sell it, gift it, or do anything else without referring to her husband. Except in situations where there is extreme distress, such as famine or illness, the husband has no right to use this property. Even in such circumstances, the husband is morally bound to restore the property or its value as soon as he is in a position to do so.[278] If husband or in-laws are given the streedhana for safe keeping, this is entrustment of property and if the same is dishonestly misappropriated or sold, the husband or in laws have committed criminal breach of trust. If the *streedhan* or personal property has been jointly kept, the court will presume that it has been kept in the custody of the husband and that the wife has entrusted the property. She does not lose her ownership rights over the property just because she has allowed it to be used jointly and refusal to return or misappropriation will amount to the offence under Section 406. The wife does not have to show any special agreement to prove that the property was entrusted.[279]

Prior to this interpretation, a woman who was sent out of her matrimonial home without her belongings had to take recourse to only civil remedies. Further since the Dowry Prohibition Act makes both the giving and receiving of dowry an offence, most of the woman do not take action under this law, though it also states that the dowry belongs to the woman. By incorporating the concept of Streedhana, and interpreting it to mean even articles which were given to her by her husband and his relatives and the dowry, woman now have a swifter and cheaper recourse under law. On the other hand the criminal law provision relating to adultery does not give the wife the right to prosecute her husband. This has been interpreted by the court as a provision, which is to protect marriage and not women, while also holding that women are protected under the present provision, as they cannot be prosecuted. The Supreme Court felt that an aggrieved woman had recourse to divorce proceedings.[280] Similarly in order to bring a successful prosecution of bigamy, the court has held that the second marriage should be proved, and mere admission by husband or his living together with another woman who purports to be his wife would be insufficient to prove bigamy. This makes it impossible to prove bigamy in most cases and in the case of both these occurrence, a woman is left with the choice of civil remedy only.

277 Rashmi Kumar v. Mahesh Kumar Bhada, (1997) 2 SCC 397.
278 Pratibha Rani v. Suraj Kumar, (1985) 2 SCC 370.
279 Rashmi Kumar v. Mahesh Kumar Bhada, (1997) 2 SCC 397
280 Sowmithri Vishnu vs. Union of India, 1985 (Supp) SCC 137; Revathy vs. Union of India, AIR 1988 SC 835

Cruelty to Married woman and Dowry Deaths

Section 498A and 304B which deal with cruelty to a married woman and dowry deaths have been enacted to combat with domestic violence. Section 498A was challenged in Sushil Kumar Sharma's case where the Supreme Court upheld constitutional validity of the provision and held that mere possibility of misuse did not render a provision invalid.[281] Dowry has the same meaning as defined in the Dowry Prohibition Act and is not confined to only that given at the time of marriage. Hence any demand made after marriage too, will be covered by the definition of dowry. However in K. Prema S. Rao vs Yadla Srinivasa Rao[282], the court held that when the husband harassed the deceased wife to transfer the land given to her by her parents in marriage ritual, it cannot be said to be in connection with the marriage and would not constitute dowry demand and husband could not be said to be guilty of causing dowry death. In the instant case, the husband was convicted for cruelty under Section 498A and abetment of suicide under Section 306. The dowry death provision applies only to married women. However in Reema Aggarwal v. Anupam[283], the Supreme Court held that even in cases of lack of valid marriage, the 'husband' would not be allowed to take shelter behind a smoke screen that there was no valid marriage and hence the question of dowry would not arise. Persons who contract marriages ostensibly and cohabit with women in the purported exercise of their role and status as 'husband' would come under the purview of Section 498A and 304B of the IPC. The Supreme Court has in a series of judgments, held that "soon before her death" is a relative term and no time limit can be fixed for the same. The court looks at the proximate and live link between the effect of cruelty based on dowry demand and the death concerned as the event should not be remote in time.[284] The limitation for the offence under Section 498A starts from the last act of cruelty but where the complaint was lodged within time but there was delay in taking cognizance of the complaint and in investigation and filing of chargesheet, the Supreme Court condoned the delay and held that the court can condone the delay in the interest of justice.[285]

Rape

Rape is an offence under the Indian law and has been defined by Section 375 of the Indian Penal Code and its punishment is given in Section 376. In 1983, following the campaign by women's groups and legal activists, there were substantial changes made in the criminal law relating to rape. Apart from the

281 Sushil Kumar Sharma vs Union of India (2005) 6 SCC 281: AIR 2005 SC 3100

282 2003 CrLJ 69

283 AIR 2004 SC 1418

284 Kaliyaperumal vs State of Tamil Nadu, (2004)9 SCC 157, Vidhya Devi vs State of Haryana (2004)9 SCC 476; Harjit SIngh vs State of Haryana MANU/ SC/0209/2005; Kamesh Panjiyar @ Kamlesh Panjiyar vs State of Bihar, AIR 2005 SC 785: (2005) 2 SCC 388

285 Ramesh vs State of Tamil Nadu, AIR 2005 SC 1989; Also see Arun Vyas vs Anita Vyas, (1999) 4 SCC 690

changes in Section 376, stipulating the minimum sentence, which can be reduced by the convicting court for reasons to be specially recorded, the incorporation of Section 376(2) recognising certain aggravated forms of rape and imposing higher penalties for them and adding Section 376A to D which made sexual intercourse not amounting to rape in certain situations culpable. Amendments in the Indian Evidence Act were made and Section 114A was included which shifted the burden of proof in cases of rape covered under Section 376(2) where the court shall presume that sexual intercourse was without a woman's consent if intercourse was proved and the woman stated that it was without her consent. These amendments were campaigned for in the wake of the cases of rape by police officers. The changes were demanded to bring public officials within the purview of the law and make cases of apparent consensual intercourse between persons in situations where the accused was in a position of institutional authority vis-a-vis the rape victim which are difficult to prove due to the institutional force against proper investigation and thereby decrease the chances of successful prosecution. Easier to prove, as in such cases Section 114A would shift the burden of proving that the intercourse was without the consent of the woman on the man once the woman stated that she did not consent. The other changes in the incorporation of Section 376B to D resulted in making consensual intercourse between a man in certain positions of authority with a woman in the custody of such male an offence in recognition of the fact that this consent was in reality no consent. The other change was the inclusion of Section 376A, which made marital rape, though of a separated couple, an offence. These changes were brought in with other changes in the Dowry Prohibition Act and the inclusion of Section 498A and Section 304B in the Indian Penal Code.

The explanation to Section 375 states that penetration is necessary ingredient of rape. This should be penetration by the penis and not of objects though partial penetration is held to be sufficient to prove the offence[286]. Absence of semen or spermatozoa in the vaginal swab was not sufficient to acquit the accused and negate the version of the victim, according to the Supreme Court in State of Tamil Nadu vs Suresh[287]. Refusal to mention that the sexual intercourse occurred would result in the registering of the offence of outraging the modesty of a woman (Section 354 IPC), which is an offence punishable with two years imprisonment. Attempt to commit rape is also an offence. If rape was not committed, then the courts go into the facts of the case to determine as to whether there was the intention to commit rape or to outrage the woman's modesty. There is a thin line between the two and most cases of attempt, end up as convictions under Section 354 IPC instead of Section 376 read with Section 511 (which makes attempt to commit an offence an offence and punishes the same with half the term provided for the main section).

286 State of Uttar Pradesh vs Babul Nath (1994) SCC (Cri) 1585
287 AIR 1998 SC 1044

One of the important issues in a rape trial is the issue of consent. The offence hinges on the consent or its lack on the part of the victim, and apart from the victim there are generally no eye-witnesses to the offence, given its nature. Hence injuries are considered a proof of resistance and lack of consent on the part of the victim. Here the proof of injuries is through medical evidence. Given the difficulties in medical evidence due to the exigencies of rape cases, and understanding that lack of resistance is not a proof of consent, in a series of judgments, the Supreme Court has held that its absence is not indicative of lack of consent. In State of Maharashtra vs Chandraprakash Kewalchand Jain[288] the Supreme Court held that the evidence of prosecutrix is to be judged in the backdrop of the particular fact-situation in which she was placed. The absence of resistance by the prosecutrix is required to be viewed in the context of the sense of awe attached to the authority and her helplessness. Generally, an Indian woman would not make false allegations of rape against any person, so as to attach stigma to her character and disrepute to her family. In Dilip vs State of Gujarat,[289] the Gujarat High Court held that absence of injuries in a case where the court held that since the accused had posed themselves to the victims as police officers, they were demoralised and hence their lack of resistance could not be said to mean consent. In State of Himachal Pradesh vs Mange Ram[290], the Supreme Court held that when the prosecutrix submitted due to terror, it did not signify consent. In Balwant Singh vs State of Punjab[291] the Supreme Court held that it cannot be said that the resistance should be such that it causes injury to the victim and that absence of injuries on the body of the prosecutrix would not falsify case of rape against the accused. In State of Rajasthan vs N.K.[292], the Supreme Court held that absence of injuries on the body of the prosecutrix did not signify consent. In State of Himachal Pradesh vs Gian Chand[293], the Supreme Court held that absence of injuries on the private parts of the accused also did not absolve the accused from the charge of rape. In Vishnu vs State of Maharashtra[294], the Bombay High Court held that "absence of violent or stiff resistance may as well suggest helpless surrender to the inevitable due to sheer timidity".

In Uday vs. State of Karnataka[295] the Supreme Court held that it appeared that "the consensus of judicial opinion is in favour of the view that the consent given by the prosecutrix to sexual intercourse with a person with whom she is deeply in love on a promise that he would marry her on a later date, cannot be said to be given under a misconception of fact. A false promise is not a fact within the meaning of the Code. We are inclined to agree with this view, but

288 AIR 1990 SC 658
289 1999 Cri.L.J 704
290 2000 Cri.L.J 4027
291 AIR 1987 SC 1080
292 2000 Cri.L.J 2205
293 (2001) 2 LRI 1416
294 (1998)3 LJ 287
295 AIR 2003 SC 1639

we must add that there is no strait jacket formula for determining whether consent given by the prosecutrix to sexual intercourse is voluntary, or whether it is given under a misconception of fact. In the ultimate analysis, the tests laid down by the Courts provide at best guidance to the judicial mind while considering a question of consent, but the Court must, in each case, consider the evidence before it and the surrounding circumstances, before reaching a conclusion, because each case has its own peculiar facts which may have a bearing on the question whether the consent was voluntary, or was given under a misconception of fact. It must also weigh the evidence keeping in view the fact that the burden is on the prosecution to prove each and every ingredient of the offence, absence of consent being one of them." In Deelip Singh Alias Dilip Kumar v. State of Bihar[296], the Supreme Court took the view that prosecturix had taken a conscious decision to participate in the sexual act only on being impressed by the accused who promised to marry her. But accused's promise was not false from its inception with the intention to seduce her to sexual act. But in Yedla Srinivasa Rao vs State of AP[297] the Supreme Court held that where the accused first committed rape on victim against her will and consent but subsequently, he held out a hope of marrying her and continued to satisfy his lust, it was apparent that the accused had no intention to marry and it became further evident when Panchayat was convened and he admitted that he had committed sexual intercourse with the victim and also assured her to marry within two days but did not turn up to fulfil his promise before the Panchayat. This conduct of the accused stood out to hold him guilty. The Court held that what is a voluntary consent and what is not a voluntary consent depends on the facts of each case. In order to appreciate the testimony, one has to see the factors like the age of the girl, her education and her status in the society and likewise the social status of the boy. If the attending circumstances lead to the conclusion that it was not only the accused but prosecutrix was also equally keen, then in that case the offence is condoned. In the present case in view of the facts as mentioned above the Court was satisfied that the consent which had been obtained by the accused was not a voluntary one which was given by her under misconception of fact that the accused would marry her but this is not a consent in law.

Generally the law relating to rape has led to the development of criminal law on delay in lodging FIR. The Supreme Court of India in State of Punjab vs Gurmit Singh[298], held that in sexual offences delay in the lodging of the FIR can be due to variety of reasons particularly the reluctance of the prosecutrix or her family members to go to the police and complain about the incident which concerns the reputation of the prosecutrix and the honour of her family. It is only after

296 MANU/SC/0948/2004

297 2006(9)SCALE692: MANU/SC/8531/2006

298 1996 Cr.LJ 1728

giving it a cool thought that a complaint of sexual offence is generally lodged. Even if there were some delay in lodging FIR in respect of offence of rape, if it is properly explained and the explanation is natural in the facts and circumstances of the case, such delay would not matter. In this the victim did not disclose the offence to her teachers or classmates, but to her mother upon reaching home. This conduct of the victim girl was held to be natural and her evidence could not be disbelieved on grounds that she did not disclose the incident to the first person she came across. This has been reiterated in later judgments too.[299]

The other areas where the rape law has impacted criminal jurisprudence is regarding conviction based on the sole testimony of witness and the law relating to compensation to the victims of crime because of the nature of the offence and the paucity of evidence in such crimes which are personal in nature and not committed openly.[300]. In State of Punjab vs Gurmit Singh[301], the Supreme Court of India held that failure of the investigating officer to carry out proper investigation, should not affect the credibility of the witness and sometimes corroboration may not be forthcoming on material particulars due to failure on the part of the investigating agency to collect material evidence. In Sheikh Zakir vs State of Bihar[302], the Supreme Court held that non-examination of the police officer who refused to register the complaint when the victim first approached the police was not necessary to prove the reason for the delay as the Complainant had stated the reason for the delay in her FIR and a police officer who had not performed his duty was not likely to come to court and depose of the same. In Balwant Singh vs State of Punjab[303] the Supreme Court held that in the case of gang rape of a woman, when the Police disbelieved the prosecution story and treated the case as cancelled had no relevance especially since the police had withheld the report of examination by the Chemical examiner of the vaginal swabs of the prosecutrix as to the presence of semen and spermatozoa, and upheld the conviction of the accused.

The Supreme Court in Delhi Domestic Working Women's Forum vs. Union of India[304] laid down the following guidelines to assist the victims of rape:

1. The complainants of sexual assault cases should be provided with legal representation. It is important to have someone who is well acquainted with the criminal justice system. The role of the victim's advocate would not only be to explain to the victim the nature of the proceedings, to prepare her for the case and to assist her in the police station and in court but to

299 State of Rajasthan vs N.K. 2000 Cr.LJ 2205; State of Himachal Pradesh vs Gian Chand (2001) 1 LRI 1417;

300 See Kamalanantha vs State of Tamil Nadu, (2005)5SCC194

301 1996 Cri.LJ 1728

302 AIR 1983 SC 911

303 AIR 1987 SC 1080

304 (1995) 1 SCC 14

provide her with guidance as to how she might obtain help of a different nature from other agencies, for example, mind counselling or medical assistance. It is important to secure continuity of assistance by ensuring that the same person who looked after the complainant's interests in the police station represents her till the end of the case.

2. Legal assistance will have to be provided at the police station since the victim of sexual assault might very well be in a distressed state upon arrival at police station, the guidance and support of a lawyer at this stage would be of great assistance to her.
3. The police should be under a duty to inform the victim of her right to representation before any questions were asked of her and that the police report should state that the victim was so informed.
4. A list of advocates willing to act in these cases should be kept at the police station for victims who did not have a particular lawyer in mind or whose lawyer was unavailable.
5. The advocate shall be appointed by the court, upon application by the police at the earliest convenient moment, but in order to ensure that victims were questioned without undue delay, advocates would be authorised to act at the police station before leave of the court was sought or obtained.
6. In all rape trials anonymity of the victim must be maintained, as far as necessary.
7. It is necessary, having regard to the Directive Principles contained under Article 38(1) of the Constitution of India to set up Criminal Injuries Compensation Board. Rape victims frequently incur substantial financial loss. Some, for example, are too traumatised to continue in employment.
8. Compensation for victims shall be awarded by the court on conviction of the offender and by the Criminal Injuries Compensation Board whether or not a conviction has taken place. The Board will take into account pain, suffering and shock as well as loss of earnings due to pregnancy and the expenses of childbirth if this occurred as a result of the rape.

Till such Criminal Injuries Compensation Boards are set up, the trial courts have been empowered to award compensation including interim compensation pending trial to the victims. In Bodhisattwa Gautam vs Subhra Chakraborty[305] the Supreme Court reiterated these principles and further said that if the court trying an offence of rape has jurisdiction to award compensation at the final stage, there is no reason to deny the court the right to award interim compensation, which should also be provided in the Scheme.

305 AIR 1996 SC 922. Also see Dinesh vs State of Rajasthan, (2006) 3 SCC 771

Apart from the IPC, there are several other criminal legislation, which deal with issues related to women. One of these is Section 125 of the CrPC that provides for maintenance of wives, children and parents. This section provides for maintenance upto the sum of Rs.500 per month to a relative who is unable to maintain her or himself when the person whom he/she is dependent upon refuses to fulfil this obligation voluntarily. This provision is meant to prevent vagrancy. A wife including a divorced wife, a minor legitimate or illegitimate child, a child who is a major but unable to maintain himself/herself due to physical or mental disability and a parent are entitled to maintenance under this section. The application for maintenance can be made before the Magistrate within whose jurisdiction the applicant resides, the respondent resides or they last resided together. If the maintenance order is not complied with, the Magistrate can issue a warrant for levying fine against the respondent for the amount due and may sentence the person to imprisonment for a term which may extend to one month or until payment if sooner, is made. A wife will not be entitled to maintenance if she is living in adultery, or if she refuses to live with her husband without any sufficient reason or if they are living separately by mutual consent. Where the husband offers to maintain his wife on condition of her living with him, and the wife refuses to live with him, the Magistrate may consider the grounds for refusal before passing order of maintenance. If the husband has committed bigamy or is living in adultery, it shall be just ground for the wife's refusal to live with him.

The legal system takes a paternalistic view of women and women's issues. Women are seen as victims to be protected, and not citizens who require rights. The judgments of the courts also reflect this view. While it is commendable that the legal system is sensitive to some of the problems faced by women and is aware of the fact that most women are oppressed and denied their rights, it does not seek to give women a greater control over their lives nor does it tackle the issue of exploitation head on.

Offences Against Public Tranquillity

These offences are contained in Chapter VIII of the IPC. They are important for the maintenance of public order and are resorted to by the State to quell any direct action strategies. All these offences are cognizable and bailable except where another offence is committed by the mob that is non-bailable.

Section 141 defines an Unlawful Assembly as an assembly of five or more persons whose common object is:

1. To overawe by criminal force, or show of criminal force to the Central or any State Government or Parliament or the Legislature of any State, or any public servant in the exercise of the lawful power of such public servant; or

2. To resist the execution of any law or of any legal process; or
3. To commit any mischief or criminal trespass or other offence; or
4. By means of criminal force, or show of criminal force to any person, to take or obtain possession of any property, or to deprive any person of the enjoyment of a right of way, or of the use of water or other incorporeal right of which he is in possession or enjoyment, or to enforce any right or supposed right; or
5. By means of criminal force or show of criminal force to compel any person to do what he is not legally bound to do, or to omit to do what he is legally entitled to do.

Criminal force has been defined by Section 350 of the IPC as intentional use of force against any person without the person's consent, in order to the committing of any offence or to cause injury, fear or annoyance to the person against the person to whom the force is used.

An assembly, which is peaceful and does not resist the execution of any law by the law enforcing authorities, is not an unlawful assembly. An assembly, which is not unlawful when it assembled, may become subsequently unlawful, and whoever intentionally joins an unlawful assembly or continues in it after it turns unlawful is a member of it. If an offence has been by any member of an unlawful assembly in persuasion the common object, or such as the members of the assembly knew to be likely to be committed in persuasion of that object, every member of the assembly at the time of commission of that offence would be guilty of the offence. (Sections 142 and 149) Hiring, engaging, employing or promoting or conniving at the hiring, engaging or employing or any person to become a member of any unlawful assembly will make the person liable for prosecution as a member of an unlawful assembly (Section 150).

Common object is broader than common intention, but mere presence does not lead to a presumption of common object. It has to be proved by the prosecution. This is generally proved by any overt act of the person, in his doing or omitting to do something, and making a distinction between leaders and followers. A sudden fight would not make every person liable. Participation in an unlawful assembly is punishable under Section143 with imprisonment upto six months or fine or both. Joining or continuing in an unlawful assembly knowing that it has been commanded in the manner prescribed by law to disperse is punishable with imprisonment upto two years or fine or both (Section 145). Knowingly joining or continuing in any assembly of five or more persons likely to cause a disturbance of the public peace, after it has been lawfully commanded to disperse, is punishable with imprisonment upto six months or fine or both. Joining an unlawful assembly being armed with deadly weapon or with anything which, is used as a weapon of offence, or is likely to cause death, is punishable with imprisonment upto two years or fine or with both

(Section 144). When an unlawful assembly or its member in persuasion of the common object uses force or violence, every member is guilty of rioting which is punishable with imprisonment upto two years or fine or both (Sections 146 and 147). Rioting with a deadly weapon is punishable with imprisonment upto three years or fine or both (Section 148).

These provisions apart from being substantive sections, can also be read along with other provisions for offences committed in furtherance of the common object. When a murder is committed by a member of the unlawful assembly in furtherance of a common object, then if the members of the unlawful assembly knew that the offence of murder was likely to be committed in persuasion of the common object and if death had been caused in persuasion of common object then every member of the unlawful assembly would be liable for offence of murder. These offences provide for vicarious liability for the acts of a mob on the members of the mob. The member of a mob cannot take a defence that a particular offence was not committed by him if it was committed by another member in pursuance of the common object of the mob. There is no need to prove common intention to commit the offence or any act which results in the abetment of the offence and hence is broader in its scope. In Mizaji and Anr. v. The State of U.P.[306], the Supreme Court explained the meaning and scope of the section when it stated that " The first part of Section 149 IPC means that the offence committed in persuasion of the common object must be one which is committed with a view to accomplish the common object. It is not necessary that there should be a preconcert in the sense of a meeting of the members of the unlawful assembly as to the common object; it is enough if it is adopted by all the members and is shared by all of them. In order that the case may fall under the first part, the offence committed must be connected immediately with the common object of the unlawful assembly of which the accused were members. Even if the offence committed is not in direct persuasion of the common object of the assembly, it may yet fall under Section 149 if it can be held that the offence was such as the members knew was likely to be committed. The expression 'know' does not mean a mere possibility, such as might or might not happen.... For instance, it is a matter of common knowledge that when in a village a body of heavily armed men set out to take a woman by force, someone is likely to be killed and all the members of the unlawful assembly must be aware of that likelihood and would be guilty under the second part of Section 149. Similarly, if a body of persons go armed to take forcible possession of the land, it would be equally right to say that they have the knowledge that murder is likely to be committed if the circumstances as to the weapons carried and other conduct of the members of the unlawful assembly clearly point to such knowledge on the part of them all" In Triloki Nath and Ors. v. State of U.P.[307], the Supreme Court opined that for the purpose of attracting Section

306 (1959) Supp. 1 SCR 940
307 (2005)13SCC323

149 of the IPC, it is not necessary that there should be a pre-concert by way of a meeting of the persons of the unlawful assembly as to the common object. If a common object is adopted by all the persons and shared by them, it would serve the purpose. The common object may be commission of one offence while there may be likelihood of commission of yet another offence, the knowledge whereof is capable of being safely attributable to the members of the unlawful assembly. Whether a member of such unlawful assembly was aware as regard to likelihood of commission of another offence or not would depend upon the facts and circumstances of each case. Background of the incident, the motive, the nature of the assembly, the nature of the arms carried by the members of the assembly, their common object and the behaviour of the members soon before, at or after the actual commission of the crime would be relevant factors for drawing an inference in that behalf.[308] Common object differs from common intention as no prior concert is required. Common object can be formed at the spur of the moment. Course of conduct adopted by the members of the assembly, however, is a relevant factor. At what point of time the common object of the unlawful assembly was formed would depend upon the facts and circumstances of each case.[309] It would be enough that the members of the assembly which constitutes five or more persons, have common object and that they acted as an assembly to achieve that object. In substance, Section 149 makes every member of the common unlawful assembly responsible as a member for the act of each and all merely because he is a member of the unlawful assembly with common object to be achieved by such an unlawful assembly. At the same time, one has to keep in mind that mere presence in the unlawful assembly cannot render a person liable unless there was a common object and that is shared by that person. The common object has to be found and can be gathered from the facts and circumstances of each case.[310] In Parsuram Pandey and Ors. v. State of Bihar[311], the Supreme Court held that to attract Section 149 IPC the prosecution must prove that the commission of the offence was by any member of an unlawful assembly and such offence must have been committed in persuasion of the common object of the assembly or must be such that the members of the assembly knew that it was likely to be committed. Unless these three elements are satisfied by the prosecution the accused cannot be convicted with the aid of Section 149 IPC.

Assaulting or obstructing public servant when suppressing a riot, affray (two or more persons fight in a public place and disturb public peace -- Section 159) or unlawful assembly is punishable with imprisonment upto three years or fine or both (Section 152). Wantonly or malignantly giving provocation with intent to cause riot, is punishable with imprisonment upto one year or fine or both

308 Munivel vs State of Tamil Nadu (2006)9SCC394
309 Munna Chanda vs State of Assam (2006)3SCC752
310 Rabindra Mahto and Ors. v. State of Jharkhand JT 2006 (1) SC 137; Mohinder Singh vs State of Punjab (2006)10SCC418
311 (2004) 13 SCC 189

if the riot is committed and if it is not committed, it will be punishable with imprisonment upto six months or fine or both (Section 153).

Promoting enmity or feelings of disharmony, hatred or ill will between different groups on ground of religion, race, place of birth, residence, language, caste or community or any other ground whatsoever, or doing anything which is prejudicial to the maintenance of harmony between different religious, racial, language or regional groups or castes or communities and which disturbs or is likely to disturb the public tranquility, or training or organising the training of persons for use of criminal force or violence against any group and to cause fear or alarm or a feeling of insecurity amongst the members of any group shall be punished with imprisonment upto three years or fine or both. If such offence is committed in a place of worship, it shall be punishable with imprisonment that may extend to five years and fine (Section 153A).

Section 153B makes imputations that any class of persons cannot, by reason of their being members of any religious, racial, language or regional group or caste or community, bear true faith and allegiance to the Constitution of India or uphold the sovereignty and integrity of India, or propagating that they should be deprived or denied of their rights as citizens of India, or causing disharmony or feelings of enmity or hatred or ill will between classes, punishable with imprisonment upto three years and fine and if such offence is committed in a place of worship, it would be punishable with imprisonment upto five years and fine. The latter two provisions have been inserted in 1969 in order to deal with communal riots and to maintain the secular character of the country. The right to peaceful demonstration is a fundamental right guaranteed by Article 19(1(d) of the Constitution. The use of these provisions against assemblies engaged in morally legitimate civil disobedience harks back to the days of the British Raj and continues to be misused to date. And these provisions prove to be inadequate in dealing with the growing communal forces.

The Executive Magistrate is empowered to command any unlawful assembly or any assembly of five or more persons likely to cause a disturbance of the public peace to disperse, and if the assembly desists from dispersing, do so by force and if it is necessary to do so for the public security, use the armed forces to do so. (Sections 129 to 132 of the CrPC).

In urgent cases of nuisance or apprehended danger, where there is sufficient ground for making an order of immediate prevention or speedy remedy is desirable, the Magistrate may proceed under Section 144 and direct any person to abstain from a certain act or to take certain order with respect to certain property in his possession or under his management, if such Magistrate considers that such direction is likely to prevent or tends to prevent obstruction, annoyance or injury to any person lawfully employed or danger to human life, health or safety or a disturbance of the public tranquillity or a riot or an affray. An order under this section may be passed ex parte in cases of emergency or in cases where the circumstances do not admit of the serving in due time of a notice upon the respondent. This order may further be directed to an individual or to persons residing in a particular area or to the public in general and shall remain in force for a period not exceeding two months. Provided that if the State Government considers it necessary to do so for preventing danger to human life, health or safety or for preventing a riot or any affray, it may by notification, direct that the order remain in force for a period upto six months. The order under Section 144 can be rescinded or altered by the Magistrate or the State Government on its own motion or on the application of any person aggrieved by the same. If the application of the respondent to rescind or alter the order is rejected, after giving him adequate opportunity to be heard, the Magistrate or the State Government should record its reasons for doing so in writing.

An order under Section 144 is in the nature of an emergency proceeding. Being an administrative order, it is amenable to writ jurisdiction. An order under Section 144 is of an extraordinary character and can only be passed in serious and urgent cases when the Magistrate is satisfied that there are sufficient grounds for proceeding under the section and immediate prevention or speedy remedy is desirable to prevent the occurrences specified in the Section. A Magistrate is not entitled to issue a drastic order in wide terms without any prima facie evidence or even calling for a police report. An order that practically has the effect of a mandatory injunction in favour of one of the parties is neither justified nor warranted.[312] However a reasonable apprehension of breach of peace is enough and no overt act is necessary to justify the promulgation of the arrest. Vagueness or generality or excess of jurisdiction does not vitiate an order.[313] The disobedience of the order can be punished under Section 188 of the IPC only when the disobedience causes or tends to cause obstruction, annoyance or injury or risk of obstruction, annoyance or injury to any person lawfully employed, or danger to human life, health or safety or a riot or an affray.[314]

Code of Criminal Procedure (Amendment) Act, 2005 inserted Section 144A which gives the District Magistrate the power to prohibit carrying arms in procession or mass drill or mass training with arms. The Section states that the District Magistrate may, whenever he considers it necessary so to do for the preservation of public peace or public safety or for the maintenance of public order, by public

312 AIR 1951 Mys 17
313 1971 SC (Crl.) 36; 1971 SC (Crl.) 45
314 AIR 1956 All. 481

notice or by order, prohibit in any area within the local limits of his jurisdiction, the carrying of arms (which word shall have the same meaning as given in section 153AA of the Indian Penal Code) in any procession or the organising or holding of, or taking part in, any mass drill or mass training with arms in any public place. This public notice or order may be directed to a particular person or to persons belonging to any community, party or organisation and shall remain in force for not more than three months from the date when issued or made. However the State Government may if it considers necessary so to do for the preservation of public peace or public safety or for the maintenance of public order, direct by way of notification that a public notice issued or order made by the District Magistrate under this section shall remain in force for such further period not exceeding six months from the date on which such public notice or order was issued or made by the District Magistrate would have, but for such direction, expired, as it may specify in the said notification. This power may be delegated to the District Magistrate by the State Government, subject to such control and directions as it may deem fit to impose, by general or special order.

Removal of Public Nuisances

Under Section 133 of the CrPC, whenever a District Magistrate or a Sub-Divisional Magistrate or any Executive Magistrate who is specially empowered to do so, receives information from anyone including a police report, and on taking evidence (if any) considers that a conditional order ought to be made against a person so that:

a) Any unlawful obstruction or nuisance should be removed from any public place or from any way, river or channel which is or may be lawfully used by the public; or

b) The conduct of any trade or occupation, of the keeping of any goods or merchandise, is injurious to the health or physical comfort or the community, and that in consequence such trade or occupation should be prohibited or regulated or such goods or merchandise should be removed or the keeping thereof regulated; or

c) The construction of any building or the disposal of any substance as is likely to occasion conflagration or explosion should be stopped; or

d) Any building, tent or structure, or any tree is in such a condition that it is likely to fall and thereby cause injury to persons living or carrying on business in the neighbourhood or passing by, and that in consequence the removal, repair or support of such building, tent or structure or the removal or support of such tree is necessary; or

e) Any tank, well or excavation adjacent to any such way or public place should be fenced in such manner as to prevent danger arising to the public; or

f) Any dangerous animal should be destroyed, confined or otherwise disposed of.

The public place would include property belonging to the State, camping grounds and grounds left unoccupied for sanitary or recreational purposes. Chapter XIV of the IPC deals with offences affecting the public health, safety, convenience, decency and morals. Section 268 defines public nuisance as any act or illegal omission which causes any common injury, danger or annoyance to the public or to the people in general who dwell or occupy property in the vicinity or which must necessarily cause injury, obstruction, danger or annoyance to persons who may have occasion to use any public right. A common nuisance is not excused on the ground that it causes some convenience. The chapter makes it an offence to do any act negligently or malignantly to spread infection of disease dangerous to life (Sections 269 and 270), disobedience to quarantine rule (Section 271), adulteration of food or drink intended for sale or of drugs and their sale (Sections 272 to 275), fouling water of public spring or reservoir (Section 277), making atmosphere noxious to health (Section 278), negligent conduct with respect to poisonous substance, fire or combustible matter, explosive substance, machinery, pulling down or repairing building and animals (Sections 284 to 289) and all forms of public nuisance (Section 290).

Despite the provisions in the IPC, most of which are cognizable, the CrPC contains certain summary remedies for maintenance of public order and tranquillity, not with the purpose of punishing the wrongdoer, but for protection of life and prevention of nuisance. These remedies are almost in the nature of civil remedies though performed by the Executive armed with the powers under the CrPC the Supreme Court, in Ratlam Municipality case[315] held that action under Section 133 could be taken against the Municipal authorities to abate the nuisance caused by open drains and lack of public lavatories on the application of the citizens.

The Magistrate may also issue an injunction directing that immediate steps be taken for the prevention of any imminent and serious danger or injury to the public and on the respondent's failure to do so, the Magistrate may himself use or cause to be used any means he thinks fit to obviate such danger or prevent such injury.

The order may fix a time limit for its compliance, and if the person objects to do so, he should show cause why the order should not be made absolute. This order shall be served on the respondent in the manner of summons and if he fails to neither comply with the same nor show cause against it, he will be liable to be punished under Section 188 of the IPC (disobedience to an order lawfully promulgated by a public servant and such disobedience causes obstruction,

315 1980 Cri.L.J. 1075

annoyance or injury to persons lawfully employed or causes danger to human life, health, safety or tends to cause a riot or affray) and the order shall be made absolute. Upon the respondent's reply, the Magistrate shall take evidence in the matter as in a summons case, and may either drop the proceedings, or modify the order or make it absolute. The Magistrate can order local inspection or examination by an expert while inquiring into the matter. If the person still fails to comply with the order, the Magistrate may cause it to be performed and may recover the costs by the sale of any movable or immovable property of the respondent. The Magistrate may also make an order prohibiting repetition or continuance of the public nuisance (Sections 133 to 143).

The Juvenile Justice (Care and Protection of Children) Act, 2000

This Act replaced the Juvenile Justice Act, 1986 and made certain changes in the definition of juveniles and in the treatment provisions, though most of the sections in the earlier Act have been retained. The introduction to the Act states that it is to provide for the care, protection, treatment, development and rehabilitation of neglected and delinquent juveniles and for the adjudication of certain matters relating to and disposition of delinquent juveniles. The introduction also states that the Act was re-enacted keeping in mind the International law provisions.

Who is a Juvenile or a Child?

The definition of a Juvenile in the Act states that a juvenile is a person below 18 years of age (Section 2(k). The Act deals with two categories of Children:

Children in Need of Care and Protection

These children are those who

- Is found without any home or settled place or abode and without any ostensible means of subsistence
- Who is found begging, or who is either a street child or a working child
- Who resides with a person (whether a guardian of the child or not) who has threatened to kill or injure the child and there is reasonable likelihood of the threat being carried out or has killed, abused or neglected some other child or children and there is reasonable likelihood of this child also being killed, abused or neglected
- Who is mentally or physically challenged, ill or suffering from terminal or incurable diseases having no one to support or look after
- Who has a parent or guardian who is unfit or incapacitated to exercise control over the child

- Who does not have parent and there is no one to look after him or whose parents have abandoned him or who is missing and run away child and whose parents cannot be found after reasonable inquiry
- Who is being or is likely to be grossly abused, tortured or exploited for the purpose of sexual abuse or illegal acts
- Who is found vulnerable and is likely to be inducted into drug abuse or trafficking
- Who is being or is likely to be abused for unconscionable gains
- Who is victim of any armed conflict, civil commotion or natural calamity

These cases are referred to the **Child Welfare Committee** that should be set up in each District and should have four members of whom at least one should be a woman and one an expert on matters concerning children (Section 29). Cases before the committee can be referred by the child herself, a social worker or public spirited citizen authorized by the State Government, a registered voluntary organisation recognised by the State Government, any public servant or the Police (Section 32). The Committee can make any order for the care, protection, treatment, development and rehabilitation of the child as well as to provide for their basic needs and protection of human rights. If the Committee is of the opinion that the child has no family or ostensible support, it may allow the child to remain in the Children's Home or shelter home till suitable rehabilitation is found for him or till he attains 18 years of age (Section 33). Restoration of and protection to a child shall be the prime objective of any children's home or the shelter home. The Committee shall have the powers to restore any child in need of care and protection to his parent, including natural, adopted or foster parents, guardian, fit person or fit institution (Section 39).

Juvenile in Conflict with the Law

This means a juvenile who is alleged to have committed an offence and has not completed eighteenth year of age as on the date of commission of such offence. In all pending cases including trial, revision, appeal or any other criminal proceedings in respect of a juvenile in conflict with law, in any court, the determination of juvenility of such a juvenile shall be his age at the time of commission of alleged offence, even if the juvenile ceases to be so on or before the date of commencement of this Act and the provisions of this Act shall apply as if the said provisions had been in force (Section 20).[316] These cases are dealt with by the Juvenile Justice Board that has to be set up in every district with a

316 The amendment to the Act was introduced by the Juvenile Justice (Care and Protection of Children) Amendment Act, 2006.But this principle regarding age for consideration of juvenility being the date of offence was decided by the Constitutional Bench of the Supreme Court in Pratap Singh vs State of Jharkhand, AIR 2005 SC 2731

Metropolitan Magistrate or a Judicial Magistrate of the First Class and two social workers of which at least one must be a woman forming a Bench (Section 4). No juvenile should be tried by any other court or be kept in police or jail custody but must be kept in an Observation Home set up by or with the permission of the State Government for their temporary reception (Section 8). As soon as a juvenile in conflict with law is apprehended by police, he shall be placed under the charge of the special juvenile police unit or the designated police officer, who shall produce the juvenile before the Board without any loss of time but within a period of twenty-four hours of his apprehension excluding the time necessary for the journey, from the place where the juvenile was apprehended, to the Board. In no case should the juvenile be placed in a police lockup or lodged in a jail. If convicted, the children cannot be incarcerated in a jail but only in a Special Home set up under the Act for the re-socialisation of the child (Section 9). The orders that can be passed with regard to the Juvenile by the Board under Section 15 are:

- Go home after advice or admonition following appropriate inquiry against and counseling to the parent or guardian and the Juvenile
- Direct that the Juvenile participate in group counseling or similar activities
- Performance of community service
- Fine to be paid by parent or guardian or if the Juvenile is over 14 and earning himself
- Probation of good conduct under the care of any parent, guardian or other fit person on their executing a bond with or without surety as the Board may require for the good behavior and well-being of the juvenile for any period not exceeding three years
- Probation of good conduct and placed under care of a fit institution for the good behavior and well-being of the juvenile for any period not exceeding 3 years
- Sent to a Special Home for a period not exceeding three years or less if the Board is so satisfied.

Provided that where a juvenile over 16 years of age has committed an offence and the Board is satisfied that the offence committed is so serious in nature or that his conduct and behaviour have been such that it would not be in his interest or in the interest of other juvenile in a special home to send him to such special home and that none of the other measures provided under this Act is suitable or sufficient, the Board may order the juvenile in conflict with law to be kept in such place of safety and in such manner as it thinks fit and shall report the case for the order of the State Government. State Government may make such arrangement in respect of the juvenile as it deems proper and may order such juvenile to be kept under protective custody at such place and on such conditions as it thinks fit. Provided that the period of detention so ordered shall not exceed in any case the maximum period provided under section 15 of this Act. No juvenile shall be sentenced to death or imprisonment for any term which may extend to imprisonment for life, or committed to prison in default of payment of fine or in default of furnishing security (Section 16).

No appeal lies in case of an acquittal. special units of juvenile police are to be set up in each district to handle cases of juveniles. There shall be no joint proceeding of a juvenile and a co-accused who is not a juvenile (Section 18) and there shall be no disqualification attached to the juvenile by virtue of the conviction (Section 19) and the juvenile's name shall not be published so as to lead to his identification and such disclosure shall be punishable under Section 21 (2) with fine upto Rs. 25000.

Whenever a claim of juvenility is raised before any court or a court is of the opinion that an accused person was a juvenile on the date of commission of the offence, the court shall make an inquiry, take such evidence as may be necessary (but not an affidavit) so as to determine the age of such person, and shall record a finding whether the person is a juvenile or a child or not, stating his age as nearly as may be. Provided that a claim of juvenility may be raised before any court and it shall be recognised at any stage, even after final disposal of the case, and such claim shall be determined in terms of the provisions contained in this Act and the rules made thereunder, even if the juvenile has ceased to be so on or before the date of commencement of this Act. If the court finds a person to be a juvenile on the date of commission of the offence, it shall forward the juvenile to the Board for passing appropriate order, and the sentence if any, passed by a court shall be deemed to have no effect (Section 7A).

The State Government or the local authority shall direct that a juvenile in conflict with law who is undergoing any sentence of imprisonment at the commencement of this Act, shall, in lieu of undergoing such sentence, be sent to a special home or be kept in fit institution in such manner as the State Government or the local authority thinks fit for the remainder of the period of the sentence; and the provisions of this Act shall apply to the juvenile as if he had been ordered by the Board to be sent to such special home or institution or, as the case may be, ordered to be kept under protective care under Section 16 of this Act. Provided that the State Government, or the Board, may, for any adequate and special reason to be recorded in writing, review the case of a juvenile in conflict with law undergoing a sentence of imprisonment, who has ceased to be so on or before the commencement of this Act, and pass appropriate order in the interest of such juvenile. In all cases where a juvenile in conflict with law is undergoing a sentence of imprisonment at any stage on the date of commencement of this Act, his case including the issue of juvenility, shall be deemed to be decided in terms of this Act irrespective of the fact that he ceases to be a juvenile on or before such date and accordingly he shall be sent to the special home or a fit institution for the remainder of the period of the sentence and such sentence shall not in any case exceed the maximum period provided in section 15 of this Act (Section 64).

Offences Under the Act

- Cruelty to a juvenile -- assault, abandon, expose or willfully neglect child under custody or causing the same to be done in a manner which is likely to cause the child unnecessary mental or physical suffering punishable with six months or fine or both (Section 23)
- Employment of juvenile for begging punishable with three years and fine (Section 24)
- Giving intoxicating liquor or narcotic drug or psychiatric substance to juvenile or child punishable with three years and fine (Section 25)
- Exploitation of juvenile employee by procuring him for purposes of hazardous employment keeps him in bondage and withholds his earnings or uses such earning for his own purposes punishable with three years and fine (Section 26)

All the offences are cognizable.

Rehabilitation and Social Reintegration

The methods of achieving this listed in Chapter IV of the Act are

- Restoration to parents, adopted parents, foster parents, guardian, fit person or fit institution
- Adoption where the child is orphaned, abandoned, or surrendered through such mechanism as may be prescribed. The Act permits the court to give child for adoption to a person irrespective of marital status; or to parents to adopt a child of same sex irrespective of the number of living biological sons or daughters; or to childless couples.
- Foster care as a temporary placement of infants who are ultimately to be given for adoption
- Sponsorship to provide supplementary support to families, children's homes, special homes to meet the nutritional, medical, educational and

other needs of the children with a view to improving their quality of life

- After care organisations to take care of juveniles after they leave children's homes and special homes to enable them to lead industrious, honest and useful life

Every State Government shall constitute a Child Protection Unit for the State and, such Units for every District, consisting of such officers and other employees as may be appointed by that Government, to take up matters relating to children in need of care and protection and juveniles in conflict with law with a view to ensure the implementation of this Act including the establishment and maintenance of homes, notification of competent authorities in relation to these children and their rehabilitation and co-ordination with various official and non-official agencies concerned (Section 62A).

The Probation of Offenders Act, 1958

Probation is release of an offender under condition of good conduct instead of serving of the sentence after conviction in a case. The Act specifies the cases of such release on probation:

Section 3: Persons found guilty of offences punishable under Sections 379, 380 and 381 (Theft), 404 (Dishonest misappropriation of property), 420 (cheating) or any offence punishable with imprisonment upto two years or with fine or with both under the IPC or any other law, and no previous conviction has been proved against him and the convicting court is of the opinion that having regard to the circumstances of the case including the nature of the offences and the character of the offender, it is expedient to do so may release him on probation of good conduct after due admonition.

Section 4: Persons found guilty of offences not punishable with life imprisonment or death, and when the convicting court is of the opinion that having regard to the circumstances of the case including the nature of the offences and the character of the offender, it is expedient to release him on probation of good conduct, it may direct that he be released on his entering into a bond, with or without sureties, to appear and receive sentence when called upon during such period not exceeding three years. The Court may have conditions imposed such as residence, abstention from intoxicants or any other matter as the court may, having regard to the particular circumstances of the case consider fit to impose for preventing a repetition of the same offence or a commission of other offences by the offender. The Court should explain the terms of the order to the offender. The Court may in addition pass an order of supervision by a Probation Officer for a period not below one year to be specified in the order with such conditions as it may deem necessary. Copy of the supervision order should be given to the person released, his surety and the Probation Officer.

The offender or his surety should have a fixed place of abode or regular occupation in the area under the jurisdiction of the convicting court or where he is likely to live.

The Court should take into consideration the Probation Officer's report before passing any such order.

Section 6: A person below 21 years of age convicted of an offence punishable with imprisonment but not life imprisonment shall be released under Section 3 or 4 unless the convicting court is of the opinion that having regard to the circumstances of the case including the nature of the offences and the character of the offender, it would not be desirable that he be so released, the court should upon considering the report of the Probation Officer and any other information available to it relating to the character and physical and mental condition of the offender, pass an order of imprisonment and record its reasons for doing so.

Under **Section 5**, the Court may while releasing the offender impose costs or compensation to the victim on him

- The report of the Probation Officer is a confidential document but the Court if it considers it fit, may communicate the substance thereof to the offender and may give him an opportunity to produce relevant evidence.
- The order of release on probation may be varied in the interests of the offender and the public, and the period may be extended or diminished upto three years or any of the conditions may be altered or additional conditions may be imposed after hearing the offender and the surety, if any. If the surety refuses the variation, the offender may be required to furnish a new surety, and if he fails or refuses to do so, the Court may sentence him for the offence for which he was convicted.
- If the Court upon receiving the report of the Probation Officer considers that the conduct of the offender has been such that it is no longer necessary to keep him under supervision, discharge the bond entered into by him.
- Failure to follow the conditions, will lead to the arrest of the offender and the convicting court may either impose the sentence on him or where the failure is for the first time, then, without prejudice to the continuance in force of the bond, impose upon him a penalty not exceeding Rs 50

- All orders under the Act or a failure to pass the order of release on probation are appealable.

Who is a Probation Officer and What Are His Duties

A Probation Officer is a person either appointed or recognised as one by the State Government, or by a society recognised in this behalf by the State Government or in any exceptional case, any other person who in the opinion of the court is fit to act as a probation officer in the special circumstances of the case. A Probation Officer is a public servant.

The duties of the Probation Officer are:

- Inquire into the circumstances or home surroundings of the accused in accordance with the directions of the court in order to assist it in determining the most suitable method of dealing with him and submit reports to the Court
- Supervise probationers and other persons placed under his supervision and where necessary, try and find them suitable employment
- Advise and assist offenders in the payment of compensation or costs ordered by the court
- Assist and advise in such cases and in the manner prescribed those released under Section 4
- Perform such other duties as may be prescribed.

The Bombay High Court has held that whenever the accused is entitled to be released on probation, the Court should grant it except for reasons to be recorded in writing. Despite this large numbers of people remain in custody for petty offences for which they are entitled to probation. This is partly due to the delays in the trial of offences. People remain in custody sometimes for periods longer than they would spend if convicted due to their inability to avail bail and to engage a lawyer. Though legal aid is a fundamental right, generally lawyers are appointed when the case comes up for trial. In many cases, the accused prefer to plead guilty and avail of the set off provided under law. Probation is used sparingly and the infrastructure is inadequate in providing it to the large numbers who would be entitled to it.

APPENDIX 1

UNITED NATIONS STANDARD MINIMUM RULES FOR THE TREATMENT OF PRISONERS

Adopted August 30, 1955, by the First United Nations Congress on the Prevention of Crime and the Treatment of Offenders, UN Doc. A/CONF/611, annex I, E.S.C. res. 663C, 24 UN ESCOR Supp. (No. 1) at 11, UN Doc. E/3048 (1957), amended E.S.C. res. 2076, 62 UN ESCOR Supp. (No. 1) at 35, UN Doc. E/5988 (1977).

Preliminary Observations

1. The following rules are not intended to describe in detail a model system of penal institutions. They seek only, on the basis of the general consensus of contemporary thought and the essential elements of the most adequate systems of today, to set out what is generally accepted as being good principle and practice in the treatment of prisoners and the management of institutions.

2. In view of the great variety of legal, social, economic and geographical conditions of the world, it is evident that not all of the rules are capable of application in all places and at all times. They should, however, serve to stimulate a constant endeavour to overcome practical difficulties in the way of their application, in the knowledge that they represent, as a whole, the minimum conditions, which are accepted as suitable by the United Nations.

3. On the other hand, the rules cover a field in which thought is constantly developing. They are not intended to preclude experiment and practices, provided these are in harmony with the principles and seek to further the purposes which derive from the text of the rules as a whole. It will always be justifiable for the central prison administration to authorize departures from the rules in this spirit.

4. **(1) Part I** of the rules covers the general management of institutions, and is applicable to all categories of prisoners, criminal or civil, untried or convicted, including prisoners subject to security measures or corrective measures ordered by the judge.

   Part II contains rules applicable only to the special categories dealt with in each section. Nevertheless, the rules under section A, applicable to prisoners under sentence, shall be equally applicable to categories of prisoners dealt with in sections B, C and D, provided they do not conflict with the rules governing those categories and are for their benefit.

Information to and Complaints by Prisoners

35. (1) Every prisoner on admission shall be provided with written information about the regulations governing the treatment of prisoners of his category, the disciplinary requirements of the institution, the authorized methods of seeking information and making complaints, and all such other matters as are necessary to enable him to understand both his rights and his obligations and to adapt himself to the life of the institution.

(2) If a prisoner is illiterate, the aforesaid information shall be conveyed to him orally.

36. (1) Every prisoner shall have the opportunity each weekday of making requests or complaints to the director of the institution or the officer authorized to represent him.

(2) It shall be possible to make requests or complaints to the inspector of prisons during his inspection. The prisoner shall have the opportunity to talk to the inspector or to any other inspecting officer without the director or other members of the staff being present.

(3) Every prisoner shall be allowed to make a request or complaint, without censorship as to substance but in proper form, to the central prison administration, the judicial authority or other proper authorities through approved channels.

(4) Unless it is evidently frivolous or groundless, every request or complaint shall be promptly dealt with and replied to without undue delay.

Contact with the Outside World

37. Prisoners shall be allowed under necessary supervision to communicate with their family and reputable friends at regular intervals, both by correspondence and by receiving visits.

38. (1) Prisoners who are foreign nationals shall be allowed reasonable facilities to communicate with the diplomatic and consular representatives of the State to which they belong.

(2) Prisoners who are nationals of States without diplomatic or consular representation in the country and refugees or stateless persons shall be allowed similar facilities to communicate with the diplomatic representative of the State which takes charge of their interests or any national or international authority whose task it is to protect such persons.

39. Prisoners shall be kept informed regularly of the more important items of news by the reading of newspapers, periodicals or special institutional

publications, by hearing wireless transmissions, by lectures or by any similar means as authorized or controlled by the administration.

Books

40. Every institution shall have a library for the use of all categories of prisoners, adequately stocked with both recreational and instructional books, and prisoners shall be encouraged to make full use of it.

Religion

41. (1) If the institution contains a sufficient number of prisoners of the same religion, a qualified representative of that religion shall be appointed or approved. If the number of prisoners justifies it and conditions permit, the arrangement should be on a full-time basis.

(2) A qualified representative appointed or approved under paragraph (1) shall be allowed to hold regular services and to pay pastoral visits in private to prisoners of his religion at proper times.

(3) Access to a qualified representative of any religion shall not be refused to any prisoner. On the other hand, if any prisoner should object to a visit of any religious representative, his attitude shall be fully respected.

42. So far as practicable, every prisoner shall be allowed to satisfy the needs of his religious life by attending the services provided in the institution and having in his possession the books of religious observance and instruction of his denomination.

Retention of Prisoners' Property

43. (1) All money, valuables, clothing and other effects belonging to a prisoner which under the regulations of the institution he is not allowed to retain shall on his admission to the institution be placed in safe custody. An inventory thereof shall be signed by the prisoner. Steps shall be taken to keep them in good condition.

(2) On the release of the prisoner all such articles and money shall be returned to him except in so far as he has been authorized to spend money or send any such property out of the institution, or it has been found necessary on hygienic grounds to destroy any article of clothing. The prisoner shall sign a receipt for the articles and money returned to him.

(3) Any money or effects received for a prisoner from outside shall be treated in the same way.

(4) If a prisoner brings in any drugs or medicine, the medical officer shall decide what use shall be made of them.

Notification of Death, Illness, Transfer, etc.

44. (1) Upon the death or serious illness of, or serious injury to a prisoner, or his removal to an institution for the treatment of mental affections, the director shall at once inform the spouse, if the prisoner is married, or the nearest relative and shall in any event inform any other person previously designated by the prisoner.

(2) A prisoner shall be informed at once of the death or serious illness of any near relative. In case of the critical illness of a near relative, the prisoner should be authorised, whenever circumstances allow, to go to his bedside either under escort or alone.

(3) Every prisoner shall have the right to inform at once his family of his imprisonment or his transfer to another institution.

Removal of Prisoners

45. (1) When the prisoners are being removed to or from an institution, they shall be exposed to public view as little as possible, and proper safeguards shall be adopted to protect them from insult, curiosity and publicity in any form.

(2) The transport of prisoners in conveyances with inadequate ventilation or light, or in any way, which would subject them to unnecessary physical hardship, shall be prohibited.

(3) The transport of prisoners shall be carried out at the expense of the administration and equal conditions shall obtain for all of them.

Institutional Personnel

46. (1) The prison administration, shall provide for the careful selection of every grade of the personnel, since it is on their integrity, humanity, professional capacity and personal suitability for the work that the proper administration of the institution depends.

(2) The prison administration shall constantly seek to awaken and maintain in the minds both of the personnel and of the public the conviction that this work is a social service of great importance, and to this end all appropriate means of informing the public should be used.

(3) To secure the foregoing ends, personnel shall be appointed on a full-time basis as professional prison officers and have civil service status with security of tenure subject only to good conduct, efficiency and physical fitness. Salaries shall be adequate to attract and retain suitable men and women; employment benefits and conditions of service shall be favourable in view of the exacting nature of the work.

47 (1) The personnel shall possess an adequate standard of education and intelligence.

(2) Before entering on duty, the personnel shall be given a course of training in their general and specific duties and be required to pass theoretical and practical tests.

(3) After entering on duty and during their career, the personnel shall maintain and improve their knowledge and professional capacity by attending courses of in-service training to be organized at suitable intervals.

48. All members of the personnel shall at all times so conduct themselves and perform their duties as to influence the prisoners for good by their example and to command their respect.

49. (1) So far as possible, the personnel shall include a sufficient number of specialists such as psychiatrists, psychologists, social workers, teachers and trade instructors.

(2) The services of social workers, teachers and trade instructors shall be secured on a permanent basis, without thereby excluding part-time or voluntary workers.

50. (1) The director of an institution should be adequately qualified for his task by character, administrative ability, suitable training and experience.

(2) He shall devote his entire time to his official duties and shall not be appointed on a part-time basis.

(3) He shall reside on the premises of the institution or in its immediate vicinity.

(4) When two or more institutions are under the authority of one director, he shall visit each of them at frequent intervals. A responsible resident official shall be in charge of each of these institutions.

51. (1) The director, his deputy, and the majority of the other personnel of the institution shall be able to speak the language of the greatest number of prisoners, or a language understood by the greatest number of them.

(2) Whenever necessary, the services of an interpreter shall be used.

52. (1) In institutions, which are large enough to require the services of one or more full-time medical officers, at least one of them shall reside on the premises of the institution or in its immediate vicinity.

(2) In other institutions the medical officer shall visit daily and shall reside near enough to be able to attend without delay in cases of urgency.

53. (1) In an institution for both men and women, the part of the institution set aside for women shall be under the authority of a responsible woman officer who shall have the custody of the keys of all that part of the institution.

(2) No male member of the staff shall enter the part of the institution set aside for women unless accompanied by a woman officer.

(3) Women prisoners shall be attended and supervised only by women officers. This does not, however, preclude male members of the staff, particularly doctors and teachers, from carrying out their professional duties in institutions or parts of institutions set-aside for women.

54. (1) Officers of the institutions shall not, in their relations with the prisoners, use force except in self-defense or in cases of attempted escape, or active or passive physical resistance to an order based on law or regulations. Officers who have recourse to force must use no more than is strictly necessary and must report the incident immediately to the director of the institution.

(2) Prison officers shall be given special physical training to enable them to restrain aggressive prisoners.

(3) Except in special circumstances, staff performing duties, which bring them into direct contact with prisoners, should not be armed. Furthermore, staff should in no circumstances be provided with arms unless they have been trained in their use.

Inspection

There shall be a regular inspection of penal institutions and services by qualified and experienced inspectors appointed by a competent authority. Their task shall be in particular to ensure that these institutions are administered in accordance with existing laws and regulations and with a view to bringing about the objectives of penal and correctional.

PART II

RULES APPLICABLE TO SPECIAL CATEGORIES

A. PRISONERS UNDER SENTENCE

Guiding principles

56. The guiding principles hereafter are intended to show the spirit in which penal institutions should be administered and the purposes at which they should aim, in accordance with the declaration made under Preliminary Observation I of the present text.

57. Imprisonment and other measures, which result in cutting off an offender from the outside world, are afflictive by the very fact of taking from the person the right of self-determination by depriving him of his liberty. Therefore the prison system shall not, except as incidental to justifiable segregation or the maintenance of discipline, aggravate the suffering inherent in such a situation.

58. The purpose and justification of a sentence of imprisonment or a similar measure deprivative of liberty is ultimately to protect society against crime. This end can only be achieved if the period of imprisonment is used to ensure, so far as possible, that upon his return to society the offender is not only willing but able to lead a law-abiding and self-supporting life.

59. To this end, the institution should utilize all the remedial, educational, moral, spiritual and other forces and forms of assistance which are appropriate and available, and should seek to apply them according to the individual treatment needs of the prisoners.

60. (1) The regime of the institution should seek to minimize any differences between prison life and life at liberty which tend to lessen the responsibility of the prisoners or the respect due to their dignity as human beings.

(2) Before the completion of the sentence, it is desirable that the necessary steps be taken to ensure for the prisoner a gradual return to life in society. This aim may be achieved, depending on the case, by a pre-release regime organised in the same institution or in another appropriate institution, or by release on trial under some kind of supervision which must not be entrusted to the police but should be combined with effective social aid.

61. The treatment of prisoners should emphasize not their exclusion from the community, but their continuing part in it. Community agencies should, therefore, be enlisted wherever possible to assist the staff of the institution in the task of social rehabilitation of the prisoners. There should be in connection with every institution social workers charged with the duty of

maintaining and improving all desirable relations of a prisoner with his family and with valuable social agencies. Steps should be taken to safeguard, to the maximum extent compatible with the law and the sentence, the rights relating to civil interests, social security rights and other social benefits of prisoners.

62. The medical services of the institution shall seek to detect and shall treat any physical or mental illnesses or defects, which may hamper a prisoner's rehabilitation. All necessary medical, surgical and psychiatric services shall be provided to that end.

63. (1) The fulfilment of these principles requires individualization of treatment and for this purpose a flexible system of classifying prisoners' in-groups; it is therefore desirable that such groups should be distributed in separate institutions suitable for the treatment of each group.

(2) These institutions need not provide the same degree of security for every group. It is desirable to provide varying degrees of security according to the needs of different groups. Open institutions, by the very fact that they provide no physical security against escape but rely on the self-discipline of the inmates, provide the conditions most favourable to rehabilitation for carefully selected prisoners.

(3) It is desirable that the number of prisoners in closed institutions should not be so large that the individualization of treatment is hindered. In some countries it is considered that the population of such institutions should not exceed five hundred. In open institutions the population should be as small as possible.

(4) On the other hand, it is undesirable to maintain prisons, which are so small that proper facilities cannot be provided.

64. The duty of society does not end with a prisoner's release. There should, therefore, be governmental or private agencies capable of lending the released prisoner efficient after-care directed towards the lessening of prejudice against him and towards his social rehabilitation.

Treatment

65. The treatment of persons sentenced to imprisonment or a similar measure shall have as its purpose, so far as the length of the sentence permits, to establish in them the will to lead law-abiding and self-supporting lives after their release and to fit them to do so. The treatment shall be such as will encourage their self-respect and develop their sense of responsibility.

66. (1) To these ends, all appropriate means shall be used, including religious care in the countries where this is possible, education, vocational guidance and training, social casework, employment counselling,

physical development and strengthening of moral character, in accordance with the individual needs of each prisoner, taking account of his social and criminal history, his physical and mental capacities and aptitudes, his personal temperament, the length of his sentence and his prospects after release.

(2) For every prisoner with a sentence of suitable length, the director shall receive, as soon as possible after his admission, full reports on all the matters referred to in the foregoing paragraph. Such reports shall always include a report by a medical officer, wherever possible qualified in psychiatry, on the physical and mental condition of the prisoner.

(3) The reports and other relevant documents shall be placed in an individual file. This file shall be kept up to date and classified in such a way that it can be consulted by the responsible personnel whenever the need arises.

Classification and individualisation

67. The purposes of classification shall be:

(a) To separate from others those prisoners who, by reason of their criminal records or bad characters, are likely to exercise a bad influence;

(b) To divide the prisoners into classes in order to facilitate their treatment with a view to their social rehabilitation.

68. So far as possible separate institutions or separate sections of an institution shall be used for the treatment of the different classes of prisoners.

69. As soon as possible after admission and after a study of the personality of each prisoner with a sentence of suitable length, a programme of treatment shall be prepared for him in the light of the knowledge obtained about his individual needs, his capacities and dispositions.

Privileges

70. Systems of privileges appropriate for the different classes of prisoners and the different methods of treatment shall be established at every institution, in order to encourage good conduct, develop a sense of responsibility and secure the interest and co-operation of the prisoners in their treatment.

Work

71. (1) Prison labour must not be of an afflictive nature.

(2) All prisoners under sentence shall be required to work, subject to their physical and mental fitness as determined by the medical officer.

(3) Sufficient work of a useful nature shall be provided to keep prisoners actively employed for a normal working day.

(4) So far as possible the work provided shall be such as will maintain or increase the prisoners, ability to earn an honest living after release.

(5) Vocational training in useful trades shall be provided for prisoners able to profit thereby and especially for young prisoners.

(6) Within the limits compatible with proper vocational selection and with the requirements of institutional administration and discipline, the prisoners shall be able to choose the type of work they wish to perform.

72. (1) The organization and methods of work in the institutions shall resemble as closely as possible those of similar work outside institutions, so as to prepare prisoners for the conditions of normal occupational life.

(2) The interests of the prisoners and of their vocational training, however, must not be subordinated to the purpose of making a financial profit from an industry in the institution.

73. (1) Preferably institutional industries and farms should be operated directly by the administration and not by private contractors.

(2) Where prisoners are employed in work not controlled by the administration, they shall always be under the supervision of the institution's personnel. Unless the work is for other departments of the government the full normal wages for such work shall be paid to the administration by the persons to whom the labour is supplied, account being taken of the output of the prisoners.

74. (1) The precautions laid down to protect the safety and health of free workmen shall be equally observed in institutions.

(2) Provision shall be made to indemnify prisoners against industrial injury, including occupational disease, on terms not less favourable than those extended by law to free workmen.

75. (1) The maximum daily and weekly working hours of the prisoners shall be fixed by law or by administrative regulation, taking into account local rules or custom in regard to the employment of free workmen.

(2) The hours so fixed shall leave one rest day a week and sufficient time for education and other activities required as part of the treatment and rehabilitation of the prisoners.

76. (1) There shall be a system of equitable remuneration of the work of prisoners.

(2) Under the system prisoners shall be allowed to spend at least a part of their earnings on approved articles for their own use and to send a part of their earnings to their family.

(3) The system should also provide that a part of the earnings should be set aside by the administration so as to constitute a savings fund to be handed over to the prisoner on his release.

Education and recreation

77. (1) Provision shall be made for the further education of all prisoners capable of profiting thereby, including religious instruction in the countries where this is possible. The education of illiterates and young prisoners shall be compulsory and special attention shall be paid to it by the administration.

(2) So far as practicable, the education of prisoners shall be integrated with the educational system of the country so that after their release they may continue their education without difficulty.

78. Recreational and cultural activities shall be provided in all institutions for the benefit of the mental and physical health of prisoners.

Social relations and after-care

79. Special attention shall be paid to the maintenance and improvement of such relations between a prisoner and his family as are desirable in the best interests of both.

80. From the beginning of a prisoner's sentence consideration shall be given to his future after release and he shall be encouraged and assisted to maintain or establish such relations with persons or agencies outside the institution as may promote the best interests of his family and his own social rehabilitation.

81. (1) Services and agencies, governmental or otherwise, which assist released prisoners to re-establish themselves in society shall ensure, so far as is possible and necessary, that released prisoners be provided with appropriate documents and identification papers, have suitable homes and work to go to, are suitably and adequately clothed having regard to the climate and season, and have sufficient means to reach their destination and maintain themselves in the period immediately following their release.

(2) The approved representatives of such agencies shall have all necessary access to the institution and to prisoners and shall be taken into consultation as to the future of a prisoner from the beginning of his sentence.

It is desirable that the activities of such agencies shall be centralized or co-ordinated as far as possible in order to secure the best use of their efforts.

B. INSANE AND MENTALLY ABNORMAL PRISONERS

82. (1) Persons who are found to be insane shall not be detained in prisons and arrangements shall be made to remove them to mental institutions as soon as possible.

(2) Prisoners who suffer from other mental diseases or abnormalities shall be observed and treated in specialized institutions under medical management.

(3) During their stay in a prison, such prisoners shall be placed under the special supervision of a medical officer.

(4) The medical or psychiatric service of the penal institutions shall provide for the psychiatric treatment of all other prisoners who are in need of such treatment.

83. It is desirable that steps should be taken, by arrangement with the appropriate agencies, to ensure if necessary the continuation of psychiatric treatment after release and the provision of social-psychiatric after-care.

C. PRISONERS UNDER ARREST OR AWAITING TRIAL

84. (1) Persons arrested or imprisoned by reason of a criminal charge against them, who are detained either in police custody or in prison custody (jail) but have not yet been tried and sentenced, will be referred to as 'untried prisoners,' hereinafter in these rules.

(2) Unconvicted prisoners are presumed to be innocent and shall be treated as such.

(3) Without prejudice to legal rules for the protection of individual liberty or prescribing the procedure to be observed in respect of untried prisoners, these prisoners shall benefit by a special regime, which is described in the following rules in its essential requirements only.

85. (1) Untried prisoners shall be kept separate from convicted prisoners.

(2) Young untried prisoners shall be kept separate from adults and shall in principle be detained in separate institutions.

86. Untried prisoners shall sleep singly in separate rooms, with the reservation of different local custom in respect of the climate.

87. Within the limits compatible with the good order of the institution, untried

prisoners may, if they so desire, have their food procured at their own expense from the outside, either through the administration or through their family or friends. Otherwise, the administration shall provide their food.

88. (1) An untried prisoner shall be allowed to wear his own clothing if it is clean and suitable.

(2) If he wears prison dress, it shall be different from that supplied to convicted prisoners.

89. An untried prisoner shall always be offered opportunity to work, but shall not be required to work. If he chooses to work, he shall be paid for it.

90. An untried prisoner shall be allowed to procure at his own expense or at the expense of a third party such books, newspapers, writing materials and other means of occupation as are compatible with the interests of the administration of justice and the security and good order of the institution.

91. An untried prisoner shall be allowed to be visited and treated by his own doctor or dentist if there is reasonable ground for his application and he is able to pay any expenses incurred.

92. An untried prisoner shall be allowed to inform immediately his family of his detention and shall be given all reasonable facilities for communicating with his family and friends, and for receiving visits from them, subject only to restrictions and supervision as are necessary in the interests of the administration of justice and of the security and good order of the institution.

93. For the purposes of his defense, an untried prisoner shall be allowed to apply for free legal aid where such aid is available, and to receive visits from his legal adviser with a view to his defense and to prepare and hand to him confidential instructions. For these purposes, he shall if he so desires be supplied with writing material. Interviews between the prisoner and his legal adviser may be within sight but not within the hearing of a police or institution official.

D. CIVIL PRISONERS

94. In countries where the law permits imprisonment for debt, or by order of a court under any other non-criminal process, persons so imprisoned shall not be subjected to any greater restriction or severity than is necessary to ensure safe custody and good order. Their treatment shall be not less favourable than that of untried prisoners, with the reservation, however, that they may possibly be required to work.

E. PERSONS ARRESTED OR DETAINED WITHOUT CHARGE

95. Without prejudice to the provisions of Article 9 of the International Covenant on Civil and Political Rights, persons arrested or imprisoned without charge shall be accorded the same protection as that accorded under part I and part II, section C. Relevant provisions of part II, section A, shall likewise be applicable where their application may be conducive to the benefit of this special group of persons in custody, provided that no measures shall be taken implying that re-education or rehabilitation is in any way appropriate to persons not convicted of any criminal offence.

APPENDIX 2

BODY OF PRINCIPLES FOR THE PROTECTION OF ALL PERSONS UNDER ANY FORM OF DETENTION OR IMPRISONMENT, 1988

Scope of the Body of Principles

These principles apply for the protection of all persons under any form of detention or imprisonment.

Use of Terms

For the purposes of the Body of Principles:

(a) "Arrest" means the act of apprehending a person for the alleged commission of an offence or by the action of an authority;

(b) "Detained person" means any person deprived of personal liberty except as a result of conviction for an offence;

(c) "Imprisoned person" means any person deprived of personal liberty as a result of conviction for an offence;

(d) "Detention" means the condition of detained persons as defined above;

(e) "Imprisonment" means the condition of imprisoned persons as defined above;

(f) The words "a judicial or other authority" means a judicial or other authority under the law whose status and tenure should afford the strongest possible guarantees of competence, impartiality and independence.

Principle 1

All persons under any form of detention or imprisonment shall be treated in a humane manner and with respect for the inherent dignity of the human person.

Principle 2

Arrest, detention or imprisonment shall only be carried out strictly in accordance with the provisions of the law and by competent officials or persons authorised for that purpose.

Principle 3

There shall be no restriction upon or derogation from any of the human rights of persons under any form of detention or imprisonment recognized or existing in any State pursuant to law, conventions, regulations or custom on the pretext that this Body of Principles does not recognize such rights or that it recognizes them to a lesser extent.

Principle 4

Any form of detention or imprisonment and all measures affecting the human rights of a person under any form of detention or imprisonment shall be ordered by, or be subject to the effective control of, a judicial or other authority.

Principle 5

1. These principles shall be applied to all persons within the territory of any given State, without distinction of any kind, such as race, colour, sex, language, religion or religious belief, political or other opinion, national, ethnic or social origin, property, birth or other status.
2. Measures applied under the law and designed solely to protect the rights and special status of women, especially pregnant women and nursing mothers, children and juveniles, aged, sick or handicapped persons shall not be deemed to be discriminatory. The need for, and the application of, such measures shall always be subject to review by a judicial or other authority.

Principle 6

No person under any form of detention or imprisonment shall be subjected to torture or to cruel, inhuman or degrading treatment or punishment.* No circumstance whatever may be invoked as a justification for torture or other cruel, inhuman or degrading treatment or punishment.

Principle 7

1. States should prohibit by law any act contrary to the rights and duties contained in these principles, make any such act subject to appropriate sanctions and conduct impartial investigations upon complaints.
2. Officials who have reason to believe that a violation of this Body of Principles has occurred or is about to occur shall report the matter to their superior authorities and, where necessary, to other appropriate authorities or organs vested with reviewing or remedial powers.

3. Any other person who has ground to believe that a violation of this Body of Principles has occurred or is about to occur shall have the right to report the matter to the superiors of the officials involved as well as to other appropriate authorities or organs vested with reviewing or remedial powers.

Principle 8

Persons in detention shall be subject to treatment appropriate to their unconvicted status. Accordingly, they shall, whenever possible, be kept separate from imprisoned persons.

Principle 9

The authorities, which arrest a person, keep him under detention or investigate the case shall exercise only the powers granted to them under the law and the exercise of these powers shall be subject to recourse to a judicial or other authority.

Principle 10

Anyone who is arrested shall be informed at the time of his arrest of the reason for his arrest and shall be promptly informed of any charges against him.

Principle 11

1. A person shall not be kept in detention without being given an effective opportunity to be heard promptly by a judicial or other authority. A detained person shall have the right to defend himself or to be assisted by counsel as prescribed by law.
2. A detained person and his counsel, if any, shall receive prompt and full communication of any order of detention, together with the reasons therefor.
3. A judicial or other authority shall be empowered to review as appropriate the continuance of detention.

Principle 12

1. There shall be duly recorded:
    a) The reasons for the arrest;
    b) The time of the arrest and the taking of the arrested person to a place of custody as well as that of his first appearance before a judicial or other authority;
    c) The identity of the law enforcement officials concerned;
    d) Precise information concerning the place of custody.

2. Such records shall be communicated to the detained person, or his counsel, if any, in the form prescribed by law.

Principle 13

Any person shall, at the moment of arrest and at the commencement of detention or imprisonment, or promptly thereafter, be provided by the authority responsible for his arrest, detention or imprisonment, respectively with information on and an explanation of his rights and how to avail himself of such rights.

Principle 14

A person who does not adequately understand or speak the language used by the authorities responsible for his arrest, detention or imprisonment is entitled to receive promptly in a language which he understands the information referred to in principle 10, principle 11, paragraph 2, principle 12, paragraph 1, and principle 13 and to have the assistance, free of charge, if necessary, of an interpreter in connection with legal proceedings subsequent to his arrest.

Principle 15

Notwithstanding the exceptions contained in principle 16, paragraph 4, and principle 18, paragraph 3, communication of the detained or imprisoned person with the outside world, and in particular his family or counsel, shall not be denied for more than a matter of days.

Principle 16

1. Promptly after arrest and after each transfer from one place of detention or imprisonment to another, a detained or imprisoned person shall be entitled to notify or to require the competent authority to notify members of his family or other appropriate persons of his choice of his arrest, detention or imprisonment or of the transfer and of the place where he is kept in custody.
2. If a detained or imprisoned person is a foreigner, he shall also be promptly informed of his right to communicate by appropriate means with a consular post or the diplomatic mission of the State of which he is a national or which is otherwise entitled to receive such communication in accordance with international law or with the representative of the competent international organisation, if he is a refugee or is otherwise under the protection of an intergovernmental organisation.

3. If a detained or imprisoned person is a juvenile or is incapable of understanding his entitlement, the competent authority shall on its own initiative undertake the notification referred to in the present principle. Special attention shall be given to notifying parents or guardians.
4. Any notification referred to in the present principle shall be made or permitted to be made without delay. The competent authority may however delay a notification for a reasonable period where exceptional needs of the investigation so require.

Principle 17

1. A detained person shall be entitled to have the assistance of a legal counsel. He shall be informed of his right by the competent authority promptly after arrest and shall be provided with reasonable facilities for exercising it.
2. If a detained person does not have a legal counsel of his own choice, he shall be entitled to have a legal counsel assigned to him by a judicial or other authority in all cases where the interests of justice so require and without payment by him if he does not have sufficient means to pay.

Principle 18

1. A detained or imprisoned person shall be entitled to communicate and consult with his legal counsel.
2. A detained or imprisoned person shall be allowed adequate time and facilities for consultation with his legal counsel.
3. The right of a detained or imprisoned person to be visited by and to consult and communicate, without delay or censorship and in full confidentiality, with his legal counsel may not be suspended or restricted save in exceptional circumstances, to be specified by law or lawful regulations, when it is considered indispensable by a judicial or other authority in order to maintain security and good order.
4. Interviews between a detained or imprisoned person and his legal counsel may be within sight, but not within the hearing, of a law enforcement official.
5. Communications between a detained or imprisoned person and his legal counsel mentioned in the present principle shall be inadmissible as evidence against the detained or imprisoned person unless they are connected with a continuing or contemplated crime.

Principle 19

A detained or imprisoned person shall have the right to be visited by and to correspond with, in particular, members of his family and shall be given adequate opportunity to communicate with the outside world, subject to reasonable conditions and restrictions as specified by law or lawful regulations.

Principle 20

If a detained or imprisoned person so requests, he shall if possible be kept in a place of detention or imprisonment reasonably near his usual place of residence.

Principle 21

1. It shall be prohibited to take undue advantage of the situation of a detained or imprisoned person for the purpose of compelling him to confess, to incriminate himself otherwise or to testify against any other person.

2. No detained person while being interrogated shall be subject to violence, threats or methods of interrogation, which impair his capacity of decision or his judgment.

Principle 22

No detained or imprisoned person shall, even with his consent, be subjected to any medical or scientific experimentation, which may be detrimental to his health.

Principle 23

1. The duration of any interrogation of a detained or imprisoned person and of the intervals between interrogations as well as the identity of the officials who conducted the interrogations and other persons present shall be recorded and certified in such form as may be prescribed by law.

2. A detained or imprisoned person, or his counsel when provided by law, shall have access to the information described in paragraph 1 of the present principle.

Principle 24

A proper medical examination shall be offered to a detained or imprisoned person as promptly as possible after his admission to the place of detention or imprisonment, and thereafter medical care and treatment shall be provided whenever necessary. This care and treatment shall be provided free of charge.

Principle 25

A detained or imprisoned person or his counsel shall, subject only to reasonable conditions to ensure security and good order in the place of detention or imprisonment, have the right to request or petition a judicial or other authority for a second medical examination or opinion.

Principle 26

The fact that a detained or imprisoned person underwent a medical examination, the name of the physician and the results of such an examination shall be duly recorded. Access to such records shall be ensured. Modalities therefore shall be in accordance with relevant rules of domestic law.

Principle 27

Non-compliance with these principles in obtaining evidence shall be taken into account in determining the admissibility of such evidence against a detained or imprisoned person.

Principle 28

A detained or imprisoned person shall have the right to obtain within the limits of available resources, if from public sources, reasonable quantities of educational, cultural and informational material, subject to reasonable conditions to ensure security and good order in the place of detention or imprisonment.

Principle 29

1. In order to supervise the strict observance of relevant laws and regulations, places of detention shall be visited regularly by qualified and experienced persons appointed by, and responsible to, a competent authority distinct from the authority directly in charge of the administration of the place of detention or imprisonment.

2. A detained or imprisoned person shall have the right to communicate freely and in full confidentiality with the persons who visit the places of detention or imprisonment in accordance with paragraph 1 of the present principle, subject to reasonable conditions to ensure security and good order in such places.

Principle 30

1. The types of conduct of the detained or imprisoned person that constitute disciplinary offences during detention or imprisonment, the description

and duration of disciplinary punishment that may be inflicted and the authorities competent to impose such punishment shall be specified by law or lawful regulations and duly published.

2. A detained or imprisoned person shall have the right to be heard before disciplinary action is taken. He shall have the right to bring such action to higher authorities for review.

Principle 31

The appropriate authorities shall endeavour to ensure, according to domestic law, assistance when needed to dependent and, in particular, minor members of the families of detained or imprisoned persons and shall devote a particular measure of care to the appropriate custody of children left with out supervision.

Principle 32

1. A detained person or his counsel shall be entitled at any time to take proceedings according to domestic law before a judicial or other authority to challenge the lawfulness of his detention in order to obtain his release without delay, if it is unlawful.

2. The proceedings referred to in paragraph 1 of the present principle shall be simple and expeditious and at no cost for detained persons without adequate means. The detaining authority shall produce without unreasonable delay the detained person before the reviewing authority.

Principle 33

1. A detained or imprisoned person or his counsel shall have the right to make a request or complaint regarding his treatment, in particular in case of torture or other cruel, inhuman or degrading treatment, to the authorities responsible for the administration of the place of detention and to higher authorities and, when necessary, to appropriate authorities vested with reviewing or remedial powers.

2. In those cases where neither the detained or imprisoned person nor his counsel has the possibility to exercise his rights under paragraph 1 of the present principle, a member of the family of the detained or imprisoned person or any other person who has knowledge of the case may exercise such rights.

3. Confidentiality concerning the request or complaint shall be maintained if so requested by the complainant.

4. Every request or complaint shall be promptly dealt with and replied to without undue delay. If the request or complaint is rejected or, in case of inordinate delay, the complainant shall be entitled to bring it before a judicial or other authority. Neither the detained or imprisoned person nor any complainant under paragraph 1 of the present principle shall suffer prejudice for making a request or complaint.

Principle 34

Whenever the death or disappearance of a detained or imprisoned person occurs during his detention or imprisonment, an inquiry into the cause of death or disappearance shall be held by a judicial or other authority, either on its own motion or at the instance of a member of the family of such a person or any person who has knowledge of the case. When circumstances so warrant, such an inquiry shall be held on the same procedural basis whenever the death or disappearance occurs shortly after the termination of the detention or imprisonment. The findings of such inquiry or a report thereon shall be made available upon request, unless doing so would jeopardize an ongoing criminal investigation.

Principle 35

1. Damage incurred because of acts or omissions by a public official contrary to the rights contained in these principles shall be compensated according to the applicable rules or liability provided by domestic law.
2. Information required to be recorded under these principles shall be available in accordance with procedures provided by domestic law for use in claiming compensation under the present principle.

Principle 36

1. A detained person suspected of or charged with a criminal offence shall be presumed innocent and shall be treated as such until proved guilty according to law in a public trial at which he has had all the guarantees necessary for his defence.

2. The arrest or detention of such a person pending investigation and trial shall be carried out only for the purposes of the administration of justice on grounds and under conditions and procedures specified by law. The

imposition of restrictions upon such a person which are not strictly required for the purpose of the detention or to prevent hindrance to the process of investigation or the administration of justice, or for the maintenance of security and good order in the place of detention shall be forbidden.

Principle 37

A person detained on a criminal charge shall be brought before a judicial or other authority provided by law promptly after his arrest. Such authority shall decide without delay upon the lawfulness and necessity of detention. No person may be kept under detention pending investigation or trial except upon the written order of such an authority. A detained person shall, when brought before such an authority, have the right to make a statement on the treatment received by him while in custody.

Principle 38

A person detained on a criminal charge shall be entitled to trial within a reasonable time or to release pending trial.

Principle 39

Except in special cases provided for by law, a person detained on a criminal charge shall be entitled, unless a judicial or other authority decides otherwise in the interest of the administration of justice, to release pending trial subject to the conditions that may be imposed in accordance with the law. Such authority shall keep the necessity of detention under review.

General clause

Nothing in this Body of Principles shall be construed as restricting or derogating from any right defined in the International Covenant on Civil and Political Rights.

APPENDIX 3

BASIC PRINCIPLES FOR THE TREATMENT OF PRISONERS

Adopted and Proclaimed by General Assembly Resolution 45/111 of 14 December 1990

1. All prisoners shall be treated with the respect due to their inherent dignity and value as human beings.
2. There shall be no discrimination on the grounds of race, colour, sex, language, religion, political or other opinion, national or social origin, property, birth or other status.
3. It is, however, desirable to respect the religious beliefs and cultural precepts of the group to which prisoners belong, whenever local conditions so require.
4. The responsibility of prisons for the custody of prisoners and for the protection of society against crime shall be discharged in keeping with a State's other social objectives and its fundamental responsibilities for promoting the well-being and development of all members of society.
5. Except for those limitations that are demonstrably necessitated by the fact of incarceration, all prisoners shall retain the human rights and fundamental freedoms set out in the Universal Declaration of Human Rights, and, where the State concerned is a party, the International Covenant on Economic, Social and Cultural Rights, and the International Covenant on Civil and Political Rights and the Optional Protocol thereto, as well as such other rights as are set out in other United Nations covenants.
6. All prisoners shall have the right to take part in cultural activities and education aimed at the full development of the human personality.
7. Efforts addressed to the abolition of solitary confinement as a punishment, or to the restriction of its use, should be undertaken and encouraged.
8. Conditions shall be created enabling prisoners to undertake meaningful remunerated employment which will facilitate their reintegration into the country's labour market and permit them to contribute to their own financial support and to that of their families.
9. Prisoners shall have access to the health services available in the country without discrimination on the grounds of their legal situation.
10. With the participation and help of the community and social institutions, and with due regard to the interests of victims, favourable conditions shall be created for the reintegration of the ex-prisoner into society under the best possible conditions.
11. The above Principles shall be applied impartially.

HUMAN RIGHTS LAW NETWORK

1) **Andaman & Nicobar Islands**
Human Rights Law Network
AB-31- Aberbeen Bazar Babu Lane
Port Blair - 744101
Tel : 03192-230756
Email: tmail portblair.hrln@gmail.com

2) **Andhra Pradesh**
Human Rights Law Network
House No. 1-9-312/5/2
Opposite Sree Play School
Achyutreddy Marg, Vidya Nagar
Hyderabad -500 044
Tel : 040-27661883
Email: hyderabad@hrln.org

3) **Arunachal Pradesh**
Human Rights Law Network
Quarter # 7, Type IV
Raj Niwas Area, Itanagar,
Tel : 0360-2292561
Mobile : 09436050907
Email : arunachal@hrln.org
hrlnarunachal@yahoo.co.uk

4) **Bihar**
Human Rights Law Network
M3- 15, Sahdeo Marg
Sri Krishna Pury
Patna - 800001
Mobil : 9430919317
Email : ravinad@gmail.com

5) **Chhattisgarh**
Adv. Bose Thomas
Vill + P. O. Patora
Via. Utai, District Durg - 491107
Mobile : 09425567095

6) **Gujarat**
Human Rights Law Network
B-5, Sushil Nagar Society Near Octroi Naka
Opp. Gandhi Labour Institute
Drive-in-Road, Ahmedabad-380052
Tel : 079-7475815
Email : ahmedabad@hrln.org

7) **Himachal Pradesh**

(i) Human Rights Law Network
Vimal Sadan, Near Co-operative Bank
Chotta Shimla-171002
Tel : +91-0177-2621108
Email : shimla@hrln.org

(ii) Kamlesh General Store, 1st Floor,
Vpo Sidhbari, Teh. Dharamsala
Distt. Kangra
Email : ranajitender@rediffmail.com
Mobile : 094180 18983

8) **Jammu & Kashmir**
Human Rights Law Network
Bee Dee House, First Floor,
Near Maulana Azad Urdu University
Kursoo Rajbagh, Srinagar, Kashmir
Pin - 190001
Mobile : 09906667957
Email : hrln_kashmir@yahoo.com

9) **Karnataka**
Human Rights Law Network
No. 20, Park Road,
Tasker Town, Shivajinagar
Bangalore -560051
Tel : 080-65624757
Email : bangalore@hrln.org

10) **Kerala**

(i) Human Rights Law Network
TC-25/2952, Old GPO Building
Ambujavilasom Road
Thiruvananthapuram 695001
Tel: +0471-5581466, 2460652
Email: trivandrum@hrln.org
kandalilsandhya@yahoo.com

(ii) 41/3661, Amples Building
Amulya Street, Off Providence Road
Kochi - 682018
Tel : 0484-2390680
Email : kochi@hrln.org

11) **Madhya Pradesh**

(i) Human Rights Law Network
10 - B 1st Floor Aman Complex
Govind Garden(Near Apsara Talkies
& Punjab National Bank) Above Nobal
Electronic, Govimdpura
Bhopal-462023
Tel: 0755 - 4700012
Email : bhopaL@hrln.org

(ii) 81, Beniganj, Mahal Road
Chhattarpur, Tel: 07682 - 247473

(iii) K.P. Gongore (Advocate)
54/4, Malviya Nagar,
Near AB Road, Indore - 452 008
Mobile: 09826034053

12) **Maharashtra**
   (i) India Centre for Human Rights & Law
   1st Floor, Motiwala Mansion
   56, Dontad Street (Damar Galli)
   Masjid (West) Mumbai - 400 009
   Tel : 23439651 / 23436692

   (ii) C/o YMCA
   140, Mahatma Gandhi Road
   Nagpur – 440001
   Tel : 0712 – 2524834, 2524 789
   Mobile : 09860818422

13) **Manipur**
Human Rights Law Network
KVIC Building 2nd Floor
Opposite Videocon House
Paona Bazar, Imphal – 795 001
Tel : +91-0385-2442165
Email : manipur@hrln.org
hrln_manipur@yahoo.com

14) **Nagaland**
C/o Prodigal's Homenscb Building,
4th Floor East Wing,
Dimapur –797112
Mobile : 09862254954

15) **Orissa**
Human Rights Law Network
Flat 403-B, Rashmi Vihar Apartment
Budheswari Colony, Cuttack Road,
Bhuvaneswar – 751006
Tel : 0674-2314260,
Mob: 98610 23282
E-mail : bhubaneswar@hrln.org

16) **Punjab & Chandigarh**
Human Rights Law Network
House No. 2439 Sector 37
Chandigarh–160036, Tel:0172-23094478
Email: chandigarh@hrln.org

17) **Haryana**
Mr. Raj Kumar
Village Naraina
Tehsil. Samalka
District Panipat
Haryana –132150
Mobile : 9315551130

18) **Rajasthan**
Human Rights Law Network
12, 1st Floor Navjivan Complex
Station Road, Jaipur–302006
Tel : 0141 – 2371324
Mobile : 09414788415
E-mail: jaipur@hrln.org

19) **Jharkhand**
Human Rights Law Network
Hiran Bala Niwas,
East Jail Roadnear Plaza Chowk,
Dist. Ranchi – 834 001
Email : Vasavi.santosh@gmail.com
Mobile: 09431103047

20) **Sikkim**
Human Rights Law Network
2nd Floor, Satey Bazar
Above Mahesh Saloon
Upper Sichey, Near District Court
Gangtok–737-101
Tel : +91-03592-203557
Email : sikkim@hrln.org

21) **Tripura**
Human Rights Law Network
Binoy Reang, Colnel Bari,
Near Colnel Chowmuni
Agartala, Tripura (West) – 799 001
Tel No. (O) 09436463916
Email – hrlntripura@yahoo.com

22) **Tamil Nadu**
Human Rights Law Network
319/155, IInd Floor Linghi Chetty Street
Chennai – 600 001, Tamilnadu
Tel : (O)044-2524 3246 (M) 09841091674
Email : dgita@yahoo.com, chennai@hrln.org, hrlnchennai@yahoo.co.in

23) **Uttar Pradesh**
   (i) Human Rights Law Network
   20 A, Hastings Road, Ashok Nagar,
   Allahabad 211 001
   Tel : 0532- 242 1893

   (ii) O J-19/66 Bari Bazar
   P.S. Jaitpura, Varanasi – 221 002
   Tel : +91-0542-586676/688
   Email : varanasi@hrln.org

24) **Uttarakhand**
Human Rights Law Network
Ishwari Bhawan West Pokharkhali,
Ranidhara Road,
Almora - 263601
Mobile : 09412092159
Email : almorah@hrln.org

25) **West Bengal**
Human Rights Law Network
Sohini Apartment
Flat 1A, 3 Parbati Chakrabarty Lane
Kalighat, Kolkata - 700 026
Tel : +91-33- 30967154, 24546828
Email : kolkata@hrln.org,
hrln_cal@hotmail.com